James Thomson Callender

The history of the United States for 1796

Including a variety of interesting particulars relative to the federal government

James Thomson Callender

The history of the United States for 1796
Including a variety of interesting particulars relative to the federal government

ISBN/EAN: 9783744749244

Printed in Europe, USA, Canada, Australia, Japan

Cover: Foto ©ninafisch / pixelio.de

More available books at **www.hansebooks.com**

THE HISTORY

OF THE

UNITED STATES

FOR 1796;

INCLUDING A VARIETY OF

INTERESTING PARTICULARS

RELATIVE TO THE

FEDERAL GOVERNMENT

PREVIOUS TO THAT PERIOD.

PHILADELPHIA:

FROM THE PRESS OF *SNOWDEN & M'CORKLE*,

NO. 47, NORTH FOURTH-STREET.

1797.

CHAPTER I.

First session of the fourth Congress.—Resolution proposed by Mr. S. Smith for checking the British treaty.—Hints respecting that paper.—Attempts to involve America in a French war.—Sketch of the state of France, by Edmund Burke.—Contrast between her and the United States.—Scanty pay of the Federal army.—Fatal effects of a rupture with France.—Camillus.—His mistakes as to the state of Europe.—Mr. Pinckney.—His opinion of the advantage of delaying a British treaty.—Attempts to irritate France.—Extreme danger of doing so.—Real authors of the misunderstanding.—Montgaillard's prediction.—Notice to the patrons of a certain gazette.—Concluding remarks,   1

CHAPTER II.

Character of Mr. Gallatin.—Connecticut poetry.—Major Jackson.—John Watts.—The Boston Federal Orrery.—Curtius.—His exaggerated statement of British resources.—Remarks on paper money.—*Causes of the preference of Britain to France in the federal party.*—*Democratical conspiracy developed by Curtius.*—*Defence of Jefferson, Madison, Giles, Parker, Christie, &c.*—*Fables from Pittsburgh.*—*Curious presentment by a grand jury in Georgia.*—*Purity of Boston,* 31

CHAPTER III.

Federal artifices to promote a French quarrel.—*Howe's landing at the head of Elk.*—*Jacobins not worse than other people.*—*Burgoyne's picture of the British East-India Company.*—*Recent stoppage of the bank of England.*—*Robespierre eclipsed by Pitt.*—*Amount of the yearly rental of Britain.*—*Note on the state-house of Hartford.*—*Number of the public creditors of England.*—*The triumph of Camillus.*—*Moral certainty of American indemnification for British piracy.*—*Mercantile apathy for the sufferings of American seamen.*—*Impressment at Jeremie.*—*Pinckney.*—*Jay.*—*Neck or nothing forgeries of Pitt.*—*Dependence of the British West-Indies on the United States.*—*Fallacies of Camillus.*—*What Jay should have said to Grenville,* 74

CHAPTER IV.

British piracies on American shipping in 1796.—*Case of the schooner John.*—*Of Capt. Samuel Green.*—*British privateers built in the United States.*—*Skirmish in Port Jeremie between the Americans and Capt. Reynolds.*—*Impressments by the Severn, the Hermoine, and the Regulus.*—*Twelve Americans whipt.*—*Case of the brig Fanny.*—*Of the ship Bacchus.*—*The Swallow.*—*The Paragon.*—*The*

Voluptas.—The Lydia.—The Hannah.—Fray at Liverpool ; and rout of a press-gang.—The Friendship.—The Ocean.—Letter from Samuel Bayard.—The brig Polly.—Vigilance of the American tories.—The Hannah of Baltimore.—The ship Dina, of New-York.—The ship Polly, Captain Mayo, - - - - - - - 122

CHAPTER V.

Federal plan for a French War.—Specimen of French justice.—The Sea Horse.—The Musquito.—Remarks on the British treaty by Mr. Gallatin.—Reply by Mr. Tracy.—Hints on the western insurrection.—Case of the brig Maria Wilman, captain Oaks.—The schooner William, captain Scott. Despotic influence of the tories in American seaports.—Elegant style of some of their publications. The Polly, captain Wade.—The Edward and William, captain Jones.—The Ariel.—The brig Sisters.—Capture of the brig Jay, by the French, and barbarous treatment of the captain.—Mr. JAY'S INSTRUCTIONS.—*Extracts from them* NEVER BEFORE *published.—Proofs of his* neglect *of orders.—Anecdotes relative to the British treaty,* - - - - - - 151

CHAPTER VI.

British depredations continued.—Mercantile selfishness.—The brig Fame.—The schooner Andrew.—Joshua Whiting.—The brig Columbia.—The sloop Dove.—The May Flower.—The Eliza.—Murder of captain Bosson.—Snuff Excise.—Memoirs of ALEXANDER HAMILTON, *late Secretary of the*

Treasury.—His singular mode of correspondence with certain persons.—Remarks on his connection with Reynolds, - - - 189

CHAPTER VII.

Farther observations on the correspondence between Messrs. Hamilton and Reynolds.—Singular mode of secrecy in framing the federal constitution, and of discussing Jay's treaty.—Defence of General Mason.—Report to President Adams, by Mr. Pickering, on French captures.—Singular style of that paper.—Defamatory charge by Judge Iredell to a grand jury in Virginia.—Their pitiful presentment.—Defence of Mr. Cabell.—Curious letter to Mr. John Beckley.—Observations on the PURITY *of the federal government.—Specimens of the mode of travelling in America.—A trip to New-York,* - - - - 228

CHAPTER VIII.

Proceedings of Congress.—Affair of Randall and Whitney.—Plan of appointing a short-hand writer.—Debates on the federal city.—Act of Appropriation.—Debates on the call for Jay's instructions.—Strange answer of the President.—Appropriations for the British treaty.—Explanation of the conduct of Mr. Muhlenberg.—Singular multiplicity of petitions in favour of appropriating for the British treaty.—Rise of the session.—Summary of events till the end of the year 1796, 277

IN January laſt, I publiſhed *The American Annual Regiſter for 1796*. My collection of materials required more room than had been expected, and it was found neceſſary to cloſe the volume without completing the plan.

Some gentlemen, who wiſhed to ſee the publication proceed, offered to aſſiſt by ſubſcriptions for a ſecond volume. But this was unſuitable, becauſe perſons who had not ſeen the former one could not with propriety be aſked to ſubſcribe for a continuation of it. I therefore began the ſame taſk over again under a different title page. The ſubject was fertile, and repetitions of what had been ſaid already have been avoided with ſo much care that they do not, in whole, extend to near half a page.

On the appearance of the former volume, certain critics complained of my ſtile. The roughneſs of their own, in the inſtant of condemnation, afforded the beſt apology for the faults of mine. But moreover theſe refined literati were the patrons and prompters of William Cobbet. He had ſpoke of me, with his wonted politeneſs, in ten or twelve pamphlets. It was proper, as it ſeems, that I ſhould be ſilent, becauſe the two chaplains of Congreſs, the ſecretaries of ſtate and of the treaſury were in the number of his auxiliaries or admirers. I would not injure Mr. Cobbet by comparing him with his employers. The bench and jury who aſſaſſinated lord Stafford were ſtill more execrable than Titus Oates.

In this catalogue of the patrons of genius we find Mr. Robert Liſton. The Britiſh ambaſſador, not contented with paying Mr. Cobbet for his labours, receives a daily bundle of his gazettes. No perſon poſſeſſing the feelings of a gentleman would ſuffer that commodity to come within his door. Such intermeddling from a foreign envoy would not be endured by any independent country in the world, unleſs in the United States of America. A French envoy at London, or an Engliſh ambaſſador at Paris, never ſets up a newſpaper to recommend his measures. Neither the old monarchy nor the present republic of France, would, for a single day, have endured such a connection. In London, where the spirit of national independence is understood and felt, the first news of the Morning Chronicle being supported by a French pension, would level the printer's office with the pavement. But Mr. Liston goes farther. He corresponds with internal traitors. He is detected, and the most despicable, or rather the most prostituted of all cabinets, hath accepted of his refusal to reveal their names. To trace the conspiracy, Congress appoints a committee of five members. Of these, three are tories, and one of them is Robert Goodloe Harper, the intimate friend of Liston, the adviser of a Spanish war, and of the conquest of Mexico. This is a new way to discover plots.

When the fifth number of this book was published, Mr. Alexander Hamilton printed, in Mr. Fenno's gazette, a denial of his connection with Reynolds. He has now come from New-York to complete a satisfactory statement. Like the pot whitewashing the kettle, he has already received from Mr. Wolcot a certificate of his virtue. He is, at present, also soliciting Mr. Monroe and Mr. Muhlenberg, on both of whom he had heaped mountains of calumny. Mr. Hamilton entreats them, to attest his *innocence*, that is to say, their belief of his having *debauched Mrs. Reynolds*.

The variety of articles transmitted for revisal and publication was unexpected, and many have been delayed for want of room. The denial of access to subscribers appeared an ungracious task. A compliance with their wishes made it necessary to shorten the latter part of the narrative, and to leave out some entire chapters that were prepared for the press. This gives to the volume a miscellaneous texture, which the rigid remarker is entitled to condemn. At another time, I shall perhaps do better.

A report has been circulated, that Mr. John Beckley is the author of this volume. He did not frame a single sentence of it. He is unacquainted with my hand writing, and I could not be sure to distinguish his.

Philadelphia, July 19th, 1797.

History of the United States, &c.

CHAPTER I.

First session of the fourth Congress.—Resolution proposed by Mr. S. Smith for checking the British treaty.—Hints respecting that paper.—Attempts to involve America in a French war.—Sketch of the state of France, by Edmund Burke.—Contrast between her and the United States.—Scanty pay of the Federal army.—Fatal effects of a rupture with France.—Camillus.—His mistakes as to the state of Europe.—Mr. Pinckney.—His opinion of the advantage of delaying a British treaty.—Attempts to irritate France.—Extreme danger of doing so.—Real authors of the misunderstanding.—Montgaillard's prediction.—Notice to the patrons of a certain gazette.—Concluding remarks.

AT the beginning of the year 1796, the fourth Congress of the United States were in their first session. On the 4th of January, Mr. Samuel Smith laid on the table of the Representatives a resolution in these words: "That from and after "the   day of   it shall not be lawful "for any foreign ship or vessel to land in the "territories of the United States any goods, wares, "or merchandize other than the produce of that "country to which *the ship or vessel belongs.*" This proposal was professedly pointed at the treaty of commerce with Britain, which had been signed at London on the 19th of November, 1794, by Mr. John Jay, as envoy on the part of America. Mr. S. Smith opposed that instrument. He said in Congress, that, within two years, it might be expected to destroy the shipping of this country. The fifteenth article of the treaty has these words: "Nor shall any prohibition be imposed on the exportation or the importation of any articles to or from the territories of the two parties respectively, which shall not equally extend to all other nations." Thus the resolution was in strict harmony with the conditions of the treaty; yet, if the United States shall ever carry it into execution, the treaty itself will, in some measure, be at an end. Britain could find a thousand effective ways of expressing her disgust at this regulation, which would incommode her much more than the other maritime states of Europe. Still she would have less reason to complain than any nation in the world, because the resolution is grounded on the principle assumed in the English act of navigation*.

The treaty in question has produced many volumes of elaborate investigation. Since the new constitution, no other subject has excited so general an effort of the ingenuity, the eloquence, and

* On the 2d of September, 1793, the French Convention passed a similar act. Its operation is only suspended on account of the war. By the first article, no foreign commodities can be imported into France, but in French vessels, or in those of the country which produces them, or of the country from which they are usually first exported. By the second, no foreign vessel can convey from one port of France or her colonies to another, any of their produce. Third, every French vessel must have her officers and three-fourths of her crew Frenchmen. It is amazing that the court of Versailles did not adopt this rule an hundred years ago. It will, in a short time, double or quadruple the number of French seamen. Were other omens averted, this law is an epitaph on the naval supremacy of Britain. See an eloquent report by BARRERE.

the paffions of America. It was this emergency which marked out the prefent year as more eminently deferving of hiftorical notice. The matter itfelf daily grows in importance, as this tranfaction has brought the United States to the verge of a French war. Few have leifure to read, and ftill fewer have information or even capacity adequate to comprehend a great part of the complicated arguments employed for or againft it. To attempt a detail of the topics on each fide would be a voluminous, and by this time, almoft an ufelefs undertaking. The public has already become fatiated with effays, letters, memorials, replies, obfervations, features, reports, addreffes, views, vindications, defences, paragraphs, refolutions, petitions, explanations, proceedings of town meetings, motions, and fpeeches. Within the fhort fpace of eighteen months, the argument has entirely fhifted its place. The ftrefs of the debate can be no longer about whether the Britifh treaty is advantageous or prejudicial to American commerce; but whether it is worth preferving at the rifk of a French war. That the Directory of Paris have this object fomewhat in their eye is moft likely. The recall of their ambaffador, citizen Adet, was a broad intimation of their defign. In Europe, fuch a ftep is the profeffed fignal for hoftilities. It is as certain that a party in this country are folicitous of driving the United States into that conteft. If a croud of other evidences could be forgotten, their abfence is fupplied by the letter from fecretary Pickering to Mr. Pinckney our ambaffador to the French republic. At the fame time, attempts are conftantly made to decry the power of France. When a French general chances to retreat, the newfpapers of the party teem with exultation. The republic at large is invariably reprefented as a rendezvous of ruffians, a nuisance to civilized society. It is impossible that the French should fail of being offended at such unprovoked insolence. They hire no gazettes in Paris to revile America. They do not fill libraries in censuring our political characters. Yet our federal prints attack, on every occasion, both the republic and all her friends, in the most vulgar style of abuse. Even the ministerial prints of London, the organs of Rose and Dundas, are, by many degrees, less insolent in their invective, and less brutal in their reproach*.

Before going farther, we shall glance at the character and actual state of the French, whom Mr. Pickering and his friends are so anxious to degrade. In preparing for a quarrel it is essential to be acquainted with the talents and resources of your antagonist. The situation of our citizens, thinly dispersed over an immense continent, affords a peculiar avenue to deception. It has been employed with diligence against the republic. On a topic

---

* For instance, a late correspondent in the Gazette of the United States writes thus: "That contemptible and drunken vagabond "Tom Paine, who is notoriously destitute of every honest principle, religious, moral, or political, has crowned his career of impudence and falsehood, &c.—This creature of avaricious poverty and deranged ambition, would set the world on fire, if he could find sixpence by the light, and advocate the climate and government of hell to be popular there.—He was, at the commencement of our troubles, a decided friend to the measures of Great Britain." After the war, "his first attack was upon the *tranquility* of Great Britain: but here he was disgracefully defeated." [It will be time enough to speak of his *defeat* when the bank of England begins to pay its notes in gold and silver. The present paper-money plan is like trying to cross the Atlantic in a cork jacket.] "I regret there was found any man in the United States so base and hostile to the peace and honour of his country, as to publish this letter of infamy;" the letter from Paine to general Washington, printed by Mr. Bache. The peace of the country runs no hazard, and as little awaits the honour of the general. On the 14th of December, 1796, Dr. Ames observed in Congress, that "the character is fixed in *history!*" Paine, therefore, has come too late.

of such universal importance candid explanation can hardly be tedious. No better authority will be required than that of Edmund Burke. Two letters from him on this head have been recently printed. A few detached sentences, extracted from whole sheets to the same purpose, will place the resources of France in a just light, and shew what the United States have to expect in a contest with her. "Out of the tomb of the murdered monar-
"chy in France, has arisen a vast, tremendous,
"unformed spectre, in *a far more terrific guise* than
"any which ever yet overpowered the imagi-
"nation and subdued the fortitude of man.—The
"republic has actually conquered the finest parts of
"Europe, has distressed, disunited, deranged, and
"broke to pieces all the rest.—We have not in the
"slightest degree, impaired the strength of the com-
"mon enemy, (France), in any one of those points
"in which his particular force consists.—The re-
"gicide has received our advances with scorn*!—
"If things should give us *the comparative happi-
"ness of a struggle*, I shall be found dying by the
"side of Mr. Pitt.—Spain is a province of the ja-
"cobin empire.—Her crown is a fief of regicide.—
"We have not considered, as we ought, the dread-
"ful energy of a state in which the property has
"nothing to do with the government.—The disco-
"very is dreadful, the mine *exhaustless*.—A repub-
"lic of a character the most restless, the most en-
"terprising, the most impious, the most fierce and
"bloody, the most hypocritical and perfidious,
"the most bold and daring that has ever been seen,
"or indeed that can be conceived to exist!"

Mr. Burke is far from being singular in his pa-
nic. Major Cartwright, in his work, entitled, *The*

---

* The letters were published before Malmesbury went to Paris.

Commonwealth in Danger, shews the folly of England depending for safety, solely on her fleet. The French may give battle by sea, be defeated, and lose twenty ships of the line, without material injury. They know that the English must be crippled and return to port. The road is then open, and they disembark in Britain what troops they please. The major adds, that, previous to the victory of the 1st of June, 1794, admiral Howe was reviled for not beating the French fleet; but even then, he only did so because the French came purposely in his way. They also, by sacrificing a few ships of the line, gained their object. This was to secure the arrival of an American convoy with provisions. Arthur Young, a third writer of eminence, has demonstrated the depth of his despair by the following proposal; viz. that England should raise an army of five hundred thousand men; and that they, as well as their officers, must all be *men of property*. He says that nothing else can save the country from a French conquest. This was above two years ago*. These authorities confirm the lamentations of Mr. Burke. As to his picture of what France can perform, we may judge by what she hath suffered. In March, 1795, Dumourier printed at Hamburgh, a very interesting pamphlet on the state of the war. He therein says, that, in December, 1794, a report was laid before the Convention of the number of soldiers whom France had lost by her three campaigns. They were stated at six hundred and fifty thousand. Dumourier adds, that this computation was by one-third part less than the truth; and that, including emigration, famine, and the scaffold, France had

* See An Idea of the present State of France, printed sometime previous to March, 1795.

then loft twelve hundred thoufand men, in the flower of life, befides aged perfons, women and children. Compared with this havoc of the human fpecies, the wafte of any other modern war is but trifling. The king of Pruffia eftimates that the war of 1756, which lafted seven years, deftroyed, in the whole, and in all parts of the world, only about a million of foldiers. To the twelve hundred thoufand Frenchmen we may fafely add eight hundred thoufand from the allied armies; fince the latter were equally numerous with the republicans, and befides were beaten. We have thus about two millions of deaths, in two years and four months, or above eight hundred thoufand per annum; fo that the prefent war is at leaft five times more deftructive than that of 1756.

No other nation or government that the world ever faw, could have fupported fuch enormous loffes as the French have endured; yet their ftrength appears undiminifhed, and every campaign adds to the catalogue of their conquefts. It is not lefs than madnefs for a party in America to be hiring newfpapers to revile fuch a terrible people. They are not only moft formidable from their phyfical ftrength, but from the peculiar ftructure of their government. "It is fyftematic;" fays Mr. Burke, " it is fimple to its principle; it has unity and con-
" fiftency in perfection." [Congrefs have refufed to impofe a land tax. Nay fome of them, with furprifing hardinefs, declare fuch a meafure impracticable, though land taxes are at this moment paid in perhaps every ftate of the union. Pennfylvania has three or four. Oppofed to this frivolity, this puppet-fhew of legiflation, obferve what Burke tells of France:] "In that country, entirely to cut off a
" branch of commerce, to extinguifh a manufac-
" ture, to deftroy the circulation of money, to

"violate credit, to suspend the course of agriculture, even to burn a city or to lay waste a province of their own, does not cost them a moment's anxiety.—Going straight forward to its end, unappalled by peril, unchecked by remorse, despising all common maxims and all common means, that hideous phantom overpowered those *who could not believe it possible she could at all exist!*"

This is the sort of enemy whom we may chance to encounter, as the price of the British treaty, and the epistle of Mr. Pickering. When in parliament, Mr. Burke was considered as the best informed member of the House of Commons. He has long been the oracle of English aristocracy. He is a pensioner to Pitt, and would be sorry to overcharge the picture of French power.

It is serving America, to make a short comparison between the relative force of the two nations. The French, in only four years, have overcome the German empire, Spain, Portugal, Italy, and the Netherlands, comprehending not less than fifty millions of people. The United States, white, black and yellow, have not five millions. The French have drubbed three British kingdoms, with their population of fourteen millions, and crushed numerous conspiracies and rebellions in the heart of their country. The revolt of La Vendee alone cost as much fighting as passed in America during the revolution. Pichegru, in one campaign, did what Marlborough, though constantly victorious, could not accomplish in ten.

In 1794, France maintained nearly eleven hundred thousand fighting men, and was, in 1795, to have sixty thousand cannoneers*. In 1797, America, by the report of Oliver Wolcott†, was to

* Carey's edition of Guthrie's Geography, vol. ii. p. 699. † P. 18.

UNITED STATES.

require an army of three thousand five hundred and twenty-four men, including officers, cadets, artificers, and twenty-seven surgeons. Even this handful cost infinite haggling in Congress*; and the greatest anxiety how they were to be paid. The French are the best appointed troops, perhaps, in the world. From an immense distance, they have been often transported in waggons to the field of battle. The pay of American regulars is absolute beggary. The privates have a ration per day worth twenty cents, or seventy two dollars and eighty cents a year. Their pay is four dollars per month, or forty-eight dollars a year. An annual suit of clothes are valued at twenty-five dollars, so that the accounts stands thus;

	Dolls.	Cts.
Rations,	72	80
Pay,	48	
Clothes,	25	
Total,	145	80

Every man who can handle an axe may gain double the sum, and have his victuals into the bargain. For such a pittance our soldiers, in war, penetrate the wilderness to fight an enemy who give no quarter. In peace they are cooped up in garrisons from whence they dare not stray above a gun shot, and where they have been often in the utmost distress for necessaries. Thousands of horses, in attempting to carry supplies through the desart, have consumed their loads, and died of hunger†. General Wayne, it is said, lost his life at lake Erie, for want of two ounces of castor oil.

Such is the present balance by land between the

* The particulars will appear in the next volume.
† Mr. S, Smith stated this, last winter, in Congress.

regular forces of France and the United States. They are as one man to three or four hundred. Our expences equal or exceed our revenues. Congress have refused to attempt a land tax. All other sources are about exhausted; and a war with France, by the ruin of our commerce, would certainly cut off a great part of those arising from it. Nine parts in ten of the public taxes proceed from the duties on impost and tonnage. In the land tax debates of Congress, last winter, Mr. Harper strangely said, that, if at war with France, our trade would not, in his opinion, suffer more than it does already. He inferred that our revenues would not, by that event, be materially reduced.

If we look at the sea there is no prospect of success in a contest with France. We have on the stocks three frigates. Of their navy an exact account cannot here be given, but it has, for a century, been the second in Europe. It lately was said to contain three hundred and thirty-seven vessels. An hundred and twenty one were ships of the line. Of these the least carry seventy four guns*. They would, in a contest with America, be seconded by Spain, Portugal, and Holland. Against this immensity of numbers, our Lilliput squadron would be like three pismires in the gullet of a crocodile, or three grains of chaff in the charge of a six pounder. But then our privateers can destroy their commerce! Yes. And they shall destroy ours. Thus, as Henry Fielding says, we sell a blind horse and receive a bad note in payment. Our seaport towns, from Portland to Savannah, will be successively transformed into a range of bonfires. The shutting up of the Mediterranean and the western waters would compose but an atom in the Alps of our calamity.

* Carey's edition of Guthrie's Geography, vol. ii. p. 696.

In a ſtruggle with France alone, unſupported by her allies, we could not muſter a tenth part of her force either by land or ſea. Mr. Pitt computed, in the Houſe of Commons, that the campaign of 1794, coſt the republic an hundred and fifty millions ſterling. Ours with the Wyandots were eſtimated at a million of dollars yearly. The burden produced infinite diſcontent, and an earneſt deſire of peace. France, at an annual charge three or ſix hundred times greater, continues to fight and to conquer, to trample every enemy, and to dictate the terms of every peace. To contend, if we can help it, with this republican Typhœus would, in raſhneſs, reſemble the laſt ſtruggles of Jeruſalem and Palmira. On the altars of Titus and Aurelian we might read with probability the proſpect before us.

As a political writer, Alexander Hamilton holds the ſame rank in America that Burke enjoys in England; and it would be injuring the logic of his party not to give his opinion. Camillus, No. vii. was publiſhed in the ſummer of 1795, and contains a ſurvey of Europe extremely different from that of Mr. Burke. "It cannot be denied that ſhe (Britain) "is triumphant on the ocean; that the acquiſitions "which ſhe has made upon France are hitherto "*greater* than thoſe which France has made upon "her." The reduction of two or three iſlands in the Weſt Indies is not worth notice in this conteſt, where the independence of Britain is in imminent danger. When No. vii. was written, the French had conquered Holland, and the Auſtrian Netherlands. "Holland," ſays Mr. Burke, "is to England a "matter of value *ineſtimable*.*" By the conqueſt of the low countries, France forms a ſemicircle around the Britiſh iſlands. Hence, while the fleet

* Letter I.

of England lies wind-bound at Spithead, or is in any other given situation, the French, by taking an opposite point of the compass, can, at their leisure, disembark an army on the coast of Britain, or Ireland. For excluding them, an hundred ships of the line and an hundred canoes would be of equal importance. This, by the way, points out the folly of a favourite British maxim, that *he who is master by sea is master by land*. While the Netherlands, therefore, continue a part of the republic, it is frivolous to speak of British conquests in the East or West Indies, or indeed any where else. They signify no more

"Than Cæsar's arm, when Cæsar's head is off."

" If, on the one hand, she (Britain) owes an im-
" mense debt, on the other she possesses an immense
" credit, which there is no symptom of being im-
" paired. British credit has become, in a British
" mind, an article of *faith*, and is no longer an ob-
" ject of reason." [Thus Camillus tells us that the creditors of England are fools. The prospects of a merchant are not very hopeful, when no man of prudence will trust him. Yet such is the condition of England as described by its advocate.] " Her
" government possesses, internally, as much vigor,
" and has as much national support, as it perhaps
" ever had at any former period of her history.
" Alarmed by the unfortunate excesses in France,
" most men of property cling to the government,
" and carry with them the great bulk of the nation,
" almost the whole of the farming interest, and
" much the greatest proportion of other industri-
" ous classes."

Mr. Burke has the advantage of being on the spot;

and he diffents entirely from Mr. Hamilton. He eftimates the number of Britifh citizens who think for themfelves, at four hundred thoufand. Of thefe he computes that eighty thoufand are " pure " jacobins, utterly incapable of amendment.— " On thefe, no reafon, no argument, no example, " no venerable authority, can have the flighteft in- " fluence. They defire a change, and they will have " it if they can.—This minority is great and formi- " dable. I do not know whether, ifI aimed at the to- " tal overthrow of a kingdom, *I fhould wifh to be en-* " *cumbered with a larger body of partifans**." The London Courier, of the 26th of December, 1796, affirms, that thefe two letters were publifhed by the connivance of *the minifter*. Burke has penfions to the effective amount of about four thoufand pounds fterling, fo that this fuppofition becomes highly probable. Thus the authority of Pitt is fuperadded to that of Burke, and they explode the opinion of Camillus. Each fucceeding campaign is an additional nail driven into the head of monarchy. Every new tax makes a number of new enemies. Here we perceive three diftinct caufes for a Britifh revolution. Thefe are, a fuperior and implacable enemy on the continent, whofe local pofition makes a Britifh navy ufelefs; a national debt, which by this time approaches to four hundred millions fterling, and of which the very intereft can be paid only in paper; and a party within the country whofe enmity cannot be extinguifhed, and who, by the confeflion of their enemies, are abundantly numerous for the deftruction of any government in the world. " Among her allies," fays Camillus, " are the two " greateft powers of Europe, France excepted ; " namely, Ruflia and Auftria. Spain and Sardinia

* Letter I.

"make a common cause with her." The two latter have been turned by France into mere stepping stones in her path to the dominion of Europe. Russia never gave any help, more or less, to the crowned coalition. Catharine is now dead; and her son has declined any concern with it. But even if he did send an army to the Rhine, Britain would be obliged to pay them. As for Austria, Jasper Wilson, in his celebrated letter to Mr. Pitt, says, that, before the present war began, the Emperor was offering nine per cent for money, so that by this time he must be as much entangled in debt as England herself. Nothing but arbitrary power could enable him to pay even a single regiment. This will not hold out long. "She (France) cannot, without great dif-
"ficulty, from their geographical position, make
"any farther acquisitions upon the territories of
"Austria." Carnot is a better geographer than Mr. Hamilton. Since this prediction, Moreau and Jourdan have penetrated into the heart of Germany. They have subdued a multitude of its princes, and were within a small matter of reaching Vienna. As to Italy, Buonaparte has eclipsed every commander since Telesinus and Sylla engaged under the walls of Rome. Hear what Burke says: "The over-
"running of Lombardy, the subjugation of Pied-
"mont, the possession of its impregnable fortresses,
"the seizing on all the neutral states of Italy, our
"expulsion from Leghorn, instances renewed for
"our expulsion from Genoa, Spain rendered sub-
"ject to them and hostile to us, Portugal bent un-
"der the yoke, half the empire over-run and rava-
"ged*." This is the picture of 1796. Yet, in reliance on the political foresight of Camillus, a numerous party in the United States have filled, and

* Letter I.

continue to fill *their* newspapers with scurrilous calumnies against *the* French nation. They insulted her ambassador, even after he had been recalled; and, as if this had not been enough to ensure a rupture, Mr. Pickering sent a letter to Mr. Pinckney in France which is more in the tone of a libel than a diplomatic paper. When the blind lead the blind, we know the sequel. With regard to Europe, Mr. Hamilton is, in all his views, mistaken. This lamp of political wisdom, has conducted America to the edge of a precipice from which General Washington saw fit to retire. It is of consequence to expose the sophistry of Mr. Hamilton, that our *enlightened* citizens may see by what ignorance they have been led into the present crisis. We shall, on this account, pick up two or three others of his mistakes.

"Britain and her possessions are *essentially safe*," says Camillus, " while she maintains a decided " maritime superiority." Burke, in one of his letters, speaking of the war of 1689, says, that " in " two years three thousand vessels were taken from " the English trade." In every war, the commerce of Britain suffers prodigiously. The present state of the West Indies shews that a superior fleet cannot always preserve her islands. Witness the recapture of Guadaloupe, the conflagration of St. Vincents, Grenada, and St. Lucia! But the expedition of Hoche, to Ireland, is the best refutation of Mr. Hamilton. Some people speak of the British navy as if it could be present every where at the same time. If twenty-five thousand Frenchmen had disembarked at Bantry bay, a march of two days would have brought them to Corke, a city as large as Philadelphia, disaffected to government, and besides entirely defenceless. Another week would be sufficient for reaching Dublin. The temper of its citizens appears by a letter from the viceroy.

He boasts of having a militia of two thousand barristers, attornies, merchants, and such people. But these men would not mount guard, if they durst employ the poorer classes to do so for them. Dublin has between two and three hundred thousand inhabitants, and if the bulk of them had been well affected, the militia might have amounted to twenty thousand. His lordship says that the whole militia of the island are about twenty-five thousand. This is a pitiful portion in a population of four millions*. It is hard to say whether the catholics of Connaught or the protestants of Ulster would feel the greatest impatience to join an invader. Thus the left arm of England would be cut off, without, perhaps, even the honour of a battle. This is the *essential safety* that Mr. Hamilton speaks about.

In defiance of geography and history, Camillus next endeavours to undervalue the conquest of the Netherlands. "France must be still more fa-
"tigued and exhausted even than her adversaries.
"Her acquisitions cannot materially vary this con-
"clusion; the Low Countries must have been *pret-*
"*ty well emptied* before they fell into her hands."
He has more to the same effect. They are inhabited by about six millions of industrious people, among the richest in the world. The acquisition was of immense importance. If Brussels and Amsterdam had been reduced to ashes, and if a famine

---

* His lordship tells us, that when the soldiers went off to Bantry Bay, in quest of the French, he granted their wives four pence per day till they returned. This was certainly a splendid allowance, and well worth fighting for. In a pamphlet printed in 1794, sir Henry Clinton says, that " the army is now waiting to receive a very small " share of plunder taken at the siege of *Charlestown!*"
The great take care of themselves at least. The history of *The Crimes of the Kings of England*, relates that the family of Mr. Pitt enjoy places and pensions to the amount of eighty-one thousand pounds sterling a year.

like those produced by British monopolies in Bengal, had whitened the whole country with the bones of its inhabitants, Camillus might have some reason for this insinuation. The French did not think that Holland was *emptied*, as appears from their first requisition. Among other articles, they demanded two hundred thousand quintals of wheat, seventy-five millions of pounds weight of hay, fifty millions ditto of oats, and hundred and fifty thousand pairs of shoes, two hundred thousand shirts, with straw, breeches, coats, waistcoats, overalls, hats, and so forth, all in one month, besides twelve thousand oxen to be furnished within two months. This enumeration shews the inaccuracy of Camillus, and what may be expected if the French disembark at Mud island.

" The British government maintains a proud and
" distant reserve, *repels every idea of peace*, and
" inflexibly pursues the path of war." Mr. Burke's two letters are half filled with lamentations for the debasement of England. They hold out a ludicrous refutation of Alexander Hamilton. " The
" regicides were the first," saith St. Edmund,
" to declare war. We are the first *to sue for peace.*—
" The speech from the throne in the opening of
" the session of 1795, threw out *oglings* and *glances*
" *of tenderness*. Lest this *coquetting* should seem too
" cold and ambiguous, the *violent passion* for a re-
" lation to the regicides, produced," &c. This is the *proud and distant reserve* described by Camillus.—
" I do not know a more mortifying spectacle than
" to see the assembled majesty of the crowned heads
" of Europe waiting as patient suitors in the anti-
" chamber of Regicide. They wait, it seems, un-
" til the sanguinary tyrant, Carnot, shall have snor-
" ted away the indigested fumes of the blood of
" his sovereign." The remainder of this scene

is admirably painted; but our envoy, Mr. Pinckney, is not, it appears, admitted even to the antichamber. He has been defired to quit the country. " At this fecond humiliation it might not have " been amifs to paufe and not to fquander away " *the fund of our fubmiffions.*" A report from the Committee of Agriculture at London affirms, that the lands lying wafte in Britain, could be encreafed in value by *twenty millions fterling a year!* They deferred this acquifition to manufacture French kings.—" At Bafle, it was thought proper that " Great Britain fhould appear at this market, and " bid with the reft for *the mercy* of the people-" king." This is that republic which the American emiffaries of England are fo bufy in provoking.

Mr. Burke then relates two fruitlefs applications made by England, the one at Berlin, by our friend Robert Hammond, and the other at Paris through the Danifh ambaffador. Both were rejected. " It " might be thought that here, at length, we had " touched the bottom of humiliation; our lead " was brought up covered with mud. But *in the* " *loweft deep, a lower deep* was to open for us ftill " more profound abyffes of difgrace and fhame. " However, *in we leaped!*—The queftion is not now " how we are to be affected with it in regard to " *dignity.* That is gone. I fhall fay no more about " it. Light lie the earth on the afhes of *Englifh* " *pride*!*"

We can now anfwer the query of Camillus. " How happens it that France with all her victories

---

* Britain has good reafon to be tired of this war. A late London newfpaper fays, that, from 1775 to 1782, inclufive, there were three thoufand feven hundred and forty-two bankruptcies; and from 1793 to 1796, inclufive, three thoufand fix hundred and eight. Thus *four* years of the prefent quarrel have done as much harm to the mercantile credit as *eight* years of the laft.

"has not yet been able to *extort peace !*" She never asked for it. "It is probable," says he, "the negoci-
"ation (Jay's treaty) received its first impression and
"even its general outline anterior to the principal
"part of the disasters sustained by the coalesced
"powers in the course of the last campaign (1794)."
If Jay had been warranted, as he was not, to make a treaty such as he did, its first impression would have been sketched in America before he set out. But, as lately observed*, the time chosen for making it was highly improper. Camillus, in ancient or modern annals, will hardly find that, with views merely commerical, any nation ever chose so hazardous a time for entering into a treaty. This consideration alone should have laid the bargain on its back, at least till the conclusion of a peace. It was just like building a house close to another which is on fire. During the residence of Jay in England, every post brought him news of French victories. Hence, even if the outline of his paper had been sketched before the conquest of Flanders, that decisive event should have taught him to make a pause. A suspension of signing the treaty for only three months could not have ruined America. These things were *as huge as high Olympus*. They pierced the deafest ear. They thrust themselves on the dullest understanding.

The letter of Mr. Pinckney above referred to clearly admits the advantages that might have been gained by delay. "The business, upon the whole,"
says he, " has been concluded more beneficially for
" us than I had any hope we could obtain by nego-
" ciation *six months ago*, and, in my opinion, places
" us in a more advantageous situation than we should
" have been in by becoming *parties to the war*."

* American Annual Register, Chapter 8.

If so much had been acquired by one delay of six months, reason pointed out a second postponement. Britain has been ever since going down hill, and had the affair been to begin at this time, we might have had any terms that could be desired. The latter part of the above citation obliquely implies that America had no choice between a treaty and a war. The supposition gives a poor specimen of the writer's discernment. How gladly some people would be at getting into war appears from the Aurora of the 5th of April 1797.—"A correspondent in the Centinel, "says, *that the people of this country are not YET ripe* "*for an alliance offensive and defensive with Great Bri-* "*tain,* but suggests that the event is probable." This passage points more clearly than usual at the ultimate purpose of a certain party. If the alliance above recommended were to take place, the best fortune that we could look for would be that of Ulysses in the den of the Cyclops; we should be reserved as the last morsel. If any motive can drive out of our fancy a British alliance, it is to read the recent fate of the allies of England, as described by Mr. Burke. "They (the French) have hitherto constantly de-
"clined any other than a treaty with a single pow-
"er.—In that light the regicide power finding
"each of them insulated and unprotected, with
"great facility gives *the law to them all.* By this
"system, for the present, an incurable distrust is
"sown amongst the confederates; and in future all
"alliance *is rendered impracticable.* It is thus they
"have treated with Prussia, with Spain, with Sar-
"dinia, with Bavaria, with the ecclesiastical states,
"with Saxony; and here we see them refuse to
"treat with Great Britain in any other mode."
Suppose that we shall have entered into the alliance recommended by the Centinel, and that Britain, within six months, patches up a separate peace,

while Hoche's huffars are whetting their fabres in the barracks of Dublin. America would then make but a forry figure in a folitary negociation. Befides, we cannot truft our ally. This appears by an extract from the journals of Congrefs, in the year 1779. "We are contending," fay they, againft "a kingdom *crumbling to pieces**, a nation with- "out public virtue, and a people fold and be- "trayed by their own reprefentatives; againft a "prince governed by his paffions, and a miniftry "without confiftency or wifdom; againft *armies* "*half paid*, and *generals* half trufted [thefe were "two flagrant falfehoods], againft a government "equal *only* (obferve this *only*) to plans of plunder, "conflagration, and murder, a government noted "for its violations of the rights of *religion*, juftice, "humanity, and mankind, and revolting from *the* "*protection of Providence!*"—" Our armies in Flan- "ders fwore terribly," faid uncle Toby, "but "nothing like this!" As for Providence, the people of England held frequent faft days for military fuccefs. This delicate fpecimen of the mob-ftile was part of a letter from Congrefs to their conftituents, and was draughted, at their defire, by Mr. John Jay. They fhould have faid nothing about half-paid armies, till they had been half able to pay their own. Several continental officers, on cafting up the difference between dirty pafteboard and hard filver, found, during the war, that they were fighting for about *one cent* per day†. Yet they continued to fupport the caufe, and to fink money in it. But the object of the above quotation is to point out the *confiftency* of our envoy, and how not-

---

* How does this agree with Camillus?

† This is affirmed by a gentleman, in Philadelphia who was one of them.

ably the ſtile of 1779 agrees with that of 1794. Only poor fifteen years have converted a horde of demons, for that is the amount of his billingſgate deſcription, into the moſt upright people in the world.

We have remarked on the haſte with which Mr. Jay cloſed his treaty, and how much might have been won by deferring it. But the conduct of the negociator is eclipſed by that of the great body of the people. It does not appear that the poſſibility of a rupture with France ever once came into the conception of moſt of our citizens. A majority in the Houſe of Repreſentatives of Congreſs did indeed foreſee or fear it. One of them was aſked why they did not ſtate it in their ſpeeches, inſtead of many trifles, which were advanced againſt the treaty. He replied that "they did not think it prudent. " The Hamiltonians would inſtantly have accuſed " them of encouraging the French to begin a war " with this country."

This is the very deſign of ſome of that party themſelves. When a man calls hard names at his neighbour he is underſtood as deſiring to quarrel. Mr. Monroe, American ambaſſador to France, conducted himſelf with prudence and popularity. In December 1796, he preſented letters of recall, and bade farewell to the Executive Directory, in the moſt amicable terms. His addreſs was received with reſpect and cordiality. He congratulated the nation on their victories, and their new conſtitution, in terms not as ſtrong, by twenty degrees, as thoſe of Mr. Waſhington on receiving the French flag. The Gazette of the United States, for the 29th of March, 1797, ſcolds him for this act of civility ſo contraſted to the inſolence of Mr. Pickering. " Though you could *crouch*, and *kneel*, and *lick*, and " *fawn*, on ſuch an occaſion, your fellow citizens

" can feel nothing for you but *contempt;* and for
" the Directory, who require of the United States
" an act that would proftrate them in the duft, the
" utmoft *indignation.*" There is much more in this
ftile. The alleged act referred to, is, that the Directory refufed to admit an American minifter till the United States *had redreffed their grievances.*

As for the contempt and indignation fo fiercely fpoke about, a different tone may foon be found neceffary. Mantua is at length given up. Five Auftrian armies have been deftroyed, and an hundred thoufand prifoners taken, during a fingle campaign in Italy. Compared to this work, the American revolution was mere fcratching. The Emperor cannot pay his troops with Englifh bank notes. He muft either make an immediate peace, or be dethroned. It does not appear that the United States could, in one fummer, raife five, or indeed two fuch armies, in defence of the frontier of Canada; and it is likely enough that the French may reclaim that province from England, and require this country to reftore its ancient boundaries. They would enter upon fuch a fcheme with every advantage. They have already a numerous colony of their own people in Canada, who are acquainted with it as well as the New Englanders. They have always exceeded the Britifh in the art of gaining the Indians. The war with the favages has been computed to coft yearly a million of dollars; but with a French army to fupport them, a campaign might devour fifty millions. The ceffion of Canada would be one of the leaft wonderful events of the prefent war. A great part of the people of New England have been uncomonly folicitious to exafperate the republic, and, after the treatment which they have alfo diligently beftowed on the fouthern ftates, and their numerous menaces of disjunction, the latter might chuse to give themselves but small concern in the dispute. On the south-eastern frontier, the United States are still more vulnerable. Were Victor Hughes, with three or four battalions of black troops, to land on the coast of Virginia, the horrors of St. Domingo would immediately be renewed. Georgia still continues to import negroes; a practice deserving the severest reprobation.

When we consider the terror, which France has, for three years past, inspired in Europe, the conquest of Canada, and the extension of its limits, will seem but as dust in the balance. The brutal insolence with which the republicans are treated in the Columbian Centinel, can arise only from an unacquaintance with the possible extent of danger to New England. Count Montgaillard is a French royalist. His enmity to the revolution is as sincere as that of any printer or preacher in the eastern states. In 1794, he published a pamphlet on *The Necessity of continuing the war*. " The generation," says he, " which is to invade and destroy Europe " has now reached the twelfth year of its age. It " was born in the very midst of a revolution [that " of America perhaps]; it has seen all the epocha " of this [the French] revolution; it has inhaled " all its principles, and it has sucked in every poi- " son by which it was infected.—Where is the trea- " ty of peace which can constrain this rising genera- " tion to renounce so horrible a conquest." He insists, like Burke, that the war must be continued; he even affirms, that the republic *must* be subdued. When this piece appeared, the French had not conquered Lombardy. They had not plundered one-half of Germany; and the bank of England had not stopt payment. Arthur Young, in the pamphlet already cited, speaks in the same tone. " Activity, vigour, and energy, such as the

" *world has not seen*, are exerted to spread destruc-
" tion.—The late manifestation of the French pow-
" er is too tremendous to be considered but *with
" alarm and terror*. The independence of Europe
" is at stake." He says that the war had, at that
time, cost France *thirteen hundred thousand men*.
Every nation fears her, except America, or rather
the tories, and the monied interest of our country.
William Cobbet has set up a gazette in this city,
for the express end of reviling France. He does
not conceal his design of bringing the nation into
a French war. Sincerity is always respectable, and
he cannot, as an editor, be charged with a want of
that virtue. If we are plunged into such a situation, his subscribers, and not Mr. Cobbet, must be
held accountable for the mischief that he has done.
It will be nothing wonderful, if, before three years
elapse, a French fleet shall anchor in the Delaware,
and compel Philadelphia to deliver to the republic
both him and them. Myriads of precedents of
this kind are to be found in history.

Dr. Ames once observed, in Congress, that
" this country is rising into a giant's strength." He
was right. Ten years more of peace will double the
population of the whole range of western states from
Vermont to Tennassee. Above an hundred and fifty
thousand people are annually added to our numbers, and the ratio of increase is constantly augmenting. It will soon amount to two hundred thousand yearly, or perhaps it has already reached that
proportion. This is an advantage enjoyed with
equal happiness by no other nation. The additional swarms will, for centuries to come, have no
want of room.

" The world is all before them, where to choose
" Their place of rest."

They will not, for the sake of subsistence, be compelled to bury themselves forever in mines, or unwholesome manufactories*, or to rush into mercenary regiments. Whatever profession they shall choose, a moderate portion of industry can hardly fail to supply a plentiful competence. But a foreign war, and most especially a French war, will assuredly retard, and may finally blast this fairest harvest of felicity that the human race hath ever seen. Recurring to the metaphor of Dr. Ames, it would be madness to expose the atlantean infant of America to the arm of a giant, whose limbs are completely formed, whose joints are firmly knit in his tremendous maturity of manhood. Let us forbear then to imitate, while we condemn the insolence of Genet, or to propagate the exploded calumnies of Fauchet. Let us no longer whet the edge and embitter the venom of our faith by reviling a distant nation for having, like most of ourselves, granted an universal right of conscience. To speak plainly, some of the holders of public stock, with Alexander Hamilton in their van, have excited this clamour. Witness the letters of PHOCION† ! These people tremble

---

* In England, excessive labour kills perhaps as many people as her foreign wars. See Buchan's Domestic Medicine.

† Alias, Dr. William Smith. The author of *An Examination of the late Proceedings in Congress*, as to Mr. Hamilton's conduct, says that the doctor "holds between three and four hundred shares in the " bank of the United States, and has obtained discounts *ad libitum*." The bank was incorporated by an act dated the 25th of February, 1791. A share contains four hundred dollars. Three hundred shares come thus to an hundred and twenty thousand dollars. In five years, from the 1st of January, 1792, to the 1st of January, 1797, Dr. Smith would draw nine thousand six hundred dollars per annum, at eight per cent.; in whole, forty-eight thousand dollars of interest. Add this to the principal sum, and, with the advantage of discounts, we may reckon safely, that he has netted in whole at least two hundred thousand dollars.

The world says that these shares in the bank were formed by an accumulation of Congress certificates, which the doctor bought

for their paper, which no well informed citizen will ever think of molesting; and, quite overshooting the mark, they wish to preserve it by plunging the continent into a British alliance and a French war. The latter is only another name for a second American revolution. Were Pichegru at Elkton to-morrow, many citizens would feel *more* than a spirit of resistance. The public can trace the contrivers of such a calamity; and, before opposing the house-breaker from without, they would perhaps begin with punishing those who had turned the key. It has already been proved in the Aurora, that the flambeau dispatch of Mr. Pickering contains elaborate misquotation and direct untruth. Our secretary takes the shortest way to provoke the rage of a conqueror alike inflexible in defeat and success, intoxicated with the homage, enriched with the spoils of Europe, and yet unexhausted by his thousand victories.

In this chapter the narrative of the year 1796 has made small progress, but something perhaps has been gained in point of information. The motion of general Smith, with which it set out, regarding the British treaty, introduced some reflections on the extreme hazard of a French war, and on the temerity or perfidy of those who have led the United States into so critical a situation. The authority of Edmund Burke, and other intelligent English writers, was next appealed to with regard to the power of that republic, as a counterpoise to the systematic and voluminous fallacies of Camillus. This induced naturally to a comparative view of the respective force of the two nations by land and sea; and the immeasurable infe-

---

from the continental army at eighteen pence or two shillings per pound. They may have originally cost him ten thousand dollars. As Hamilton was the progenitor of this master-piece of finance, the doctor has been active in displaying his gratitude.

riority of America was the result of examination. The shameful attempts made to widen the breach between the two countries was illustrated by additional remarks. We have closed with pointing out the peculiar advantages that America may hope for, beyond any other nation, from the continuance of peace ; and we have seen some of the motives of that party, who, under pretended zeal for her constitution, wish to disturb her tranquility. To elucidate the numberless advantages of a pacific system a great deal yet remains to be said. So much untruth and deception have been studiously heaped on the subject, that much previous labour is required to remove the rubbish, before even the foundation of a narrative can be properly sketched out. The most painful portion of the task is to bestow censure on persons or parties, and sometimes to hold up even a large majority of the nation in a light not extremely reputable. Flattery to the prejudices and vices of the public has hitherto been the bane of almost every historian. This fault shall, in the present work, be avoided as much as possible, though at the requisite expence of displeasing the violent of every party. When we sometimes stop to criticise the paragraph or essay in a newspaper, it should be remembered that to these publications the people of the United States do most universally resort for political knowledge. By seeing detected some dozens of notorious fictions in that shape, persons at a great distance from sources of accurate information may come to acquire the habit of thinking more boldly for themselves, and of demanding evidence before they believe an assertion.

The ensuing chapter will partly consist of specimens of federal composition, as a key to the projects and talents of that party. The next three chapters proceed to some remarks on the mode of suppressing the western insurrection, of repelling the savages on the south-western frontier, of compiling the present national debt, and of negociating Jay's treaty. The city of Washington, and the treatment of the late continental army, will merit and receive some investigation. These topics are intimately connected with the business of the session of Congress about to be described. Without some prefatory explanations of this kind, a reader might find himself in the same state of embarrassment, as if he were to begin a perusal of Homer, at the thirteenth book of the Iliad.

The first five introductory chapters having been employed on political subjects, we shall be prepared to go on with the journal of Congress. As variety is the soul of enjoyment, and as this work is intended for the entertainment of every class of people, an intermediate and miscellaneous chapter will be given on the present internal state of America. A swarm of books of travels, in this country will, among other articles of amusement, be brought on the tapis, and some of their injurious or absurd observations with respect to America will be candidly explained. To ourselves refutation may be unnecessary, but several copies of the present work will be sent to Europe, where it may chance to be reprinted. This part of the volume will there serve as a vindication of America against the errors of those, who either did not perceive truth, or did not chuse to tell it.

A work of the present kind has been much wanted. We complain that newspaper details are imperfect, prejudiced, and contradictory. These charges are true, but the printer cannot avoid affording foundation for them. The narrative of to-morrow is often at variance with that of to-day; and neither he nor his readers can, sometimes, be certain which to prefer. Like Penelope, an editor must frequently unravel at night the labour of the morning; while the public, amidst the shreds and fragments of information, can hardly determine what to believe or to reject.

The mere bulk of a daily newspaper makes its mode of information often intricate, and sometimes inacceslible. A folio volume of twelve hundred and forty-eight pages may damp the curiosity of the boldest reader. No one newspaper can relate every thing. The proprietor generally wishes, as far as he conveniently can, to decline publishing what his competitors have already given to the world. Almost every sheet is, likewise, half filled with advertisements which are entirely useless to most readers. These defects in newspapers cannot, by diligence or candour, be entirely shunned. But they point out the expediency of an annual compilation, where selection, brevity, and arrangement can more easily find place. Many citizens of Philadelphia take in six daily newspapers at an yearly expence of about fifty dollars. Three different prints are a common supply. Not one-half or perhaps one-tenth part of their contents are read; and they are sometimes cast into the fire without being opened. After such a waste of money, a charge of one or two dollars for a yearly publication cannot be held extravagant. The compiler of such a book has the greatest advantage in coming at a distance behind the events which he is to relate. He can expatiate on the ignorance of statesmen who, at easter, did not exactly foresee what was to happen next christmas, and which, a twelve month after it has past, he sees very distinctly. He is amazed at the dulness of newsprinters, who, with ten discordant accounts of a battle before them, did not, for some hours, distinguish the right one. With judgement and induſtry, he may write an uſeful performance; and, by ſome addreſs, he can look extremely wiſe at the expence of his predeceſſors.

CHAPTER II.

Character of Mr. Gallatin.—Connecticut poetry.—Major Jackſon.—John Watts.—The Boſton Federal Orrery.—Curtius.—His exaggerated ſtatement of Britiſh reſources.—Remarks on paper money.—Cauſes of the preference of Britain to France in the federal party.—Democratical conſpiracy developed by Curtius.—Defence of Jefferſon, Madiſon, Giles, Parker, Chriſtie, &c.—Fables from Pittſburgh.—Curious preſentment by a grand jury in Georgia.—Purity of Boſton.

"AS to Gallatin, the ſeditious Gallatin! What
"ſhall I ſay? How ſhall I deſcribe that com-
"pound of vice and depravity, that diſciple of
"meanneſs, corruption, debauchery, and idleneſs.
"He is a foreigner by birth and education." [Of courſe, he muſt be a raſcal]. "For ſome time
"after his arrival in this country, he wandered
"about the diſtrict of Maine, like Cain, a fugitive
"and vagabond, deſtitute of the means of honeſt
"ſubſiſtence.—The writer of this felt the effects
"of his own liberality for *months afterwards!*—
"Unable to pay for a lodging, or to purchaſe the
"neceſſaries of life, it was his cuſtom to ſleep in
"barns, and under the foliage of hedges, and not
"unuſually in the arms of ſome ſhameful ſtrumpet.
"The fragments of the kitchen ſatisfied the cra-
"vings of hunger. We find him next among the

"insurgents of the western counties in Pennsyl-
"vania. The late whisky rebellion there is prin-
"cipally attributed to him." There is ten times
more of this trumpery. It is copied from the Kennebeck Intelligencer; and was published about the beginning of the year 1797 to defeat the re-election of Mr. Dearborne, a member of Congress for Massachusetts. This is one sample of the federal eloquence of New England. If Mr. Gallatin had wished for an opportunity of inflaming the public, he could not have chosen a better topic than American finance. Yet his treatise on it is written in the most harmless stile, and seems to evince an unusual degree of good nature and forbearance.

About the same time with this production, the Connecticut Courant contained *Guillotina*, a series of rhimes, written by one Trumbull. They were republished in a Providence newspaper. A few lines will shew in what kind of kennel this Connecticut muse dabbles; and how wretchedly a certain party labour under a dearth of decent advocates.

"Once more my fond attentions turn,
"Where Pennsylvania's patriots burn.
"See Mifflin stretching out the laws,
"To aid the anti-federal cause."

This refers to the scandalous artifices employed in Pennsylvania to stop the arrival of the post at this city with votes for electors at the late election of President, and to the activity of governor Mifflin in detecting a variety of frauds made use of by the federal party. If Trumbull had felt any sense of common honesty, or common shame, he would not have stirred the ashes of a story so dishonourable to his friends.

" See him with Barclay, John, and Dallas,
" (Poor Pennsylvania keeps no gallows)
" Play many a democratic prank,
" In fleecing Pennsylvania bank."

One may say, with parson Adams, " I would ra-
" ther be the subject of such verses, than the au-
" thor." Several months before this piece appeared, Mr. Dallas had published a certificate that the bank of Pennsylvania was, at the time referred to, in his debt. This fact could not be unknown to the libeller of Hartford. But *old brass will make a new pan*, says the proverb. A fiction, though refuted in prose, may have a joyful resurrection in verse. The polite introduction of the gallows shews how strongly some of the federal party thirst for blood. They have given more than one intimation to that purpose. The New-York Gazette has an essay by William Wilcocks, dated the 15th of November, 1796. " Surely," says he, " the guillotine has not done *all* its du-
" ty!" He rails at the machine in France, yet recommends the setting up of another in America, for that is his plain inference. Some people should not, in common prudence, be so forward to speak of banks, till they give a satisfactory account of their connection with Alexander Hamilton, and *his* bank of the United States. " The books of
" transfer at the treasury, and the books at the
" bank, are held secret under the obligation of an
" oath, on all persons who use or inspect them, not
" to reveal the names or amount of stock hol-
" ders*." So much concealment can hardly be

---

* See An Examination of the late Proceedings in Congress, respecting the official conduct of the Secretary of the Treasury, dated 8th of March, 1793, p. 25.

for an honourable purpofe. The righteous are bold as a lion. Trumbull proceeds thus:

> "When Fauchet kept *an open mint*,
> "They doubtlefs had a finger in't."

This is another exploded untruth. The rhymer goes on at this rate through five columns of ribbaldry. The lines now cited are fufficient to fhew the claffical difcernment of his friends, and what fort of aid they will ftoop to receive. Swanwick, Giles, Gallatin, and a long lift of that party are reviled fadly. Dr. Franklin, his grandfon, Mr. Bache, and Thomas Paine meet with the fame ufage. General Wafhington, as ufual, is thoroughly foaked in the treacle of panegyric. But when the Prefident notified his intention to refign, the party foon began to change their tune. Wilcocks has faid "that the *fulfome adulation* of the Prefident on the "reception of the French flag was the *moft* derogatory part of his adminiftration*."

The charge of being a fulfome fycophant does not entirely agree with the fuperb encomiums, which Wilcocks has fo frequently plaiftered upon General Wafhington. This veering about lets us into the real character of fome people, and how little they care about the General, when his reputation ceafes to promote their private ends.

But this revolt was overbalanced by Major William Jackfon, furveyor of the port of Philadelphia. The fpeech of the Prefident, on the 8th of December, 1796, was followed up, next day, by the Major, with a puff in one of our newfpapers. It begins thus. "To attempt an illuftration of a "fubject in itfelf fo illumined as the fpeech of our "moft excellent Prefident were an arrogance

---

* Aurora, 31ft December, 1796.

" which we utterly disclaim." He goes on whitewashing for a considerable length. " The distant " settler on the Mississippi beholds with *exultation* " that his happiness forms a consideration in the " mind of the government, co-equal with that of " his fellow citizen on the Atlantic." He is equally entitled to protection; for his welfare is essential to the union. Hence exultation would be misplaced. A President and other officers of government are paid for doing their duty; and, if they fail of performing it to public satisfaction, there are, if we could only believe so, abundance of men as good as the best of them. Major Jackson here points at the Spanish treaty; but he might have reflected that the same administration, by the weakest and meanest species of trimming, has induced the danger of a French war, and if that happens, the western waters will be more completely blocked up than ever.

" Is there a seaman belonging to the United " States, or a connection of that valuable class of " citizens, whose vows are *not* offered for the " good of him, whose head and heart have been so " much occupied with their concerns?" This was an unfortunate topic. But the Major, as a military man, knows that the weakest part of a fortification has most need of defence. " Where is the " veteran whose bosom does not beat in responsive " applause to the eulogium of Washington on " military skill?" If, at the creation of the public debt, he had taken a single step to save them from indigence, if he had refused to sign the statute of limitations, and some other laws not much better[*], their bosoms would have been more likely to beat. No peculiar share of blame in this business lies on

[*] American Annual Register, chap. v. and xi.

the Prefident. The great body of the people have betrayed entire indifference about the old foldiers, otherwife fuch acts never could have paft. At the fame time money is unaccountably wafted on favages. John Watts, a Creek warrior, boafts of having taken thirty-three fcalps. In the latter part of 1796, this fellow, and a number of others, came to Philadelphia, where they feafted at an expence of four thoufand dollars*. Thus much for Major Jackfon.

Nothing is, in itfelf, more comtemptible, and nothing tends more certainly to defeat its own purpofe, than extravagant praife. Encomium never appeared in a more farcical fhape, than it has often affumed in poetry. Of this fort of writing the Bofton Federal Orrery afforded a miferable fpecimen, in the *Gratulatory Addrefs* on the birth-day of the Prefident, in February, 1796.

If a ftranger knew nothing elfe of the hiftory of the American war, than what he could glean from this copy of verfes, he would infer, that General Wafhington had fingly, and exclufively, exterminated the Britifh armies in a perfonal combat. In the laft line of the firft ftanza, this rhymer of Maffachufetts calls him the " *Godlike Wafhington.*" This is fomething worfe than mere nonfenfe. It approaches to indecency and profanation.

In the third ftanza we meet with a parallel between General Wafhington and ———: let the reader, if he can, conjecture the counter part of this comparifon! Mofes, the Jew, is introduced as not fuperior in legiflative or military merits, to the leader in our revolution. As if that were not

---

* This is ftated on the authority of Mr. Chriftopher Greenup, a reprefentative from Kentucky. The writer has not yet feen the accompt.

enough, there follows a parallel between the President and the Creator of the Universe; and though this style may seem ridiculous, incredible, and mad, it has absolutely been adopted by the bard of the *Boston Federal Orrery.* After alluding to the miraculous passage of the Red sea, he adds, that

"By *night* your pillar, and your *cloud* by day,"
"He (the President) fought your battles."

Here is an attempt to blend the services and exertions of the American colonies with the omniscient superintendancy of the Supreme Being. Effrontery or impiety cannot proceed much farther. Of such panegyrists, Dr. Edward Young has observed, that

"Their praise degrades, as if a fool should mean,
"By spitting in your face, to make it clean!"

For the sake of completeness, our author should have run a comparison of Mount *Vernon* with Mount *Sinai*, the Delaware at Trenton and the Arabian Gulph. Between such impious jargon and legitimate poetry, there is the same distinction as between the trowel of a bricklayer, and the pencil of Titian.

About the same time, another piece of excellence, too singular to be forgotten, appeared in a Philadelphia newspaper. Here it is:

" ADVICE TO COUNTRY POLITICIANS.
" Go weed your corn, and plow your land,
" And by Columbia's interest stand,
 " Cast prejudice away;
" To able heads leave state affairs,
" Give *railing* o'er and say your prayers,
 " For stores of corn and hay."

This is the first stanza of that brilliant production. American farmers are very obligingly advised to give over *railing*. The writer must by this word mean *remonstrating* against the treaty of Mr. Jay. As to *able* heads, five-sixths of the members of Congrefs are farmers, and hence this admonition applies to them. They had better, as it seems, go home and mind their ploughs. The next and concluding stanza runs, or hobbles, in the following words.

> "With politics ne'er break your sleep,
> "But *ring your hogs*, and shear your sheep,
> "And rear your lambs and calves;
> "And Washington will take due care,
> "That Britons never more shall dare
> "Attempt to make you slaves."

The felicity of the rhime in *calves* and *slaves*, proves that the auricular accuracy of this laureate keeps pace with his other qualifications. It is a very handsome compliment to the farmers of the United States to tell them that their understandings are just equal to putting a ring into the snout of a hog. The odes of Horace, and Martial's epigrams, were written in the sink of Roman tyranny; yet, they contain nothing correspondent with the abject vulgarity of this advice. The piece is, from first to last, a stupid insult on the feelings of a free country. This Philadelphian bard seems a formidable rival to the vilest sycophant that ever licked up the spittle of despotism.

The people of America boast loudly of their freedom, and of their superiority, in this respect, to every other nation; yet the spirit of servility in writing birth-day verses, exceeds all bounds.

One of the gazettes of this city, after the birthday in February, 1795, had another piece of the same shabby strain. It filled two entire columns; and, which shews the wretchedness, or rather nonentity of literary taste, it was printed, *in at least one other newspaper*.

Alluding to the friends of democratic societies, this poet calls them *sorcerers in their cells*. After raving through this comparison for a few impudent lines, worthy of Webster and his Minerva, we are told that

> "Already Washington, like Atlas stands,
> "*Alone* supporting empire with his hands;
> "*Alone*, the prop of all this vast machine,
> "The mortal hero of the immortal scene."

The genius of *Columbia* (this is the new-fangled rhyming name for America), then bounces into the following exclamation:

> "Chaos will come, when Washington expires,
> "Hide Freedom's sun, and quench her starry fires.
> "A gift so fatal, why should I retain?
> "Realms so accurst, why should my power sustain?
> "No, let these regions to the deep be hurl'd.
> "Take back, unfathom'd ocean, take your world."

A charming proposal undoubtedly! that nature shall dissolve on the death of an American president. There is reason to think that neither George the third, nor any of his predecessors, was ever saluted with such execrable buffoonery. If the decalogue had said, *Thou shalt not write nonsense*, this author must have been a dismal sinner. It is the happy privilege of an American, that he may prattle and print, in what way he pleases, and *without any one to make him afraid*.

Augustus Cæsar found it for his interest to be bountiful and grateful to Virgil and Horace. Their verses, like stepping stones across the mire, partly saved his name from that reproach, through which it has waded down to posterity. The reputation of our President requires not the help of poetical crutches. To him we may apply what the king of Prussia, in his memoirs, hath said of his brother Henry: *The highest encomium which we can bestow, is an impartial narrative of his actions*.

As a sketch of the current stile, we shall notice

one other writer of the day. Curtius published twelve letters in defence of Jay's treaty. The points now to be investigated, refer to what he says about the relative force of France and Britain, and the violent manner in which he speaks of those who differ from his political opinions.

As an evidence of the greatness of Britain, Curtius, No. vii. says, that her East-India territories " yield an annual revenue of more than eight mil- " lions sterling." Camillus, also, No. vii. lays much weight upon the ships from India to England in 1795, having cargoes " computed to be worth " between four and five millions sterling." While an alliance with that country is recommended, and such accounts given of its wealth and power, only a few words are needful to set the matter right. Three-fourths of this revenue go to the expence of supporting the government of the country; part is absorbed by investments and commercial charges, and the remainder is consumed in paying the interest of the Indian debts of the company. By the latest advices received, on the 16th of June, 1795, from India, they were owing, in that part of the world, seven millions three hundred thousand pounds sterling. This was stated in the House of Commons, on the above date, by Mr. Dundas. The company owe likewise another enormous debt in England, a part of which, under the name of *bonded*, amounted then to two millions sterling. Thus, when the company have paid the charges of government, the interest of their debts, and mercantile expences, they are, by several millions sterling, *worse than nothing*. They have been often on the brink of bankruptcy, and would have stopt payment many years ago, if Parliament had not lent them, in advance, large sums of money*. It is

---

* See Smith's Wealth of Nations.

UNITED STATES

hard to think that such an establishment can add to the real strength of a nation. Camillus and Curtius need not build much on that source of opposition to France*.

---

* As the world in general appear to be mistaken on this head, the following statements, laid before Parliament by Dundas, are inserted. They are for two different years; and shew how little England has, in reality, gained by her catalogue of Oriental crimes.

General state of revenues and charges in India.

Total of the revenues of Bengal, Madras, and Bombay, 1793-4, as above stated,	£.8,294,399
Charges of ditto, (including 66,358l. supplies to Bencoolen, &c.)	6,181,504
Revenues more than charges,	2,112,895
Interest on debts paid from this sum,	458,043
Surplus revenues,	1,654,852
Add—import, sales, and certificates,	475,994
Sums applicable to investments, payment of commercial charges, &c. (exclusive of 20,000l. gained by issuing notes,	2,130,846

Estimates for 1794-5.

Total revenues of Bengal, Madras, and Bombay, estimated 1794-5,	£.7,790,807
Total charges, ditto, (including 104,632l. supplies to Bencoolen, &c.)	5,923,063
	1,867,744
Deduct interest on debts, per No. XVI.	437,047
Estimated surplus revenue,	1,430,697
Add No. XV. Estimated sales of imports, and amount of certificates,	380,669
Amount estimated to be applicable to investments, payment of commercial charges, &c. &c.	1,811,366

On the 24th of May, 1791, Charles Fox said, in the House of Commons, that the company's debts amounted to sixteen millions eight hundred thousand pounds sterling. These details agree in substance with the summary in the text. Much noise was made both

When Curtius speaks of Europe, he stumbles in the same way as Camillus. " Great Britain, though " her army was destroyed in the Netherlands, re- " tains *all* her activity and resources*. Govern- " ment has not been compelled to distress her trade " to man her navy." She never manned twenty sail of the line, at one time, without distressing trade. A general press is the sure consequence of such an equipment. The scarcity of seamen has been very great. Again. " Her debt has indeed " been augmented; but still immense sums of mo- " ney (of *paper* he should have said) are offered, " and the only question with government is, whose " *money* shall be received on loan." That is on account of the extravagant premiums. As for money, all the gold and silver coin in England would not pay above one-nineteenth part of the debts that she has contracted. If the island could be divided into three equal shares, it would require one of them to satisfy the public creditors. " Britain, " at this moment, maintains as commanding an at- " titude among the powers of the earth, as *at any* " *former period.*" Only two pages before, Curtius had said, " that her land forces were defeated and " cut to pieces, the last campaign (1794), is unde-

for and against Jay's conduct on account of the stipulations respec- ting the East India trade. When it is observed how little even the East India company can make, who are masters of India itself, a sus- picion may be excited, that this branch of commerce was not worth much contention. American ships can sail to China, without leave of England; and that is the most important branch of the Oriental market.

* To fill up these armies, the country was, in some places, half depopulated. On the 24th of March, 1795, Mr. Sheridan inform- ed the House of Commons, that one magistrate had attested twen- ty-one thousand recruits. About the same time it was stated in the house, that Manchester, since the war began, had lost twelve thousand people.

" niable; and there is no queſtion that any com-
" bat by land would be decided *in favour* of
" France." When England won the battles of
Blenheim, Quebec, and Minden, ſhe was equally
ſuperior *at ſea*. Curtius has no ground to compare
the preſent attitude to that of any former period.

With the ſame judgment this writer rejects all
danger of a Britiſh revolution. If England cannot
be happy enough to make a peace, ſhe will be ex-
cluded from every port in Europe, as ſhe is at preſent from two-thirds of them; and then her commerce and her power muſt decline together. It is
worth while to conſider the effects of this turn in
her affairs on the ſituation of America. One of the
conſequences muſt be the exploſion of her paper
money. The quantity in circulation may be in
England about three times, and in Scotland ſixty
times greater than that of gold and ſilver. This
is a rough gueſs. Every year of war augments
the quantity of paper. The firſt effects of a national bankruptcy would be an utter deſtruction of
credit. Currency would again be reſtricted to
the precious metals; and they would increaſe to
three, four, or five times the value that they now
bear. The ſilver ſix-pence, which, in London,
would not, laſt winter, buy a pound of beef, will
then purchaſe three, four, or five pounds, as was
the caſe fifty or an hundred years ago. Hence it
follows, that the manufactures of Britain will fall
ſurpriſingly in their prices, becauſe the ſame quantity of labour that formerly was worth half a guinea, will then probably be offered for three or four
ſhillings, or leſs. Another cauſe muſt cheapen Britiſh exports. The country being rid of public
debt, will, of courſe, caſt off a great proportion of
her taxes; for, at this time, including the expence
of the collection of revenue to pay its intereſt, the

debt requires about sixteen millions sterling per annum. Even now the manufactures of the United States cannot, in many cases, bear a competition in point of cheapness with those of Britain. But a sudden fall of one-half of the former rate, or perhaps a still greater reduction must put an end to them, unless their cost can also be lessened. The price of so many commodities having sunk so fast, they will, of course, drag all other kinds of property after them, till matters shall be restored to their common level, because the situation would be too forced and unnatural for any length of endurance. The price of flour, for example, could not long continue at eight or ten dollars, in America, while England raised it for two or three. The value of lands, houses, and personal labour sinking with such rapidity would produce numerous failures, and the quantity of money afloat being more than was wanted, the precious metals, as on similar occasions, would drive paper out of the market. This must, in some degree, give a check to banking. Another class of people would suffer essentially, and that is the holders of public stock. From its nature the fall would be more severely felt in this than most other property. Land, when equally ploughed, will yield as large a crop as now, whatever might be the want of money. The scarcity of houses in the sea port towns, would prevent them from standing empty. Good tradesmen are always needful and must be paid a subsistence. But stock being entirely unproductive of itself, unless as to the interest paid by the public, its decline in price would operate as a real loss, since it is only worth what it can bring in the market.

Thus the ruin of the British system of funds, and paper money, would run the hazard of shaking the same systems in the United States. This appears to be the reason why persons connected with them have such a violent prepossession for British success, and so strong an aversion to the ascendancy of France. The destruction of public credit in that country, soon after the revolution began, and the mixture of despotism and anarchy which have since prevailed, inspired every holder of stocks with horror. A considerable number of these public creditors were from the eastern states, and but few from the southern. The whole influence of the fiscal corps, was directed against the French revolution. As a requisite counterpoise, the party wished to cast America into the arms of Britain. The bankers and stock-holders were joined by two other classes. The one of these consisted of British tories, who had been permitted to continue here in the war, or who had returned since the end of it. Another order of men, in whom the motives of the former were often blended, had frequent occasion for the discounting of bills, to support their credit. Within a few years, since banks became numerous, there has arisen an extreme spirit of mercantile speculation, which could only expand its flight on the wings of paper-money. All these sorts of people, with a few exceptions, and all on whom they had influence, joined in reprobating the French revolution. Alexander Hamilton has always been considered as the leader of this party. His official powers gave him a very considerable sway in the management of the public funds, and the bank of the United States. Under him, the party have acted, or are thought to have acted with system and spirit. But while they were thus loudly declaiming, and often with justice, against the shocking barbarities perpetrated in France, many of them have forfeited their pretensions to purity, by promoting, to the utmost of their skill, a civil war among the United States themselves, and likewise a quarrel with the republic. Their designs have been gradually developed by the course of events; and it has at length been fairly confessed, both by their words and actions, that they are willing to go to war with France. They dread her example as contagious for the destruction of their financial fabric, which they constantly mention not by its proper name, but as the *constitution*.

Having premised these particulars, we shall now quote some of the expressions that Curtius adopts in his twelfth letter. " There is a confederation " of characters, from New-Hampshire to Geor- " gia, arrayed in opposition, either to the consti- " tution of the United States, to its administration, " or to particular men in office. The opposition " of the principal men *in this confederacy* can be " traced to some known causes, originally of a " personal nature. Disappointment in application " for some office, or the failure of some favourite " scheme in their political system, has converted " many of the friends of the late revolution into " determined opposers of the general system of the " present administration."

This charge is daily repeated in an infinity of different shapes. No facts are specified by Curtius, except an indistinct reference to Genet. " The con- " duct of this ambassador is entirely unexampled " in the history of civilized nations[*]." He was received with tumultuous hospitality, and childish exultation. But when it was discovered that he wanted to plunge the nation into a war with Britain, this envoy instantly sunk into neglect. Curtius says, " that his views were counteracted by the President, " seconded by *the northern states*." One would

---

[*] Carey's edition of Guthrie's Geography, vol. ii. p. 294.

imagine that the militia of New-England had been ordered to march, that the legiflatures had taken fome important ftep, or at leaft that their members in Congrefs had introduced fome motion to the houfe, which led the way for recalling the French minifter. Not one of thefe circumftances ever happened. The impertinence and indifcretion of Genet were, in a few months, vifible to all men of fenfe. His importance fhrunk immediately to nothing. As to *feconding*, it was manifefted in no way by New-England, unlefs fcurrilous newfpaper paragraphs deferve that name. Even this commodity was as plentifully beftowed at New-York and Philadelphia, as at Bofton. The reign of Genet was very fhort. He arrived in this city on the 17th of May, 1793, and his recall was folicited by the American Secretary of State in a letter dated the 16th of Auguft following. This letter, though different indeed from the ftile of Timothy Pickering's epiftle to Pinckney, was as fharp as decorum would permit. The one haggles like a rufty knife. The other cuts like a razor. The next news from France was, that, if Genet had returned home, Robefpierre would have made him look out at *the little national window*. Even the letter defiring his recall was not fo much as wrote by a native of New-England, though Henry Knox, as Secretary at War, was then a member of the American cabinet. Neither did Alexander Hamilton, though alfo in office, write any part of it; for the difpatch has none of his entangled periods. It was drawn by Thomas Jefferfon of Virginia. The ftory of the Prefident being *feconded by the northern ftates* is, therefore, an entire falfehood.

The hiftory of Genet has been thus examined, becaufe it is the only fact to which Curtius refers. We now go back to his quotation, and fhall begin with what he calls *a confederation of characters arrayed against the constitution, &c.*

The most eminent personage of the party accused is Thomas Jefferson, the single man who assisted the President in driving Genet out of office. But if the democrats, as, for the sake of distinction, we must call them, were so violently attached to Genet, they must have held his antagonist Jefferson in the utmost abhorence. Yet this is so far from being the case, that, at the distance of four years, their respect and friendship are unabated. Thus, as to Genet, the charge against the great body of the democrats involves a gross contradiction. Whether a few individuals do still admire what he did, cannot be worth enquiring. If he was often in the wrong, he was sometimes in the right. The wretched attack made upon him by John Jay and Rufus King was only fit for two old women in a chimney corner. It disgraced the national character of America, by shewing what weak men had been elected as a chief justice and a senator.

Curtius speaks of *the principal men in this confederacy*, and *their disappointment in application for some office*. Neither can this apply to Jefferson. He had been ambassador to France. He was then Secretary of State. Little more was to be had. Sometime after he resigned his office. The resignation was voluntary. This appears from the choice of a successor to him. Randolph was of the same party and principles; which proves that the President only chose him because Jefferson would no longer keep the office.

As to the failure of *some favourite scheme in their political system*, of this also Mr. Jefferson stands clear. His retirement was heard of with general regret. Nay, so much does he possess the confidence of every state in the union, that Mr. Adams was perhaps the only man on the continent who could have had a tolerable chance against him for the presidency. It is singular that the principal person of a confederacy against government should possess the esteem even of its friends.

We must enquire among the representatives in Congress for the second leader of the confederation of characters. This is James Madison, esq. of Virginia. Mr. Vans Murray said, some years ago, in Congress, that he might be called the father of the present constitution. It would be strange if he was already impatient to strangle his own offspring. Of the private character of the man it is needless to speak, for the stock-holding newspapers confine themselves to an incomprehensible jargon about conspiracies. He certainly had no hand in promoting the popularity of citizen Genet. He was in Virginia during the period of the citizen's importance. It is doubtful if they were ever in the same room together. The classical elegance, and logical acuteness of Madison bear the same resemblance to the scampering fustian of Genet which Madeira has to ditch-water. It is impossible that two persons so contrasted in every thing intellectual could have agreed, for a single day, in any confederation. Besides, Mr. Madison is in close friendship with Mr. Jefferson, who put an end to the citizen. *Disappointment in application for some office* cannot be imputed to this gentleman, unless the office can be named which he was disappointed of obtaining. Very few places in the gift of the President would have been a temptation. Mr. Jefferson did not, as Secretary of State, save money. By absence from his estate, he very likely lost as much as he received for residing in Philadelphia. If Mr. Madison had undertaken an office in this city worth two thousand dollars a year, it would have been of no pecuniary advantage to him, while his plantation was lying half wasted for want of his presence. But none of the federal hacks has ever pretended that Mr. Madison met with a repulse in solicitation. They say that he has been in the pay of France. Yet he just now despitefully gives up his seat in Congress, thus robbing the accusation of the last rag which covered its nakedness. He never had a cent from the government of this country, excepting his six dollars per day. As to *favourite schemes*, Mr. Madison, at least for the last four years, has been as often in a majority as out of it.

Thus we have got over the first and second heads of the confederation. The third in order is William B. Giles, another Virginian. Almost all which has been said of Mr. Madison suits him. He never applied for any office. Perhaps the executive has not one to bestow, that, in a pecuniary light, would deserve his acceptance. He has an independent fortune. He is a lawyer of eminence. He could make a handsome income by his profession, if he chose to stay at home, and mind that only. He could live on his own farm in Virginia for a tenth part of the money which he must spend in attending Congress. To such a man six dollars a day, or any place that the executive could give him, is not an object; and nothing but sheer ignorance can excuse a party writer for holding such language about him.

If we look over the other members who have often voted in opposition to executive oracles, the same observations as to personal independence apply to perhaps every one of them. For instance, Gabriel Christie is a merchant in Havre de Grace, a village at the mouth of the Susquehannah. If he wants to recommence planter, he has a large farm of his own a few miles up the river, in one of the moſt healthy and deſirable ſpots in Maryland. Such a man could gain nothing by confuſion, nor could the executive offer him almoſt any poſt poſſeſſing a lucrative temptation. An office in Philadelphia, or any where out of his own country, with a ſalary of fifteen hundred dollars a year would be as a feather. The caſe is ſimilar with Meſſrs. Baldwin, Blount, Heath, Page, Parker, New, Nicholas, Macon, M'Dowell, Carnes, Venable, Preſton, and others. They have either independent property, or lucrative profeſſions, or both. They could gain nothing by diſturbing government. They never made the ſmalleſt attempt of the kind; nor has any of the ſcribblers, who abuſed them in wholeſale, ever pretended to ſpecify a ſingle fact, and much leſs to bring evidence of a ſingle fact, that looked like a confederacy againſt government. Such malicious nonſenſe may do very well for a Connecticut tavern, a Kennebeck Journal, or a town meeting of Stockbridge, when our patriotic citizens are toaſting *John Jay and the papers!* It may ſuit Samuel Dexter in a circle at the dancing ſchool, or Daniel Buck in an addreſs to ſome mob, who are ringing the town bells for joy at his return to Vermont.

After the words *ſeconded by the northern ſtates*, Curtius proceeds thus. " But the party which *ori-*
" *ginally* rallied under that man, (Genet) ſtill ex-
" iſts, and forms a league co-extenſive with the
" United States, connected in all its parts, and act-
" ing by a ſingle impulſe." Dr. Swift, ſpeaking of Gulliver's Travels, ſays, that they contained *a lie at every ſecond word.* If a ſingle word could convey an untruth, Curtius would be an unrivalled maſter in that ſort of brevity. The party, ſuch as it is, exiſted in all its vigour, for ſeveral years before Genet landed on this continent, a fact known

to every perfon who has croffed even the threfhold of American hiftory. As for the *fingle* impulfe, if the *confederates* were always to behave to each other with common civility, there might be fome poffibility of the charge being true. But they are conftantly differing among themfelves on ferious topics. For example, Colonel Parker, on the 10th of February, 1797, made an able and earneft fpeech in defence of the three frigates. He was fupported, *manibus pedibufque*, by John Swanwick, who, if cartloads of flander can beftow diftinction, fhines like a ftar of the firft magnitude in the democratical zodiac. They were oppofed by three of their confederates, Meffrs. Chriftie, Nicholas, and Giles. The poor frigates were kicked about, as if they had been fo many wafhing tubs. Nicholas wifhed them to rot on the ftocks, as an inftructive monument of national folly. Chriftie did not care if they were reduced to afhes. Giles declared that he always had oppofed, and always fhould oppofe them, in every ftage, and every fhape. This is only one inftance out of fifty or an hundred, that occur in every feffion, where the gentlemen ftigmatized as acting by a fingle impulfe, do fhew very plainly that they value not one farthing the opinions of each other; but fpeak immediately from their own caprice or conviction. We go back to Curtius.

" Thus, in the infancy of our empire, the bane of
" all republics, is already diffufed over our coun-
" try, and *poifons the whole body politic!*" [It is natural that weak or ignorant people fhould find their heads half cracked, while they hear of fuch terrible phantoms.] "Faction is a difeafe, which has pro-
" ved fatal to all popular governments; but in Ame-
" rica it has affumed an afpect more formidable than
" in *any other country*." [He affigns fome foolifh reafons, and then adds:] " But in America, faction

" has affumed confiftency and fyftem. It is *a con-*
" *fpiracy perpetually exifting*, an oppofition organi-
" zed and difciplined, for the purpofes of defeat-
" ing the regular exercife of the conftitutional pow-
" ers of our government, whenever a meafure does
" not pleafe the *fecret* leaders of the confederacy."

Curtius ought to name thofe fecret leaders, and to give fome traits of the progrefs of this confpiracy. In his labyrinthian ftile, it is impoffible ever to take a faft hold. He is one of the moft decent writers of the federal party; and this is the univerfal way in which they make an affault on private characters. In the laft four years of chiming, they have hardly advanced four intelligible affertions. Their charges glide from the grafp of ftraight inquiry, like the fhade of Anchifes from the embrace of his fon. The Tom Thumb tale about Fauchet bribing Randolph, has been fafely conducted to its grave in the American Annual Regifter. As for the weftern infurrection, Findley, in his hiftory of it, has fhewed that Gallatin was fo far from being an infurgent, that he had a principal fhare in preventing mifchief. It is deplorable that a party fo pregnant with charges fhould be fo unfortunate in their few attempts at fpecification. " Already," fays Curtius, " are the heads of our govern-
" ment denounced as traitors; already is our coun-
" try threatened with civil war:—If the oppofers
" of *the treaty* can poffibly embroil our country in
" civil war, it will be effected."

There is a confiderable famenefs in the dialect of the Hamiltonians. Their conftant cry is the danger of a civil war; and the ufual menace a disjunction of the eaftern from the fouthern ftates. This railing comes exclufively from the eaftern and fome parts of the middle ftates. To the fouth of Pennfylvania no newfpaper embattles itfelf againft the

Yankees. Of the three daily prints in Baltimore, not one is attached closely to either party. A majority of the inhabitants voted for Jay's bantling. In the whole country, down to Georgia, you meet with no gazette lying and raving in the stile of Curtius and the Columbian Centinel. The Virginians encourage no newsprinter to balance accounts in black ball with Webster; or to proclaim the people of New-England bankrupts, swindlers, conspirators, and traitors. They are not, with the monotony of a magpie, eternally croaking about the danger of rebellion. Their souls do not sit so much upon thorns as those of their eastern fellow citizens. There appears to be less vinegar in their composition. At least, by judging from the state of the press, in these opposite quarters of the union, a bystander would make that inference. Envy may have some share in this barking. The population of Massachusetts and Connecticut is stationary, and their territory is but small. From New-York, inclusive, all the states to the southward, excepting three*, have an immense extent of new land, which holds out the certain prospect of augmented wealth, population, and importance.

The relative proportion of exports from the middle and southern states has augmented greatly, and must continue to do so. Boston, formerly as populous as Philadelphia, hath still but about twenty thousand inhabitants, while those of its late rival have augmented to sixty thousand. New-York, which formerly was much its inferior, hath fifty thousand. But Baltimore is the most provoking instance of recent ascendency. This town arose, but as yesterday, from a marsh; and rivals or eclipses the wealth and population of the metropolis of New-

---

* New-Jersey, Delaware, and Maryland.

England. Virginia is twelve times larger than Maſſachuſetts; and has already double her population. So great a difference of numbers did not exiſt in the cenſus, of 1775, and it is hourly augmenting.

"Like ancient ladies when refus'd a kiſs,"

Theſe two New-England ſtates are not perhaps pleaſed to foreſee the decline of their conſequence. Whatever may be the cauſe, the rancour of many of their citizens againſt the ſouthern ſtates appears to be of the bittereſt kind. Judging from the Columbian Centinel, a foreigner might be led to believe that the latter have ſubſcribed a ſolemn league of revolution; that troops have been raiſed, and magazines formed; that half our citizens are preparing to butcher the reſt; that Madiſon is a ſecond Cataline, and Giles a Cæſar Borgia. A conſiderable minority in New-England agree with the politics of Virginia. In May, 1794, the inhabitants of Boſton held a very numerous town-meeting, at which, by a great majority, they agreed to recommend to Congreſs to prolong the embargo. An additional ſixty days of famine would have put an effectual end to Britiſh piracies in the Weſt Indies; and would likewiſe have been of more ſervice to France than an aid of ten thouſand land forces, and ten ſhips of the line. A copy of the Boſton reſolutions, ſigned by the town clerk, was tranſmitted not only to their repreſentative, Dr. Ames, but a ſecond alſo, ſuperſcribed to Mr. Madiſon, Colonel Parker, and Mr. Giles. This told pretty plainly that they truſted the three latter gentlemen farther, in that inſtance, than their own repreſentative. Perhaps, however, this town-meeting conſiſted likewiſe of *conſpirators. Aves unius generis facile congregantur.* The fooliſh word *jacobin* is rung in endleſs changes;

while Curtius gravely declares that " private " affociations are formed and extending their influ- " ence over our country." All this is the vileſt traſh imaginable.

The calumny of the federal patriots is not confined to the ſouthern ſtates. The whiſky riots in the weſ- tern counties of Pennſylvania have ſupplied them with a happy fund for declamation. Of their la- bours in this line, accept the following ſpecimen.

In a Philadelphia newſpaper of the 8th of March, 1796, there is inſerted an extract of a letter, dated Pittſburgh, the 25th of February preceding, which contains unexpected intelligence: The extract extends to one third of a column, and repreſents the weſtern counties, as having relapſed into a ſtate of anarchy. " It is generally believed," ſays the writer, " that near half the men in this country " have croſſed the river to take poſſeſſion of what- " ever land they could get. *This town is almoſt* " *empty!* Some large parties are gone with an in- " tent to clear all before them, where the land is " good. Reports from the woods ſay, that a ſtrong " party coming to a houſe, they turn out the weak- " er, and a ſtronger coming on turn them out, ſo " that ſome houſes *change their owners two or three* " *times a day.*" This makes about a fourth part of the extract, which is all exactly in the ſame ſtyle, though ſome paſſages ſoar quite above comprehen- ſion.

No farther intelligence about this tumult reach- ed us, till the 28th of March brought forth a ſe- cond extract of an epiſtle from Pittſburgh, dated the 12th of March. It corroborates the former news, affirming that " *the poor people are paſ-* " *ſing the Alleghany in legions with their families* to " reſide, and eſtabliſh actual ſettlements," &c. Both letters, but the ſecond in particular, have a multiplicity of ranting bombastical phrases, which would be apt to make their veracity suspected. Both of them speak much about a Mr. ——, who is doing some inexplicable wonders. Both contain a profusion of such egregious nonsense, and malicious falsehood, that they are in themselves, an hundred and fifty degrees beneath animadversion.

No further notice was taken in any newspaper about this insurrection. Hence it is natural to infer that both pieces came from the same pen, and that both were written with one rascally view, that of spreading a false alarm among the people in the Atlantic regions of the union. If such revolutionary wonders were going forward, beyond the mountains, it was strange that nobody should hear about them but one correspondent. It is the business of every good citizen, to pluck up by the roots such incendiary slander. There seems a double barbarity in ripping open the scar of a wound that is but just skinned over.

The bad effect of such reports was very well described in Congress by Mr. Baldwin. On the 1st of December, 1794, this gentlemen observed that in a country so extensive as America, and where the people are so widely scattered, it was a work of immense difficulty to have a regular and accurate account of the measures of government communicated through every part of the union. It can scarcely be conceived, said he, by those who have no call to visit the interior and more retired parts of the country, how much the peace of society is disturbed by the malicious propagation of political falsehood. The most wicked lies are kept in circulation, for months together, and before they can be effectually contradicted, the people have become almost frantic. For example, Mr. Baldwin mentioned, (and editors of newspapers in every part of the union, ought to quote this part of his obfervations, as a *caveat* in future,) that it had been afferted that a poll tax of forty fhillings per head, has been laid on all the inhabitants, that the excife has been extended to *wheat*, to *looms*, and to inftruments of hufbandry, and that the late draughts of the eighty thoufand militia, are fold to France to carry on the war! It is probable, that riots and infurrections are fomented by thefe rumours more than by all other caufes. If a conftant and regular publication of all that is done could reach every part of the United States, it would be an effectual, and, perhaps the only cure for thefe mifchiefs. The people of this extenfive country have, for thefe ten years, enjoyed all the effential benefits of fociety, on very eafy terms. A man with five or fix hundred acres of land is fcarcely called upon for a dollar of taxes in a year. Perhaps no people on earth ever enjoyed fo fully the advantages of fociety with fo few burdens. Is it not a diftreffing confideration, that when we have fo few real evils, we fhould create to ourfelves imaginary ones, that give us fo much ufelefs uneafinefs? Some wrong meafures have taken place, and hereafter will take place, and nobody can expect that any kind of conduct will give *univerfal* fatisfaction*.

But a very fmall difference is perceivable in the fcale of morality from one end to another of America. Of this remark the Yazoo bufinefs afforded a notable inftance. By an act paft in January, 1795, a junto in the affembly of Geor-

---

* In the courfe of the difcuffion of this day, Mr. Hillhoufe having fpoke for fome time, Mr. Dayton rofe next. He began by remarking, that it could not be expected that he was to make any obfervations on what had been faid by the member juft fitten down, as *he did not hear ten words which the gentleman faid*. This was owing to noife made by members in the houfe.

gia fold to four companies of land-jobbers some vacant lands of that state. On the 2d of March, 1795, Mr. Harper said in Congress that the sale covered thirty millions of acres of the finest land in the world, and most admirably situated for commerce and emigration. It might, every foot of it, be made worth half a dollar per acre. Its settlement would tend to open the Mississippi navigation. These *thirty millions* of acres had been sold, he said, for *five hundred thousand dollars!* A more villainous transaction cannot be conceived. Yet, strange to tell! many persons in the religious town of Boston were deeply concerned in buying from these purchasers. The newspapers said that the speculators of that place had agreed to give some millions of dollars for a part of this booty. The reader knows that the bargain hath since been set aside, but that does not lessen the infamy of those connected with it. The following extract from the presentment of the grand jury of Chatham county in Georgia, at the October term of 1796, gives an entertaining picture of the parties concerned.

"We further and abominably present those abo-
"minable and iniquitous grants of pine barren
"land, which have been palmed upon foreigners
"and northern citizens, the plats of which have
"been decorated generally with timber not found
"on them; and most of the pretended tracts sold
"are not in existence, to the injury of the cha-
"racter of the state, and the honest citizens thereof;
"nine-tenths of whom behold the speculation with
"the utmost abhorrence, considering the measure
"calculated to injure their reputation and to cheat
"the unwary, to add to the pelf of a few men, who
"are void of principle and honour, and who would
"sacrifice their country and its rights to increase
"their own property. We are sorry to say, that

"among those characters, are those high in office in the United States; and two judges thereof, to wit, James Wilson of the Supreme Court of the United States, and Nathaniel Pendleton, of the District Court of this state, together with James Gunn, Senator from this state to Congress, have been foremost in influencing the legislature which passed the pretended Yazoo law, bartering the rights of this state, and the most fertile tract in the United States, for a mere song; and which, if it were to be deemed legal, those concerned have sold for ten times as much, which the state, by proper management, might have put into her treasury.

"We congratulate our fellow citizens, however, on the virtue of the last legislature, which declared the said pretended sale, constitutionally null and void, as fraudulent and corrupt, and we hope our fellow citizens at large, will now exhibit their virtue, by sending such men only to the next legislature, as are known to be free from speculation, and will respect our rights by continuing and confirming the annulling law. It is only by a firmness of conduct in the citizens at large, on this important occasion, that our rights can be respected in Congress, and at home; that this species of gambling can be discountenanced, and speculating sharpers be defeated, which is as much to be desired, on account of morality and our rising generation, as the future repose of society, and the reputation of our growing community.

"We further present on this head the attempt by Alexander Moultrie and others to drag this state into the federal court, to answer a suit in equity, under a former pretended Yazoo sale. We abhor both speculations alike, and we recom-

"mend to the officers of the ſtate, who may have been ſerved with copies of the bill filed in the ſaid ſuit, to make no anſwer thereto until the next meeting of the legiſlature, who we hope will remonſtrate to Congreſs on this ſubject. We cannot ſuppoſe the ſtate liable to be ſued, and in this caſe we hope ſhe will preſerve her dignity, by refuſing an anſwer, particularly in a court where the judges have been guiding the laſt ſpeculations, and where ſhe can conſequently expect no juſtice. We hope that the amendment to the conſtitution, ſo unanimouſly entered into by Congreſs, againſt the ſuability of a ſtate, will not be leaped over to anſwer the vile purpoſes of the moſt infamous ſpeculation."

The above preſentment gives no ſublime notion of American juriſprudence, even at its fountain head. What follows will ſhew the pollution of ſome of its inferior ſtreams. In a work like this, the wrongs of the poor ought not to be overlooked; and the ſtory is inſerted at this place leſt, in the ſubſequent preſs of matter, it might chance to be forgotten. The particulars are taken from a letter addreſſed to the printer of the Georgia and Auguſta Chronicle, dated Hancock county, 30th of April, 1796, and ſigned Henry Boyle. They ſerve to ſhew what outrages may be perpetrated, in this country, under the ſanction of public juſtice.

Sometime in laſt fall, Abner Pierce was committed to jail, and as it ſeems in Hancock county, on ſuſpicion of ſtealing a mare, the property of Ward Darnel. He remained in irons till the ſitting of the ſuperior court, *but could not have his trial.* The only evidence againſt him was the oath of Darnel, while two other perſons ſwore that they were witneſſes to his having received the mare from Darnel, in virtue of a mutual agreement. After being confined for a confiderable time, public juftice had not leifure *to do its duty*, by giving him a trial.

This poor man was on the point of lying in jail till the next fuperior court; " confequently," fays the letter, " as the imprifonment would have amoun-
" ted to nearly twelve months, lying fummer
" and winter in the dungeon, chained in irons,
" without one bit of fire to thaw the froft off his
" frozen limbs, and only one oath againft him, two
" in his favour, humanity fhrinks at the idea*."
What makes the affair ftill worfe, the prifoner had a wife and two fmall children. They had neither cow nor horfe, nor any vifible means of fubfiftence,

---

* What ufe could there be for keeping the man in irons? A good ftone wall would have anfwered well enough. But perhaps the prifon was made of boards. About forty years ago, a wooden jail in Virginia, with a prifoner for debt confined in it, took fire. The alarm fpread. The jailor, in haftily turning the key, fpoiled the lock. The prifoner, feeing all efforts for his releafe to be in vain, ftript off his clothes, thruft them through the bars of the door, which was of iron, and bade the keeper carry them, as being all which he had, to his family. He then retired to a corner of the prifon, lay down, and perifhed in the flames.

If a man was to be kept a twelve-month in irons, and then to be hanged, for ftealing *one* horfe, what fhall we make of the old Congrefs, and their agents, who forcibly pilfered fo many that are yet unpaid for? Nay, what is to be faid of the third and fourth Congrefs, who have rejected many fcores or hundreds of fuch claims, *after admitting them to be juft?* At the fame time, we are giving John Adams, FOURTEEN THOUSAND DOLLARS to buy furniture for his houfe. The latter motion went through the Reprefentatives by fixty-three votes againft twenty-feven. It was impoffible to withftand the pathos of Mr. Samuel Sitgreaves, when defcribing the crazy bedfteads, the broken chairs, the ragged linen, the moth-eaten curtains, the rufty faucepans, and the fractured waterpots, that General Wafhington was to leave behind him in Market-ftreet. But, had it been a foldier with a wooden leg, who, refiding at the diftance of three hundred leagues, had only juft heard of the ftatute of limitations; or had it been a widow, like Ami Darden, whofe only horfe had been dragged from her plough, while her children were ftarving, Mr. Sitgreaves might as well have addreffed the north-weft wind.

except his labour. Four perſons entered themſelves as ſecurities to the amount of twelve hundred dollars, that this Abner Pierce ſhould attend at the next ſuperior court. Mr. Boyle, who ſubſcribes this letter, was one of the juſtices of peace who granted his liberation. For ſuch an office of benevolence and of equity, he has been abuſed in a newſpaper, and publiſhed, in his own defence, the letter above abridged.

The following is another anecdote of oppreſſion, and of ſo ſingular a kind, that it ought to be recorded for the honour of the eighteenth century. A negro man from the coaſt of Guinea had been ſold to a farmer on the ſouthern line of North-Carolina. In the fall of 1793, he applied to a black boy and girl, the property of an adjacent planter, to give him ſome victuals. In return he aſſured them that he would perform a charm to ſoften the ſeverity of their maſter. He gave them a callibaſh full of the feathers and claws of birds, mixed with negro men's nails. This was buried under the threſhold of the planter's door. He was, at that time ſick, or fell ill ſoon after; and having ordered the boy to be puniſhed for ſome offence, the latter ſaid that, if he was pardoned, he would tell what had made his maſter ill. The concealment was immediately diſcovered, along with ſome of the ſame materials which had been ſtuck about the ſick man's bed. The necromancer was conſequently taken up. This was on a Saturday. He was tried on the next Monday, by a jury of three free-holders, convicted of witchcraft, and hanged on the Tueſday. The boy and girl were whipt and branded in the forehead with a red hot iron. One of theſe children was eleven, and the other thirteen years of age. The ſtory has made noiſe, and an indiſtinct account of it, with ſome remarks, appeared in the newspapers, a confiderable time after the perpetration of the murder. The narrative is here given on the authority of a gentleman of veracity in Pennfylvania, who was on the fpot foon after. A neighbouring magiftrate obferved to him that he had no doubt as to the guilt of the prifoner. He was forry for being from home at the time of the execution, as he fhould have made his own negroes attend it. He added, by way of confolation, that the owner of the flave would not be any great lofer by the affair, becaufe the ftate was to grant him feventy pounds of damages*.

We fhall clofe this chapter with a few mifcellaneous remarks. In the profound debates of December, 1796, about *whether Americans were the freeft and moft enlightened people in the world*, Dr. Ames faid that, by all which he could learn, the people in Europe who *could* read were but as numerous as thofe in America who could *not* read. In plainer words, he meant to ftate that the people in the new world had twenty times more commonly a decent education than thofe in the old one. Mr. Giles agreed with him in thinking that Americans were wifer than the reft of mankind, but he did not believe it modeft or becoming to divulge the fecret; for a fecret it hitherto has been, and, fince the refolution was negatived, it is likely to remain fo. The very morning after the doctor made the above remark, Mr. Bache printed a decifive fpecimen of the fuperiority of the American intellect. A woman in New-Hampfhire was accufed, and perfecuted for being a witch. A man who had beaten her, was, juft before this debate, brought to trial. The wicked bench laughed at the charge of witch-

* In Jamaica, feveral black people have been executed for witchcraft.

craft. In revenge, a mob of the wifeſt men on earth were on the point of pulling down the court houſe.

Connecticut is uſually held up as the mirror of true republicaniſm, the centrical point, the very focus of federal virtue. Take the following inſtance. In ſpring, 1796, during the debates on the Britiſh treaty, a newſpaper of that ſtate, which has been already cited*, had the following moſt extraordinary paragraph.

"*We are informed, by a gentleman from the up-*
"*per part of the county of Hampſhire, that a regi-*
"*mental review was held, if we are not miſtaken,*
"*at Conway. As the people were informed that*
"*ſome communications of a political nature, were to*
"*be made to them, upon the parade, a very general*
"*attendance was obſerved, of all ages, from ſixteen*
"*years to ſixty. The communications were read to*
"*them while under arms, and they were then cal-*
"*led upon to expreſs their ſentiments, which was*
"*done without any heſitation. The unanimous voice*
"*of the people preſent was, that,* before they would
"ſubmit to a proſtration of the conſtitution, *by the*
"*preſent majority in the Houſe of Repreſentatives,*
"they would MARCH TO PHILADELPHIA ; up-
"hold the conſtitution and the Preſident ; and cauſe
"the treaty with Great Britain to be carried into ef-
"fect."

It would have been curious to ſee this army ſet out from Hartford with Trumbull, as a ſecond Alcæus at their head, chanting the pæan of battle. Before they had got within an hundred miles of this city, Pennſylvania might perhaps have furniſhed them with materials for a Connecticut Æneid; and truly the cauſe to be celebrated, and the bard

* American Annual Regiſter, chap. ix.

who was to sing, were two objects so worthy of each other, that the world has not seen a more suitable conjunction.

All the intemperate expressions of democratic societies, and *Aqua vitæ* reformers, do not come within sight of the effrontery and insolence of this single paragraph. A body of men assemble in arms at a review. They declare that they will march to Philadelphia, overbear the majority of the House of Representatives, and uphold the constitution, and the President. By the way, it was time that a public servant of such dangerous popularity should be removed from his office. The resignation of General Washington merits the inexpressible gratitude of his country. But what better was the Conway review than the meeting at Braddock's field? Indeed it was much worse; for the whisky boys did not, like this federal gang, make an explicit avowal of rebellion.

If the description drawn by Morse of New-Englanders be faithful, nothing but such behaviour is to be looked for. " They are indeed," says he, " often jealous to excess; a circumstance which is " a fruitful source of imaginary grievances, and of " *innumerable suspicions, and unjust complaints against* " *government*.—A very considerable part of the peo- " ple have either too little or too much learning to " make *peaceable subjects*. They know enough, " however, to make them think that they know a " great deal, when in fact they know *but little*.— " Hence originates that restless, litigious complain- " ing spirit, which forms a dark shade in the cha- " racter of New-England men*." This is the account given by one of their own parsons.

Morse hath obligingly announced his own princi-

---

* The American Geography, London edition of 1792, p. 146.

ples. "The clergy (of Connecticut) who are nu-
"merous, and as a body very respectable, have hi-
"therto preserved a kind of *aristocratical* balance
"in the very democratical government of this state;
"which has happily operated as a check upon the
"overbearing spirit of *republicanism**." What a
precious deliverance that must be! It is not sur-
prising that this state vomited up, during the revolution, such a multitude of the most inveterate cut-
throat tories.

"In New-England," says Morse, "learning is
"more generally diffused among all ranks of peo-
"ple than *in any other part of the globe*†." His
universal geography shews how little Morse himself knows about many parts of the globe. He
farther adds that "another very valuable source of
"information to the people is the newspapers, of
"which not less than thirty thousand are printed
"every week in New-England‡." Philadelphia
has now, besides other prints, eight daily newspapers. They work off about forty thousand sheets
of paper in a week‖; so that the people of this city must be still wiser if possible, than the New-Englanders; who have only one daily newspaper in
the whole country.

But newspapers, and especially some of those in
New-England, do not always tend to illuminate;
they often mislead. Thus, about the memorable
month of April, 1796, a number of the Columbian
Centinel had an article that begins thus.

"MR. RUSSEL,

"I send you another extract from Philadelphia,
"*too important* to be kept private. You may there-
"fore insert it," &c.

* The American Geography, London edition of 1792, p. 219.
† Ibid. p. 145. ‡ Ibid.
‖ In the first session of the fourth Congress, the House of Repre-
sentatives cost the public for newspapers, *twelve hundred dollars!*

This important packet is by far too long, as well as too stupid, for republication entire, but a few detached parts may serve as a specimen.

The writer sets out by alluding to the *disgraced* situation of Congress and our country. A majority in the house are " lifted *under* Madison and Galla-
" tin; or rather Gallatin and Madison, for the lat-
" ter has *become so changed* as to be only a second
" to the former, a devoted tool to him in *overturn-*
" *ing the government.*——A majority of the house
" are arrayed, *under such* leaders, to oppose and
" *pull down the President.* Their aim is to *destroy*
" *the executive,* to usurp to the house all the power
" given by the constitution to them exclusively."

The House of Representatives, or a majority of them, have never been *lifted* under Mr. Madison or any body else; as little has Mr. Madison been lifted under Mr Gallatin, as *a devoted tool* to aid him in *overturning the government.* No reason is assigned, and no proof is offered, that a majority in Congress had any such design; and the result shewed that a majority of the representatives would submit to ratify the treaty. What then becomes of their pretended *enlistment?*

As for *pulling down* of the President, the expression is highly impertinent, and intended only to inflame the feelings of the public. Did a British House of Commons ever scruple, or did they even forbear, to discuss the merits of a foreign treaty? No! And yet it seems that to do so in America is to *pull down* the President, and *overturn* the constitution. If the conduct of Congress in making this enquiry was culpable, the constitution is *de facto* overturned already. It is laid in ruins at the feet of the executive. The writer goes on to tell us that, since 1781, Mr. Madison has been *a devoted tool to the French interest and government,* the ab-

ject tool or *the active hireling* of the tyrant of the day. He is charged with *unwearied endeavours* to plunge this country into the present war *in aid of France.*

There is more ribbaldry to the same purpose, and all equally impudent and nonsensical. What must be the *state of mind* among the readers of this honest *Centinel*, if they digest such a morsel? An hundred legislators never yet assembled, without often differing in opinion from each other. The people without doors are also much divided on almost every great topic, and we may as well conceit them to be bribed as their representatives.

If the citizens of New-England are so much wiser than their neighbours, it must certainly appear in the choice of their representatives in Congress. The superiority is not always conspicuous. In the debate on the snuff excise, in spring 1794, some members from that part of the union, and especially Mr. Sedgwick, affirmed, that a land tax was injust and *impracticable*, and that Americans *would never submit to it**. It was impossible for any member to give a more consummate proof of ignorance or stupidity. The constitution of Massachusetts itself, the very state that sent Mr. Sedgwick to the house, authorises the assembly " to impose and levy pro-
" portional and reasonable assessments, rates, and
" taxes, upon all the inhabitants of, and persons re-
" sident, and *estates* lying within the said common-
" wealth†." Such taxes are actually paid, yet Mr. Sedgwick has often declared that they never could be raised. This conveyed a gross reflection upon the country. In point of argument, the gentleman might as well have whistled yanky doodle to the le-

---

* The words were taken down at the time, by the author.
† Part 2d. chap. i. sec. i. article 4.

gislators of America. This remark has no reference to Messrs. Henderson, Harper, and a certain venerable majority in the second session of the fourth Congress.

While the people of Massachusetts have been so anxious about the preservation of the federal constitution, they should revise their own. Morse says, " that the religion of Massachusetts is established, " by their excellent constitution, on a most liberal " and *tolerant plan.*" The present horrible oppression of baptists, and other sectaries, contradicts this assertion*.

When the Trojan fugitives, driven ashore on the coast of Africa, solicited aid from the queen of Carthage, Dido, in her answer, tells them, that, *acquainted with misfortunes, she had learned to succour the miserable.* A higher authority than that of Virgil, has also declared, that, *by the sadness of the countenance the heart is made better.* A shoal of metaphysicians, moral philosophers, and divines, in volumes of five hundred or a thousand pages, have likewise told us, that adversity softens and refines the heart.

By far the greater part of the world is full of misery; government, a few of the republics excepted, is nothing but robbery reduced to a system. Life itself has emphatically, and justly, been termed *a vale of tears.* These truths are not only trite, but they have been stale, and even mouldy, for twenty centuries.

Now, as adversity is so common every where, and so supreme an antidote for thawing the ice of selfishness, as poets have loaded avarice with ridicule in this world, and as divines have menaced it with perdition in the next, our natural conclusion, from

---

* See American Annual Register, chap. ix.

these powerful and coalescing causes, must be, that this blessed planet is pregnant with sympathy, charity, liberality, and the entire bead-roll of benevolent sensibilities. Amen.

These remarks have occurred on reading the account of a very melancholy affair which took place in the latter end of February, 1796, at Hingham, in the state of Massachusetts. The following particulars of it are abridged from a letter written by one of the professors in the university at Cambridge, dated the 23d of February, and printed in a late Boston newspaper.

About two months before the date of the letter, a young foreigner called on this professor, and introduced himself by saying, that he wanted to become acquainted with some scientific man. The subject which he brought on was pneumatics and mechanics. He conversed with the professor fluently, in French, Dutch, and Latin. After a conference, of which part is related, he took his leave, and, by agreement, paid a second visit to the professor in three days. We shall now quote *verbatim* a part of the account of him, as given by the writer of the letter.

" From his good figure, polite and easy manners,
" I concluded he was some unfortunate emigrant
" from the continent of Europe, probably in the
" service of the monarchy, *who, destitute of money*
" *and friends*, chose to apply some of the principles he had learnt at college, to the purpose of
" *procuring subsistence* by a novel exhibition. *On*
" *this account*, I never asked him his name or nation?"

On what account? He was destitute of money and friends, and he wanted to procure subsistence by the exhibition of a novel mechanical apparatus;

and, *therefore*, this American philosopher did not venture to ask him his name or nation.

"'Twas pitiful! 'twas wond'rous pitiful!"

That the professor in a college should be capable of mean ungentlemany conduct, we know by frequent personal experience; but, that any man should wish to bring himself forward to the public in so humiliating a point of view, is rather uncommon. Is it a crime to be in want of money? Is it culpable to attempt earning subsistence by exhibiting an apparatus of mechanism? Both these *liberal* and *manly* doctrines are avowed by this Cambridge professor. Such treatment of a foreigner, a man of learning, and, above all, a fellow creature in distress, is disgraceful not only to the individual who acted so, but, from his alacrity in telling the story, it reflects a sarcasm on the country to which he belongs. A reader in Europe will be tempted to think very meanly of the general cast of our ideas. Was the professor afraid that this foreigner would eclipse him in the eyes of his pupils, by his intended shew? How easy would it have been for the professor to have found employment of some decent kind for a well educated man, who understood four languages! It is trusted that every reader will heartily despise such a frost-bitten pedagogue.

The chilling reception that he encountered, was undoubtedly the reason why this ill-fated wanderer fell into despair, and shot himself. He left a letter addressed to the professor, wherein he states, that his want of money, and the failure of his plans for obtaining subsistence, had determined him to put an end to his life.

The professor speaks of him thus:

" The writings and drawings which he left di-
" rected to me, are so far from evincing a derang-
" ed mind, that they intimate a cool and vigor-

"ous intellect; being executed not merely with
"taste, but mathematical exactness.—I have never
"heard any thing against his character, but have
"seen some evidences of his humanity, in giving
"freedom to his slave, after binding him to a trade
"by which he could get his living." How much
is it to be regretted that a man so gifted, should
have met with such beastly treatment!

The professor concludes by citing the exit of
this gentleman as a proof, that "*nature*, without
"the commanding voice of *religion*, has left the
"noblest of her works imperfect." What part of
the christian religion taught this person to keep a
stranger at a distance, because he is in distress? To
repel such sordid ideas, and to extend the feelings
of humanity, is the only intelligible or rational
purpose of religion.

The name of this victim to rashness was *Iberkin*.
He was probably a German, there is, at least, such
a name in Prussia. The letter-writer is Dr. Benjamin Waterhouse, Professor of Medicine at Cambridge. Leyden gave him education; Rhode-Island
had the dishonour of his birth.

The people of New-England boast much of their
superior hospitality to strangers; of which this
anecdote holds up a shocking sample.

Before this sorry pedant speaks a second time of
religion, let him read the parable of *the good Samaritan*. In the Levite, *who passed by on the other
side*, he will trace the intellectual pedigree of his
own mind. When such a character presents itself to
mankind, as a paragon of *piety*, it is both our right,
and duty to wrench the vizor from the features of
deformity, and to administer that typographical
drubbing, which has been so hardily courted, and
so richly deserved.

L

CHAPTER III.

Federal artifices to promote a French quarrel.—Howe's landing at the head of Elk.—Jacobins not worse than other people.—Burgoyne's picture of the British East-India Company.—Recent stoppage of the bank of England.—Robespierre eclipsed by Pitt.—Amount of the yearly rental of Britain.—Note on the state-house of Hartford.—Number of the public creditors of England.—The triumph of Camillus.—Moral certainty of American indemnification for British piracy.—Mercantile apathy for the sufferings of American seamen.—Impressment at Jeremie.—Pinckney.—Jay.—Neck or nothing forgeries of Pitt.—Dependence of the British West-Indies on the United States.—Fallacies of Camillus.—What Jay should have said to Grenville.

AMONG other artifices employed by the federal party to exasperate the people of this country against the French republic, one is, their assertion that the United States were indebted for the aid of France to the personal benevolence of Louis. This is constantly held up as a reason for detesting the revolution; and mountains of ribbaldry have, from that ground, been discharged on its authors. Some notice has already been taken of this error*. Mr. Burke, in the letters above quoted, goes fully through it. He says that even when Louis came to the throne, "the revolution strongly operated "in all its causes." The politicians of France had been compelled to despise their kings. "From "quarrelling with the court, they began to com-

* British Honour and Humanity, p. 14. American Annual Register, chap. viii.

"plain of *monarchy itself ;* as a fyftem of govern-
"ment too variable for any regular plan of nation-
"al aggrandizement. They obferved, that, in
"that fort of regimen, too much depended on the
"perfonal character of the prince.—They compa-
"red with mortification the fyftematic proceedings
"of a Roman Senate with the fluctuations of a
"*monarchy.*—What cure for the radical weak-
"nefs of the French *monarchy,* but in *a republic?*
"Out the word came; and it never went back.—
"The different effects of a great military and am-
"bitious republic, and of a monarchy of the fame
"defcription were conftantly in their mouths."
After a long detail of circumftances, Edmund goes
on in thefe words: "Thefe fentiments were not pro-
"duced, as fome think, by their American alli-
"ance. The American alliance was produced by
"their *republican* principles and *republican* policy."
Several pages are fpent on this fubject, and every
thing proves that the alliance of France with America was the work of the republican party,
not of the king. After this explanation, no man
who prefers truth to fiction will deafen the public
about their obligations to Louis, or the guilt of
putting him to death. It was at worft not more
criminal than the unavenged murder fo lately committed in the jail of Philadelphia*. We print weekly whole columns of reproach againft French armies; yet, when five thoufand of thefe troops marched down Front-ftreet, in their way to the capture
of Cornwallis, it is ftill remembered with what
proftration of gratitude they were welcomed by
the furrounding citizens. The French ambaffador
was looked up to as a tutelar divinity. His landing
from Europe was announced by the difcharge of
cannon, by fire-works and illuminations. His pre-

* American Annual Regifter, chap. X.

fence was essential at every public entertainment. He was the arbiter of politics, of fashion, and of taste. But our turn has been served, and citizen Adet can describe the reverse of the medal. Daniel Defoe, speaking of his country, says:

> " Ingratitude, a devil of black renown,
> " Possess'd her very early as *his own*!"

Yet there is nothing quite so paltry as this conduct of ours, even in the fable history of England. In a comparison with British armies, the French cannot lose much. When Howe landed at the head of Elk, many persons in that neighbourhood had prepared the best entertainment which they could afford for the reception of their deliverers. They brought the English soldiers to their tables. The instant that dinner was over, the guests began to plunder. It was affirmed, at the time, that in an extent of a few miles, they took away sixteen hundred horses. It was a common practice, when one of the regulars met an American, to ask him the time of day. When he pulled out his watch, it was wrested from his fingers. The tories were so much ashamed of this treatment, that they were never heard to complain, and at the distance of twenty years, many of them are yet as firm in loyalty as ever.

Alexander Hamilton and Co. are in the habit of making comparisons between France and England to the advantage of the latter. A celebrated writer of the federal phalanx observes, that the French " have ransacked the coffers of the rich, stripped " poverty of its very rags, robbed the infant of " its birth-right, wrenched the crutch from tot- " tering old age, and, joining sacrilege to burgla- " ry, have plundered the altars of God*." All this, and much more is true; and declamations of that sort have been a powerful means with the Bri-

---

* A New Year's Gift for the Democrats, p. 1.

tish interest for exasperating the people of America. But, coming home for a comparison, the citizens of this state would not think themselves fairly painted in a picture of the Paxton boys, butchering innocent Indians in the prison of Lancaster. A few sentences will shew that, in general morality, the British are as bad as other people, and often much worse than many.

Mr. Howard says, that the annual average of executions in London only, for twenty-three years, was between *twenty-nine* and *thirty*. " In all the " seven provinces," says he, " there are seldom " more executions than from *four* to *six*." The United Provinces are, by common calculation, three times more populous than London. They should, in proportion, have *ninety* executions per annum, instead of which there are but *five*. Mr. Howard gives an hundred other facts of the same nature. This may help in ascertaining the balance of *domestic* morality.

As for politics, no jacobin can less disguise his appetite for blood and plunder than the common run of British historians. The late war against Tipoo Saib is spoke of, as follows: " No period ap- " peared more favourable *to humble Tipoo*. The " Nizam and the Mahrattas both declared them- " selves ready TO CRUSH THE RISING POW- " ER OF MYSORE*." The latter words are, as printed by the author, in *capitals*. He proceeds at considerable length, in the most sordid and insolent tone of exultation. No highwayman could speak in plainer language. To *humble Tipoo*! This creed vindicates every thing that the French have done, or can do. Thus, after the earthquake at Lisbon, Spain, might have sent an army to hum-

* Guthrie's Geographical Grammar, fourteenth London edition, p. 686.

ble Portugal. France, in the midſt of peace, might as juſtly diſembark an hundred thouſand men at Plymouth or Dover, to humble England. Thus, in all ages, has the moſt deteſtable ſophiſtry, been exerted to vindicate the commencement of unjuſt and deſtructive wars. Guthrie ſays, that this war coſt Tipoo forty-nine thouſand men. A famine deſtroyed perhaps ten times that number. Nothing but the wildeſt ignorance of hiſtory could make our citizens believe that the French are worſe than their neighbours. It is of the higheſt importance to remove this miſtake, which has become ſuch a favourite handle of party.

Of all writers, Burke is the fitteſt to be quoted on this head. "I never," ſays he, "ſhall ſo far in-
"jure the janiſarian republic of Algiers as to put
"it in compariſon, for every ſort of crime, turpi-
"tude, and oppreſſion, with the jacobin republic
"of Paris." Yet, when ſpeaking of England, this author has afforded a ſtill more complete idea of depravity. "There has not been in this century
"any foreign peace or war, in its origin, *the fruit*
"*of popular deſire*, except the war that was made
"with Spain in 1739." [This is the grand aſſertion of Paine that government dragged England into ſuch quarrels for the ſake of augmenting public debt, and pillaging the public purſe. He adds.]
"I examined the original documents.—They per-
"fectly ſatisfied me of the *extreme injuſtice* of that
"war. [This ſhews the rooted corruption of the
"people.] Some years after, it was my for-
"tune to converſe with many of the principal ac-
"tors againſt that miniſter (Walpole), and with
"thoſe who principally excited that clamour.
"None of them, *no not one*, did in the leaſt defend
"the meaſure, or attempt to *juſtify their conduct*.
"They condemned it as freely as they would have

"done in commenting upon any procceding in his-
"tory*." Every man must see that these authors
of the war of 1739, were as execrable as the French
Directory possibly can be.

This is a sufficient reply to the endless barking
of Webster and Camillus about jacobin principles.
Let us add one word more about this war of 1739.
Guthrie says, that the English took three thousand
four hundred and thirty-four prizes. They lost
three thousand two hundred and thirty-eight.
Thus we learn that a navy cannot protect an extensive commerce. English trade has, in the present
struggle, suffered still more severely. A British
navy of six hundred sail cannot secure British shipping. Six frigates have an hundred times less ca-
pability to protect the commerce of America.

In 1772, an enquiry took place before the House
of Commons, as to the conduct of the East-India
company. Burgoyne was chairman of the committee. He says, that " such a scene of iniquity,
" rapine, and injustice, such unheard of cruelties,
" such open violations of every rule of morality,
" every tie of religion, and every principle of good
" government was never before discovered; and
" that, through the whole of the investigation,
" he could not find *a single spot* whereon to lay his
" finger, it being all equally one mass of most un-
" heard of villainies, and the most notorious cor-
" ruption†." This passage occurs in the first of
more than three hundred pages, all in the same style.
By accounts transmitted from Hastings, it was proved, that, in five or six years, the servants of the
company had destroyed, starved, or driven away,
a greater number of people, than were contained,

---

* Letter I.   † Evidences of our transactions in the East-
Indies, &c. by Mr. Parker. Printed at London in 1782.

collectively, in all the British colonies. After such a review we need not be scared at the cruelty of Jacobins.

One inceſſant reproach to the French has been the breach of public credit. Our ally is deſcending, with haſty leaps, to the ſame level. On the 27th of February, 1797, the privy council of George the third, by an arbitrary order, forbade the bank of England " from iſſuing any caſh in payment, " until the ſenſe of parliament could be taken on " that ſubject." The reaſon given is, an apprehenſion of " a want of ſufficient caſh to anſwer the " exigencies of the *public* ſervice." If government had forbidden the bank to pay gold and ſilver as the intereſt of the public debt, this would have been no worſe than a ſimple confeſſion of bankruptcy. But they ſtep in between the bank and its private creditors, and ſay, " You ſhall not pay your " private debts. We muſt have the money to pay " our own ſalaries, and to ſupport our ſtanding " armies; to defray the charge of barracks built " in defiance of law; and to clear off the bills of " a prince who has defrauded his miſtreſſes, inſul-" ted his two wives, *who are both alive* *! hired " newſpapers to calumniate his mother, and at-" tempted to keep his father for life in a ſtrait waiſt-" coat."

Parliament have an equal right to interfere between any debtor and creditor in the kingdom. Thus, all the requiſitions of Robeſpierre are rivalled at a ſingle ſtroke. With equal juſtice they may ſay to every farmer, " you ſhall pay no rent to your land-" lord." Pitt is in the highway to ſubſtantiate Mr. Sedgwick's univerſal aſſeſſment†. No legiſlature on earth ever hazarded a more glaring act of

---

* Britiſh Honour and Humanity, p. 44.   † See Appendix, No. II.

iniquity. It is as extensive in its operation, as detestable in its object. Every individual in Britain will feel the effects of this stoppage. Associations of bankers and manufacturers may, and will for a time, keep up the price of paper; but the first loan wanted for 1798, will ring the knell to its interment.

The act of parliament that has followed this order of council, affects, in a tender point, the mercantile interest of the United States; and, as shall be presently explained, it strikes at one of the pillars of the British treaty. Much pains are employed to represent it as of a temporary nature, and to convince the public that credit will quickly come round to the former situation*. On this account, it cannot be regarded as desultory to state, in this place, some decisive facts, of which a few are not generally known in America.

The national bankruptcy of England is not a matter which has come suddenly to a crisis. Its inevitable approach was distinctly foreseen and described. Mr. William Morgan, an eminent writer on English finances, published, in the beginning of 1796, *Facts addressed to the people of Great Britain*. From a long series of arguments and calculations, the following particulars have been abridged.

Mr. Pitt estimates the yearly rents of all the landed estates in Britain, at twenty-five millions

---

* The tories who say so do not believe it. The rate of exchange on England was formerly above par, which is one hundred and sixty-six and two thirds per cent. It has now (May 10th, 1797,) sunk to an hundred and twenty-five, and an hundred and thirty. When a bill returns under protest from England, the indorsee is intitled to twenty per cent. of damages. People now refuse to grant such bills, unless with this proviso, that they shall not be liable to the usual penalty of non-payment.

sterling. But the land tax, at four shillings in the pound, though comprehending houses, places, and pensions, gives only one million nine hundred thousand pounds. Mr. Morgan believes that the yearly rents do not exceed eighteen millions. The actual expenses wanted, in. 1796, even for a *peace* establishment, were twenty-two millions. Thus, even a year ago, the public taxes were equal to the whole landed rents of Britain. It was, however, found difficult or impossible to raise the twenty-two millions essential for the national credit, even supposing that the war had ended in January, 1796. In February, 1795, taxes were laid to the expected amount of sixteen hundred and forty-five thousand pounds. In December following, others were also *proposed* to the amount of eleven hundred and twenty-three thousand pounds. Yet the interest of many millions of debt still remained to be *provided for*. From the first establishment of the consolidated fund, in 1786, till the commencement of the present war, the expenditure invariably exceeded the *revenue*. The deficiencies in the six years preceding the war, amounted to nearly seven millions sterling. The blank was supplied by loans, and extraordinary but casual receipts. In the first three years of the war, new taxes were laid to the amount of about four millions, and still the annual deficiencies increased. In 1795, they came nearly to *two millions*. " It is probable, there-
" fore," says Mr. Morgan, " that *annual loans*
" will become necessary, in future, to provide for
" the ordinary expences of a peace establishment ;
" and these loans, by requiring new taxes, will
" produce further deficiencies ; so that, by borrow-
" ing each year, not only to pay the deficiencies of
" the preceding year, but also the interest on the
" deficiencies in former years, the national debt

"will be increasing, at compound interest, in the
"same manner as it is reduced; but with this
"alarming difference, that the operations in the
"one case, are ten times more powerful than in
"the other. If these are likely to be the effects
"of the public debt, with the expenditure only of
"a *peace* establishment, or on the supposition that
"the war were immediately closed, what must be
"the consequences of obstinately persisting in a
"system of profusion, which, if long continued,
"would ruin any country, however unimpaired
"its strength and resources?"

Men who desire useful knowledge will not tire of this quotation. It is certainly better entertainment than to ring invidious changes on the purity of Connecticut*, and the wickedness of Virginia. Since these remarks were published by Mr. Morgan, a campaign has elapsed more disastrous, if possible, to England, than any of the former. Her situation has, uniformly, sunk from bad to worse. What, in the end of 1795, was but *expectation*, has, in 1797, been converted into *history*. Many people in America seem to be intoxicated with the superior information and abilities of Mr. Hamilton. The extravagant predictions and assertions of him-

---

* The history of the new state-house at Hartford, exhibits a delectable specimen of this commodity. The assembly possessed a claim on the state of New-York for almost fifteen hundred thousand acres of land, which are worth three or four millions of dollars. In 1795, they sold this claim for a few thousand pounds, to a private company. See American Annual Register, chap. x. If they believed their title to be groundless, they were no better than a gang of coiners, who sell bad shillings at half price. If the law-suit of this company shall be successful, New-York will hardly submit to the decision, but on the point of the bayonet. Thus it follows, that for the dirty consideration of a few thousand pounds, the legislature of Connecticut has put the union in danger of a civil war. With these facts before their eyes, and with an effrontery that transcends all description, many writers extol the superlative *federalism* of Con-

self, and his auxiliaries, about British pride, and power, and opulence, have become too despicable for refutation. If Camillus really believed what he wrote respecting them, he must have been very ignorant. If he knew more than he chose to tell, his conduct demands a harsher name. Another citation from Mr. Morgan will, perhaps, repay a perusal.

"The competition of rapacious loan-mongers to
"share in the spoils of the country, supported by
"the *fictitious* credit of paper-money, may perhaps
"enable the minister to triumph in the facility with
"which the public debts are accumulated, and the
"temporising expedient of ineffectual taxation may
"serve him as a proof of our inexhaustible re-
"sources to provide for those taxes; but a system
"founded upon delusion, must end in disappoint-
"ment and ruin. It was the boast of a French
"minister of finance, that the American war was
"carried on during his administration, without
"imposing a new tax upon the French people; and
"it was this very circumstance which produced

necticut; and poor Samuel Dexter, as one of his reasons for supporting the sugar and snuff excise, said in Congress, in 1794, that all the members of that state voted for it.

If from the assembly themselves, we turn to their constituents, the prospect does not improve. The sale of these fifteen hundred thousand acres, if the state had a real right to them, was an act of outrageous robbery on their fellow citizens; it was a second Yazoo business. When the people of Georgia found their property invaded, they elected a new assembly, erased the swindling law from the public records, proclaimed its infamous authors, and ordered their attorney-general to prosecute senator James Gunn, as one of the conspirators. This was acting like men; but the citizens of Connecticut, when in a similar situation, truckle under legislative treachery; while Pelham, and Trumbull, and Webster, and a swarm of other scribblers from that quarter, rack their ingenuity in reviling, as a race of inferior and degraded beings, the people of the southern states.

"the revolution. He borrowed immense sums an-
"nually, and endeavoured to provide for them by
"the ineffectual means of economy; for, in that
"country, taxation had then arrived at its limits.
"A syſtem of economy, under a government which
"exiſted by corruption, neceſſary failed. New
"loans became neceſſary to pay the intereſt of for-
"mer loans. The maſs of debt continued to ac-
"cumulate, till at length it overwhelmed public
"credit, and buried the government in its ruins."

As the government and the bank of England cannot at preſent command ſpecie, the next queſtion is, at what time, or from what ſource, have they a proſpect of getting it? The debts of the former are about three hundred and eighty millions ſterling. Paine gueſſes the paper of the bank of England at ſixty millions. Several other great banks had ſtopt before it, and the banks of Scotland and that of Ireland, have ſtopt ſince. In an affair of uncertainty, but of enormous magnitude, we may conjecture that eighty millions ſterling, in bank notes have been blocked up. This added to the debt will make four hundred and ſixty millions. Oppoſed to this world of paper, George Chalmers, an authority to be truſted in this caſe, ſays, that the Britiſh dominions have a circulation of twenty millions in gold and ſilver. Thus credit ſtands like an inverted pyramid, of which paper is the baſe. But ſince that calculation, the quantity of hard money has been reduced. Beſides, every guinea, and every ſixpence, will now hide itſelf. Suppoſe that the bank has at preſent in its coffers two millions ſterling, and that this money is to be reſerved for public exigencies. Two months only of the approaching campaign will exhauſt it. The caſh will dive into the pockets of thoſe who furniſh the ſupplies, and they will hold it, with the gripe of death, till the alarm has become to an issue. It is hard to see from whence money can be expected. The emperor will not replace his wages. In the mean while, confidence must by degrees decline. Tradesmen must be thrown idle, from the want of a proper medium to pay them; and, after every expedient has been tried, an universal bankruptcy will ensue. Unless France shall grant England a peace, the campaign of 1798 will require another loan. Paper cannot be sent to the East and West-Indies, even were its character found at home. The precious metals cannot be had, and public credit will of necessity expire. We see that six years before the war, the minister after every exertion, was annually borrowing great part of a million sterling to pay the interest of old debts. This practice alone would, in time, have produced insolvency; but, when there is superadded the history of the last four years, probability rises to demonstration. In 1791, Mr. Rayment published a statement of the number of the public creditors of England, taken from the books. It amounted to an hundred and twenty-seven thousand three hundred and one persons. About an hundred and twenty or thirty millions sterling have been added to the debt, so that we may now compute the creditors as being at least an hundred and sixty thousand. The bankruptcies of 1793 came perhaps to twenty millions sterling. Those made by the stoppage of paper money will be at least twenty times greater. Every man in Britain, who is worth five guineas, will be affected more or less. The shock must convulse every nerve in the mass of property. Thus much for British credit. We now come to apply these remarks with respect to Jay's treaty. The Philadelphian address to the President, thanking him for having signed it, speaks of " indemnity "(the subscribers meant to say *indemnification*) "therein stipulated for *past losses.*" The New-York chamber, in their resolutions of the 21st of July, 1795, congratulate themselves on "a fair "*compensation* for the spoliations upon our com- "merce," Curtius in his fourth letter, trusts that "just claims will be supported, and just damages "*paid!*" The fifteenth number of Camillus is occupied on this subject. He quotes the seventh article of the treaty, by which, referring to the piracies on American commerce, "his Britannic ma- "jesty undertakes to cause the same to be paid to "such claimant in *specie*, without any deduction," after the amount has been ascertained. "The plan," "says Camillus, "affords a *moral certainty* of sub- "stantial justice.—The indemnification which may "be awarded, is to be paid fully, immediately, "and without *de tour* by the British government "itself. Say ye impartial and enlightened, if all "this be not as *it ought to have been!*"

In short, the hope of recovering payment for the ships and cargoes was the greatest cause for the treaty becoming popular among American merchants. Its advocates incessantly held out this article as an object of exultation. When handling it Camillus rises above his wonted composure, and one apostrophe may well enough answer another. "Say ye impartial and enlightened, after the pre- "ceding explanation of English finances, do ye ex- "pect one farthing from the king of England? Do "ye fancy that a monarch who is fifteen months "in arrears to the wench who scours his water "closet*, whose government is three hundred

---

* On the 18th of April, 1796, Mr. Grey said in parliament, that the civil list was FIVE QUARTERS in arrears. George the Third has many millions sterling at command. His refusing to pay these arrears, proves him to be one of the meanest beings that ever disgraced human nature.

" and eighty millions sterling in debt, and who can
" pay its interest in nothing but paper, do ye fancy
" that such a person will send over his money to
" indemnify American merchants."

Dr. Ames, in his renowned speech in Congress on the treaty, delivered himself with more caution. " Five millions of dollars," said he, " and proba-
" bly more, on the score of spoliations committed
" on our commerce, depend upon the treaty. The
" treaty offers the *only* prospect of *indemnity**. Such
" redress is promised as the merchants place *some*
" confidence in. Will you interpose and frustrate
" that *hope!*" That hope, to borrow the style of Bunyan, hath since arrived in *doubting* castle, and will soon be in the grasp of giant *despair*.

One feels less for the misfortunes of some of the merchants on account of their ingratitude to their seamen. The neglect of Jay to secure an article in favour of these people, even when it was offered by Grenville, has already been stated to the public†. It was disgraceful to have accepted of such a treaty at all, without an ample compensation to every one of these men, who had been imprisoned, hand-cuffed, starved and flogged, while acting in American service. The printed resolutions of the chamber of commerce at New-York and Boston approve the treaty in general terms, without the smallest notice of this infamous omission. The *indemnity* addressers of Philadelphia drop not one word of alarm or sympathy for the dangers or sufferings of some thousands of mariners. On the 14th of April, 1797, also, when the merchants of Philadelphia

---

* This word means only *pardon for a crime*. Thus, when Charles the Second signed the act of oblivion and indemnity, the cavaliers called it an act of oblivion to his friends, and indemnity to his enemies.

† British honour and humanity, p. 41.

presented an address to Congress in favour of the treaty, that paper contains not one glimmering of compassion or even of reference to the sufferings of their seamen. Five millions of dollars, and "the " principal part of their remaining *fortunes*," form the exclusive burden of the song. Never did the sordid spirit of mercantile adventure display itself in more repulsive colours. Woe be to that country whose counsels are governed by merchants, or by priests! When the Senate saw an article about the West Indian trade which they did not like, they refused to accept it. But they overlooked this hideous chasm about seamen, though in every view of justice, honour, humanity, and even of commercial interest, it was by many degrees more important than the other. This is precisely the way in which Congress, and the country have treated their old continental soldiers; so that no part of our enlightened citizens has a title to condemn the rest.

It may be answered, *but what could you do!* The reply is ready. The immediate restoration of every American seaman, or a serious and vigorous effort to that end, should have been demanded and obtained, before making a single clause of any treaty. Farther, every one of them should have received a liberal compensation for the time during which they had been confined in British vessels. We have not heard of such compensation being either given, or sought. If any scruple was to be entertained on the part of Britain about making such reparation, it contradicted common reason to believe that negociation with such people could end in satisfaction. Figure the case that a crimp kidnaps your son on the streets of London, and sends him to the East Indies as a recruit. This offender owns the fact, and without engaging to restore the young man, he asks you to enter into an agreement for a freight of cotton or tobacco. You would not listen to such a proposal till security was given for the redemption of your son; or, if you did listen, the whole world would pronounce you an unnatural barbarian. Of British impressments, the following instance is not, perhaps, worse nor better than an hundred others. It is inserted merely as a sample.

On the 29th of July, 1795, Cyprian Cook, master of the sloop Crisis, of Norwich, in Connecticut, and Elijah Clarke, a passenger in the vessel, emitted depositions at New-London, of which here follows an abridgement. On the 4th of July, preceding, the Crisis, and above twenty other American vessels were lying at anchor in the port of Jeremie, in Hispaniola. The Hermione, an English frigate, came into the port, anchored, and sent her boats to board the Americans. Every man in the vessels, was taken away, excepting the captains and mates. They were, to the number of sixty or seventy, kept on board and fasting, during forty-eight hours. They were examined, one by one, and five only were dismissed, because, as the English captain observed, they were unfit for service. All these men were Americans born, excepting two Danes, who had been naturalized here. This outrage happened seven months and an half after signing of the treaty; and it shews how sincerely England despised our envoy and those who sent him. Tame submission to such treatment was the very excess of national disgrace. But, after Jay had declined to write an article in favour of our sailors, they were sure of meeting with the worst usage. It is strange that Jay did not burn the copy of his card, making a demand in their behalf, and of the consenting reply of Grenville. The President had very good reason to be ashamed of laying such a correspondence before the House of Representatives. It is suppo-

UNITED STATES.

fed that some thousands of American seamen have been treated like the above at port Jeremie*.

Camillus, in No. vi. points out many difficulties in the way of a complete protection for our mariners. It is likely enough that the article, if inserted, would have been broken; and real difficulties might have occurred in the business. But even decorum required such a clause. Camillus has advanced some assertions that are absolutely untrue. He says that " Great Britain has accordingly per-
" severingly declined any definitive arrangement on
" the subject; notwithstanding earnest and reitera-
" ted efforts of our government.—Our minister
" plenipotentiary, Mr. Pinckney, it is well known,
" has long had this matter in charge, and has stre-
" nuously exerted himself to have it placed upon
" some acceptable footing; but his endeavours have

---

* Some English newspapers of 1796, say, that the press gangs employed in Britain, amount to nine thousand men. A great part of these fellows are themselves sailors, and every one of them, from the nature of the service, must be robust and able-bodied. Their situation requires better wages, and better living, than that of a foot soldier. They can hardly cost the country less, in one shape or other, than two shillings sterling per day. On ship board, or in useful manufactures, they would be worth at least an equal sum. Thus each of these kidnappers sinks daily four shillings sterling, which, between positive and negative loss, they might expend or earn for society. Nine thousand men, at a loss of four shillings per head, make a sinking fund of eighteen hundred pounds sterling a day. This, multiplied by the number of days in a year, gives six hundred and fifty-seven thousand pounds per annum, for the charge of press gangs. It is an ordinary computation in Britain, that every impressed man costs, upon a medium, an hundred pounds sterling, before he is got into actual service.

Yet, in spite of this strange work, in order to man her navy, the queen of isles labours under the greatest difficulty for hands, that she has perhaps ever known. To press American seamen is very consistent with her Algerine code of *morality*, but entirely repugnant to her common maxims of *policy*. The exclusion of foreign mariners from her ports and shipping, is the great object of her act of navigation. Her breach of it arises from necessity more than choice.

"been unsuccessful." By Thomas Pinckney, and his efforts, we need not set much store. While France was in the very act of driving the allies to perdition, Jay, by the most absurd, or perfidious misconduct, put his hand to the treaty, when, if he had only waited six weeks, till the approaching conquest of Holland had been completed, he might have had almost any terms worth asking. Pinckney was silly enough to approve of his management in making so good a bargain. Neither of these precious envoys would buy largely in the funds, when there was a certainty of their tumbling. Yet they clapped up a treaty, when every moment of delay was inestimable to America. This is the scandalous way in which our business hath been transacted. The affair had hung over ten years, and then was finished at a moment of infinite impropriety. Such miserable botching the world has probably never seen before.

Camillus foresaw the objection as to the very unseasonable period of signing the treaty. In No. vii. he defends it thus. " It will be useful to go back to " the periods when the negociation began and en- " ded. Our envoy arrived in England, and enter- " ed upon the business of his mission, at the mo- " ment when there was a general elation on " account of the naval victory gained by Lord " Howe, and previous to those important successes, " which have terminated in the conquest of Holland; " and the treaty was concluded by the 19th of No- " vember last, prior to the last mentioned event, " and the defection of the king of Prussia. The " posture of things at the time of the negociation, " and not *at this time*, is the standard to try its " merits."

It will indeed be *useful to go back;* for every line of this argument is contradicted by undisputed facts.

The President's message to Congress about his having appointed Jay, was dated the 16th of April, 1794. The king of Prussia, in the beginning of that month, had published a curious manifesto stating his reasons for quitting his allies. Pitt afterwards gave him twelve hundred thousand pounds to make him return to the combat. He took the money, but never performed his promise. Instead of that, he went into Poland to besiege Warsaw. He left indeed his quota as a prince of the German empire; but they also were annihilated; along with an Austrian army, at Kaiserslautern, in a battle which lasted inclusively night and day, from the 12th to the 15th of July, 1794; in the end, the republicans plunged through the loaded Prussian batteries at the point of the bayonet. Surely, Mr. Hamilton imagines that nobody reads newspapers except himself. In November, 1794, when Jay signed this paper, Frederic William had, for many months, been abused in the daily prints of London, as a deserter from the cause of *morality*, and *regular* government. Thus Camillus stands detected of an intentional and notorious falsehood.

As to the general *elation* about lord Howe's victory, the French were equally satisfied, and with better reason. An American ambassador *ought to have been* possessed of more penetration than the porters and chairmen whom Pitt or his runners hired, upon that joyful occasion, to break the windows of John Wilkes and lord Stanhope.

Again, Camillus, says that Jay entered upon the business of his mission *previous to those important successes which terminated in the conquest of Holland.* This is another stupendous untruth, like that about the king of Prussia. A few facts and dates will prove it to be so. On the 26th of April, 1794, Pichegru totally beat Clairfait at Moucron, and killed six thousand of his troops. In the course of a few weeks, a number of other desperate battles ensued. The allies did whatever brave men, and able officers could do; but the French, by their numbers, their enthusiasm, and their talents, fairly drove them out of the field. So early as the 19th of May, 1794, the emperor printed an address to the inhabitants of Brussels, in a tone almost as dejected as the king of Prussia's farewell manifesto. The armies continued almost constantly fighting till the 26th of June, when the French gained the battle of Fleurus. This completely turned the scale. The grand Austrian army immediately sent off their baggage, and, in the course of a few days, thirty thousand people fled from Brussels. From that day forward every man in England, excepting Jay, must have foreseen the conquest of Holland. Though Jay had *entered upon the business of his mission* before the fate of Flanders was decided, it was his duty to have spun out the business and to have taken the utmost advantage of that invaluable contingency. Camillus, by advancing, in Jay's defence, the above palpable fictions, has exposed without reinforcing the weakness of the cause.

But Camillus should also have defended the Senate of Congress. They certainly did not approve of the treaty till after the defection of the king of Prussia, and the surrender of Amsterdam. They did not ratify till the 24th of June, 1795. In the above quotation, Camillus plainly implies, that, after the *defection* and *reduction*, &c. better terms might have been had. The question then comes to be *why the Senate did not stand out to get them?* They sent back an article. They should have amended and sent back others. The true reason was, first, that some of the Senators were seriously and substantially ignorant about the real state of politics in Europe; for, after the reduction of the seven United Provinces, a fear of England attacking America was "but the eye of childhood; that fears a "painted devil." Secondly, the ratification was an object of party. Jay had been sent over in despite of a majority in the House of Representatives; and to have refused the ratification of a treaty planned under the auspices of Mr. Hamilton, would have cast irrecoverable ridicule on their whole connections. For this reason twenty senators, less pardonable, if such a thing can be, than Jay himself, agreed to what he had done; and, as Junius observes, "though royal favour cannot remove moun-"tains of infamy, it undoubtedly *lessens*, for it *di-* "*vides* the burden."

But, independent of French victories, Jay must have known that Pitt, from his dreadful want of money, could not hold out for any considerable time. Much has been said as to the danger of England (forsooth!) declaring war against the United States. To shew the dreadful plight that she was in, the following particulars are taken from a series of resolutions read in the house of commons by Mr. Smith, on the 22d of February, 1796.

In September, 1795, Walter Boyd, junior, was requested by Pitt to advance him a million sterling. He did so, and by agreement, he was to draw bills on the lords commissioners of the treasury, which they were to accept. Now comes the astonishing part of the transaction. Bills for seven hundred thousand pounds were drawn in London, bearing a false date at Hamburgh, several weeks preceding the real time of framing them. Walter Boyd is not engaged in any house of business at Hamburgh, so that he might as well have pretended to draw bills from the moon. These forgeries, professing to be foreign bills, were written upon unstamped paper. "They were," says Mr. Smith, " of such a nature and description, as the " bank of England would have refused to discount " for any commercial house whatever, and such " as it would have been injurious to the credit of " any private house, to have negociated." These are civil words, but, in plain English, any other parties of such a plot, but the minister and his friends, would infallibly have been hanged.

It was plain that a government adopting such infamous expedients to raise money, must have been upon its last legs. With such facts in view, it is amazing how completely some of the ablest men in America were deceived about it. Of all the arguments in favour of the British treaty, none was more loudly repeated than the danger of a war with Britain. "War," said Dr. Ames, might be delay-" ed, but could not be prevented. The causes of " it would remain, would be aggravated, would " be multiplied, and soon become intollerable. " More captures, more impressments, would swell " the list of our wrongs, and the current of our " rage." [If England had declared war against the United States, in consequence of the representatives rejecting the treaty, she would have become bankrupt before the next Christmas.] "The " progress of *wealth* and improvement is wonder-" ful, and some will think too rapid."* [Witness the enormous bankruptcies in October, 1796, and the intolerable scarcity of money ever since. The country is thriving undoubtedly, but not the more from the extravagant spirit of over-trading] "The " vast crop of our neutrality is all seed-wheat, and " is sown again to swell, almost beyond calculation, " the future harvest of prosperity. And in this

---

* Bache's debates, vol. ii. p. 332.

UNITED STATES.

…at seems to be fiction is found to …experience." And, *in this progress*, …e United States, unless its discounts …circumspect, will go to the family- …in London, Edinburgh, and Dublin. …paper is past in Europe, and, as a …rse, its expiration in America will …or latter. In case of any serious …rance, and after the unparalelled ruin …eading England, every man here will …n metal for his bank notes. As to …*our neutrality*, the privateers of France …ave reaped a very great part of it.

…w go back to Mr. Smith's resolutions, …er proof of the utter incapacity of …me 1796, to have attacked America. …of the contractors," says he, " at the …the nation, have been so exorbitantly …to have risen even before the depo- …e thereon, to an amount greatly ex- …deposit itself, viz. on a loan of eigh- …s, to the enormous and incredible sum …*ions, one hundred and sixty thousand* …*ng.*"

…ld imagine that such a system was to …more than the gambling interest of …per month, so frequently paid of late …towns of America. Both these ways …ney resembled the resource of the …said that he could escape the gal- …ng his throat in prison.

…tance shall be given of the hurry in …s to secure the loan for 1796, and …e impatience with which the people …w the war prolonged.

…bankers of London agreed to lend a …to the minister, the custom was to

O

give them credit in the public funds to a certain amount. The current price of stock, at the time of making the bargain, determined the quantity of it to be given for the new advances of the creditors. Thus, if the three per cents were at eighty, the same proportion of them would buy ten thousand pounds, that would only buy seven thousand five hundred, if the stocks were at sixty per cent. It was hence the great aim of every premier to raise them as high as possible, before his loan, and it was usual to cast prospects of peace, into some royal speech or message, by which they were sure of being raised. But, on the 27th of November, 1795, Mr. Pitt, with a precipitancy that wears the foulest aspect, closed a loan for eighteen millions with Mr. Boyd. A message that he must have foreseen, came on the 8th of December, thereafter, from George the Third to parliament, telling his earnest desire of peace. The funds instantly got up so high that the quantity given for the loan, rose in its value, *nine hundred thousand pounds sterling*. This was just so much money lost to the public, and gained to the bankers, who probably run halves with Pitt himself. So rapid a rise in the funds, on the slender prospect of peace, shewed how very little the British were by this time disposed or indeed enabled for a war with America. " I consider all those war arguments " that have been made use of," said Mr. Christie, " as nothing more than the old story of raw-head- " and-bloody-bones, much fitter to be used by an " old woman to quiet a cross child, than to convince " any of the enlightened members of this house of " the propriety of this measure*."

Events have since proved that the dread of war was a mere chimera, as the public credit of England

---

* Bache's Debates, vol, ii. p. 351.

had become too feeble to support such a shock. But, independent of that, and admitting our legislators to have been, as many of them were, very shamefully ignorant of the state of English finance, still America had another string to her bow that would have reduced Britain to any reasonable terms. The West-India Royal Gazette, of the 7th of October, 1794, contains a memorial to Henry Dundas from the West-Indian planters and merchants. They state, at much length, how impossible it is for them to subsist unless by supplies of provisions from this country. Hence an embargo on exportation would have reduced them directly to famine. There is not room here to insert the whole memorial, though every line of it well deserves attention; but the following passages will shew how silly it was in members of Congress to stand up and make speeches about the danger of an attack from England in the shape of open war.

"The British West-India islands," says the memorial, "containing about five hundred thousand "black, and about fifty thousand white inhabi- "tants, have been for many years, greatly depen- "dant for food upon a supply of flour, rice, Indi- "an corn, oatmeal, bread, and other articles of "dry provisions, received by a speedy channel, "and in quantities proportionate to their want, "from the countries now under the sovereignty of "*the United States of America ;* by no internal re- "source can they render themselves *independent of* "*such a supply*, excepting by a total change of their "agricultural system, at the expence of their com- "merce and revenue of the mother country ; and "experience dearly bought, on such occasions, has "now sufficiently evinced, that, *by no other external* "*channel,* can such a supply, adequate to their "wants, and suited to the emergency of circum- "stances, be obtained."

With such a document staring in his face, how could a represenative pretend to say that he was afraid of Britain declaring hostilities? Or how could two-thirds of the people in this country fall into so foolish a tremor on that head? It argues very little either for the sound information, or the good sense of our citizens. The American alarm did not begin till eighteen months after the date of this memorial, till the British minister had begun to forge bills, and till the bank of England was within a year of its dissolution.

"Besides the important articles of food, timber for the purpose of building their houses and manufactories, and staves and heading, of which to form packages for their produce: horses and other cattle for agricultural uses (the indispensible vehicles of those benefits which Great Britain derives from these islands) cannot, in many cases, be obtained at all; and in *no* case, on reasonable and advantageous terms, excepting by an intercourse with *the United States of America*."

The whole paper goes on the same principles, that the British West-Indies are absolutely at the mercy of the United States.

"The British colonies of Canada, Nova-Scotia, and St. John, instead of supplying the West-India islands with timber and provisions, have, upon a fair experience, been found, nearly at all times, to consume their own productions of these articles; and, upon some occasions, even to need a supply from their neighbours of the United States."

The contents of this memorial are so pleasing as well as important, that one could wish to have it framed in glass, and hung up in every farmer's kitchen in the country, as an invincible antidote against the return of the federal mania of April and May, 1796.

Every step of investigation discovers more clearly the utter ignorance, negligence, or corruption of his excellency John Jay. This envoy might have dictated his own terms about the West-India trade, yet it was in this very quarter that he consented to a stipulation which even the capacious gulp of our Senate could not, or durst not, swallow. By the twelfth article, we were not to keep the British islands from starving by freighting any vessels larger than *seventy tons!*

" Many obstacles stand in the way of the West-
" India colonies, obtaining lumber and provisions
" from Great-Britain, or any other country in Eu-
" rope ; more particularly the precarious circum-
" stances of such a supply ; its distance in time of
" emergency, and the perishable nature of the ar-
" ticles of food, which forbids a provision of large
" stores from a resource so remote ; and even were
" it practicable for the colonies to exist under a de-
" pendance of the necessaries of life and cultivation,
" upon means so uncertain, yet the enormous ex-
" pence of those means, particularly in respect to
" lumber, must prevent their cultivating their lands
" to any beneficial purpose either to themselves, in
" the first instance, or finally to Great Britain.

" The British colonies have found, in an inter-
" course with the United States, a market for their
" superfluous produce beyond the European con-
" sumption, and particularly for the article of rum ;
" for which, at different times, the European market
" would not afford the cost of package and trans-
" port."

Thus far we have about one-fourth part of the memorial. We now plainly see that the more islands, which England conquered in the West-Indies, the more she was dependant on this country, for their means of subsistence, for timber to build houses, for staves and heading, as likewise for taking off a great part of the West-Indian productions that would not bear the expence of being conveyed to Europe. The planters and merchants proceed to complain heavily of the mode of intercourse then permitted between the continent and the islands. It is difficult to do justice to their ideas but in their own words. Here follows part of what they say.

"Since the separation of the United States from
"Great Britain, their intercourse with our islands
"having been restricted to *British vessels only*, the
"price of lumber and provisions at the West-India
"markets, under the most favourable circumstan-
"ces of peace and regular supply, has arisen from
"fifty to an hundred per cent."

This, by the way, shews the tyrannical spirit of the British government, and how every other part of the empire is sacrificed to the plan of aggrandizing the mother country. The memorial goes on in these words.

"The intercourse, while confined to British ves-
"sels, has, for various reasons, been principally
"carried on by a direct trade between the islands
"and the United States, in vessels constructed and
"fitted for the purpose, which must evidently have
"the advantage over vessels employed in the circu-
"itous trade from Great-Britain; as the last could
"not be at once proper for the transport of lumber
"from America to the islands, and for that of pro-
"duce from the islands of Great Britain; nor afford
"means of barter in rum and molasses, nor be navi-
"gated on equally advantageous terms with those
"smaller vessels, nor equally suit their expedition
"to the wants of the islands and to the state of
"markets.

"Upon the breaking out of a war with France,
"these small and defenceless vessels have either

"fallen a prey to the enemy, or been employed in other trades; and this cannot be accounted a circumstance accidental, or that admits of future remedy; since the nature of the intercourse in question forbids an establishment of regular convoys to and from all the islands at such times as may be suited to their wants; and the immense expence of outfit, seamen's wages, and insurance, discourage adventure in a trade attended with such imminent risk, and which, if a supply by such means were even possible, must swell the expence beyond those bounds which the cultivators in those islands can possibly support."

There is next stated the frequent and *invincible necessity* which the governors of the West-India islands find of opening their ports to American vessels to prevent instant starvation; and yet provisions and other articles of *immmediate necessity* are sometimes sold at three hundred per cent. beyond the average price. For this, and other reasons above stated, they solicit a more extended intercourse with America. They represent the impossibility of providing food from their lands, and the peculiar distress under which they labour during the present war. "Under such disadvantages a perseverance in the present system of their intercourse with America must form an accumulation of burden, which will entirely preclude a fair competition with their rivals in cultivation, will stimulate and assist the progress of cultivation in the Dutch and Spanish settlements, and immediately tend to the distress and ruin of the inhabitants of the British West-India colonies, and of the numerous classes of their fellow subjects in Great Britain and Ireland connected with and dependant upon them."

The memorial also represents the good policy

of encouraging America to perfevere in her agricultural fyftem, and expreffes fears that the depreffion of her intercourfe with the iflands may have a tendency of driving her to manufactures. They add, " our fyftem of exclufive poffeffion of thofe be-
" nefits has been found, in times of emergency,
" impracticable, and the participation which, at
" fuch times, we have granted to America, has
" had neither the merit of a conceffion with that
" country, nor the advantage of effectual relief to
" ourfelves."

It is needlefs to feek farther evidence of the Britifh Weft-Indies exifting wholely at our good will; and how highly England values that part of her acquifitions appears from her folicitude to extend them.

In the debate, in parliament, about the beginning of 1796, on the bill for abolifhing the flave-trade, in the Houfe of Commons, Mr. Dundas ftated the imports from the Britifh Weft-Indies, in 1795, to be as follows: eight millions eight hundred thoufand pounds fterling; revenue arifing on this amount, one million fix hundred and twenty-four thoufand; fhipping employed in that trade, fix hundred and fixty-four veffels; tonnage, one hundred and fifty-three thoufand; feamen eight thoufand; exports from Great-Britain, to the Weft-Indies, in 1794, three millions feven hundred and forty thoufand pounds, employing feven hundred veffels; tonnage, one hundred and feventy-feven thoufand; feamen, twelve thoufand; produce of the iflands imported to Britain and re-exported, three millions feven hundred thoufand pounds.

On the 10th of February, 1797, Mr. Parker, when defending the plan of building American frigates, obferved that, fince the beginning of the war, not a fingle Britifh Weft-India fleet had been homeward bound which thefe fix frigates were not ftrong enough to have taken. Such was the known track of the trade-winds that they were obliged to come *within seven days sailing of this coast.* The French were in the same condition, so that we might have been as formidable to either of these powers as Algiers is.

The stopping of this enormous trade must have ruined the credit of Britain. She would not, therefore, have been hasty in declaring war against the country, after the dreadful campaign of 1794. On the 10th of February of that year, Dorchester had, indeed, made an address to the Indians, wherein he stated the possibility of a war, in the course of the year, between England and the United States. But this was, most likely, a mere decoy for our executive. On the 26th of May following, Grenville and Dundas denied, in Parliament, any knowledge of this performance. They certainly lied, for they refused to produce a copy of Dorchester's instructions; and, as Fox observed in reply, his lordship was not a person who would hazard such a conduct without proper authority. This disavowal by Dundas and Grenville shews that they were afraid to acknowledge the speech; and that a rupture with the United States would have been regarded in the old country with universal reprobation. Grenville even pretended to deny the possibility of such a harangue having ever been delivered. What an impostor! But this agrees very well with the forgery of Boyd's Hamburg bills*.

Camillus, No. v. overlooks every circumstance of this kind that shews how much Pitt would have

* The satellites of the minister have about as much honour and honesty as himself. The Telegraph of the 30th of March, 1795, relates, that, on a late trial at Thetford, it came out that a member of Parliament pocketed three hundred pounds sterling a year for franking letters to a banking-house.

been afraid of an American war. He tries to play upon our prudence and our fears. When speaking of the claim for negroes carried away by the British from New-York, at the end of the late war, he says " no consideration of honour forbid (*forbade*) the renunciation; every calculation of interest invited to it. The evils of war for one
" month would outweigh the advantage, if, at the
" end of it, there was a certainty of attainment.
" But was war the alternative? Yes, war or dis-
" grace.—If nothing had resulted [from Jay's
" voyage, he means,] was there any choice but re-
" prisals? Should we not have rendered ourselves
" ridiculous and contemptible in the eyes of the
" whole world by forbearing them?"

The necessity that Camillus describes did not exist; though we have lost less by a shabby state of peace, than we must have done by a successful war. But wisdom would have chosen a middle course. Jay might have addressed Grenville in terms like these. " You have wronged the United States in a
" variety of shapes. Your offers of redress are eva-
" sive or insolent. We shall not declare war against
" you. There is a shorter and a cheaper way.
" America has no treaty of commerce with Eng-
" land. She cannot be accused of breaking any,
" by stopping the exportation of provisions to your
" West-India islands. We know that your fifty
" thousand whites, and five hundred thousand blacks
" cannot find bread or pork for their dinners, or
" timber to build their houses, or staves for their
" casks, or even horses or cattle, but by sending
" for them to our continent. Besides large quan-
" tities of their rum, we also take several produc-
" tions that will not bear the expence of a con-
" veyance to Europe. This market they will for-
" feit, and ninety days of an embargo in our ports

"will make them die of hunger as fast as your victims on the glacis of Tanjore*. We shall farther give notice to France that, for ready money, she may get whatever supplies she can want, on exporting them *in her own bottoms*. If you wantonly proclaim hostilities against us, we shall follow the maxim of the Celtic chief, *neither to seek the battle, nor shun it when it comes*†. Twenty thousand of our militia, would, in a few weeks, drive your handful of regulars out of Canada, and you could not, at present, spare a fleet or an army to recover it. We should thus put an end to Indian wars, by tearing up the root from whence they spring. After driving Victor Hughes out of Guadaloupe, you might burn some of our towns on the sea coast, as you did in the last war. But then we shall infallibly destroy your nine millions sterling per annum of imports from the West-Indies, and the sixteen hundred thousand pounds of revenue derived from them. This would be a mortal stroke to your finances, and so take your choice."

In No xv. Camillus treats of the compensation afforded by the seventh article of Jay's treaty for British piracies on American commerce. Since the apoplexy of British paper the word *compensation* sounds like mockery. But Camillus would have it believed that Pitt never intended the confiscation of our vessels. "These terms, *legal adjudication*, were certainly not equivalent, upon any rational construction, to *condemnation*.—Yet the British West-India courts of admiralty appear to have generally acted upon the term as synonimous to condemnation.—The British cabinet have disavowed this construction of the West-India courts; and

---

* See Burke on the creditors of the nabob of Arcot. † Fingal.

" have, as we have seen, by a special act of inter-
" ference, opened a door," &c.

The stile of Mr. Hamilton is so prolix, he has such skill at beating out his guinea into an acre of gold leaf*, that it is inconvenient to quote him at full length. But he means to have it understood, that the West-India judges acted against the understanding and wishes of Pitt. The latter must have been a very great blockhead, if he could not write a dozen intelligible lines, especially on a subject of such immense importance. But every man, Camillus and the tories excepted, can see at once the bottom of the story. The object was to seize American shipping for the treble purpose of enriching the English, of humbling America, and distressing France. Yet the orders were to be drawn in a shuffling form, that Pitt, if he should afterwards find it adviseable to disown them, as he did Dorchester's instructions, might have a chink to creep through. We may be sure that judges, and officers of the navy, acted from a perfect acquaintance with Pitt's real intention ; and, when colonel Hamilton tries to persuade us of the contrary, it is only adding insult to robbery. When the object had been attained, it was very easy for Pitt to deny his orders. In a future chapter shall be inserted a regular history of the whole of these instructions. A second set was published by the cabinet of London on the 8th of January, 1794. They were very little better than the first. A former edition, just about as bad, had been issued on the 8th of June, 1793, under which also some bucaneering was committed. Thus the court of London acted upon a system, and it was very wrong in Camillus to cast the blame on the judges in the West-Indies. As for the above *door*

---

* This can really be done.

that has been opened, it cofts two hundred and fifty pounds fterling to get in. Divine juftice never difplayed itfelf more fplendidly than by the chaftifement of Britifh pride. Since the ftorming of the Baftile, the moft aufpicious event in the annals of Europe is the fall of the bank of England.

Among the inflammatory topics of the federal party, no one has had a more powerful effect than the attempt of Genet to involve this country in hoftilities with England. The force of the objection fhall be admitted; but any other envoy, fituated like Genet, would have rejoiced in fecuring the alliance of America. This was the very part which Dr. Franklin acted at the court of France; and the ultimate confequences of his miffion overturned the French monarchy. Nothing, therefore, can be more impenetrably ftupid than to advance, as Mr. Hamilton and his hacks conftantly do, this defign of involving us in an Englifh war, as a charge of peculiar atrocity againft Genet and the republic. This was the very path formerly purfued by the United States; and it would, under fimilar circumftances, have been attempted by any nation or any ambaffador under heaven. This identical trap had been laid by the old Congrefs and Franklin for the French cabinet, fo that it was perfectly natural for France to endeavour at obtaining a retaliation. While Genet muft be condemned, Mr. Hammond was equally culpable. His perfidious and infolent propofal to Mr. Randolph, previous to the ratifition of Jay's treaty*, was more affronting to the executive feelings, if any fuch feelings exifted, than the moft frantic menaces uttered by Genet. A compliance by General Wafhington would have caft him completely into the lee-way of the

---

* American Annual Regifter, chap. viii.

British ambassador. The possession of such a secret must have been of immense value to the British cabinet. It would have been a rudder by which our executive must have steered wherever Hammond chose to lead him; for its discovery was sure to have interred even the popularity of Washington. If this disgraceful project had come from Genet, the Gazette of the United States would have played a weekly tune upon that fiddle to the end of this century. But, originating with Pitt, not a single word will be heard about it from the federal presses.

Mr. Washington has made an uncommon parade about the impartiality of his conduct between France and England. As the former saved him from the chance of ascending a gibbet, to which he had been destined by the Parliament of Britain, he cannot derive much honour from an utter oblivion of his political obligations. But the fact is, that he has preferred Britain to France. This will appear from what follows.

In 1793, when Genet came here, he was directed, by his instructions, to open negociations for a commercial treaty. They direct him to tell the American government that the executive council " are inclined to extend the latitude of the propo- " sed *commercial* treaty." Another idea was to break up the colonial and monopolizing systems of all nations, and emancipate the new world. Camillus, No. xxiv. calls the latter *a mad scheme* and *a political chimera*. These expressions betray Mr. Hamilton's general cast of thinking. His feelings are so perfectly British, and monarchical, that it seems inconceivable how he ever came to fight, as he did, for the American revolution. Mexico and Brasil are just as well entitled to freedom as New-York and Pennsylvania. Their emancipation would be an immense benefit both to the inhabitants of those countries themselves, and to mankind at large. So far from being chimerical, the event is probable*; and it would thrill with joy the heart of every man who is not completely petrified against the pleasure of seeing his fellow creatures happy. In the last age, Camillus would have defended the divine right of kings. In England, he would vindicate the Guinea trade, as in America he sighs over the memory of the Bastile; while John Jay, and Rufus King, and Jedidiah Morse, and the whole priesthood of Connecticut, heave responsive notes of sorrow†. Were these regions of the new world independent, a rapid influx of the precious metals would pour into this country; and Mr. Hamilton's bank of the United States might then be able, upon a month's warning, to give hard dollars for one-fortieth part of the notes which it hath in circulation. So far from such an emancipation being chimerical, it is next to certain of taking place. If the French do not atchieve this great event, the tide of federal population, rolling westward, will begin it in less than a century.

Returning to President Washington and Genet, we observe that the former refused to enter into any treaty, because the Senate were not sitting at the time when the French envoy made the propo-

---

* The French had actually prepared a manifesto intituled, *Les Française Libres à leurs freres de la* LOUISIANE. In one place they say, "Le despotisme Espagnol a surpasse en atrocité, en stupidité tous les despotisms connus." [Spanish despotism exceeds all others in atrocity and stupidity.] "Ce government qui a rendu le nom Espagnol execrable sur tout le continent de l'Amerique."—['This government, which has rendered the Spanish name execrable over the whole continent of America, &c.] Such orators would soon have found an audience.

† The reverend doctor has a pulpit at Charlestown, in Massachusetts. A mob in that place burnt the British treaty. Their pastor, hearing what was going on, hasted into the street to prevent them. He presently returned to his house with a black eye.

fal. Yet, in the following spring, while the Senate were in session, and without ever once consulting them, did this identical George Washington take John Jay from the bench of the Supreme Court of this country, and send him to England, where, as we all know, he made a treaty. It was impossible for the French to avoid being affronted at such duplicity. They could no longer put trust in a man capable of such naked inconsistency. Here is inserted evidence of the fact.

"The Senate being then in recess, and not to meet again till the fall, I apprised Mr. Genet, that the participation, *in matters of treaty*, given by the constitution to that branch of our government, would, of course, delay any definitive answer to his friendly proposition. As he was sensible of this circumstance, the matter has been understood to lie over, till the meeting of the Senate.—The President will meet them (the executive of France), as soon as he can do it in the forms of the constitution*."

"Gentlemen of the Senate.———I HAVE THOUGHT PROPER TO NOMINATE JOHN JAY, as envoy extraordinary from the United States to his Britannic majesty†."

* See a letter from Mr. Jefferson, then Secretary of State, to Mr. Morris, dated August 23, 1793, in *The President's Message*, &c. Carey's edition, p. 88.
† Journals of Congress, April 16, 1794.

UNITED STATES.

The President's message is of considerable length, but the few words above quoted contain its essence. In the left hand column he says, that he cannot enter into any negociation for a treaty till the meeting of the Senate. No words can be plainer or stronger than those which he employs. The opposite column speaks an opposite language. It is ungenerous to triumph over the ruins of declining fame. Upon this account, not a word more shall be said about the matter. The bare circumstances supercede any attempt either to exaggerate or demonstrate. Nothing but the necessity of explanation could have, at all, brought the subject forward.

While this sheet was going to press, (16th May, 1797,) President Adams has delivered a speech at the opening of the first session of the fifth Congress. He says that " the conduct of the government has " been just and IMPARTIAL to foreign nations." With respect to France, what has been above cited refutes the assertion. The speech consists entirely of a complaint against the republic. It forms a kind of postscript to Pickering's letter to Pinckney. Not a word escapes the President about British piracy, which continues to expand in full blossom. The very day before this speech was pronounced, the Philadelphia Gazette contained a curious example of the relative amity of France and England. The French had carried about sixteen American vessels into Jean Rabel. The British cut out these vessels, and it was expected that they would be sent to Jamaica for trial. There can be no doubt of their being tried somewhere; and the chance is, that most, if not the whole, of them will be confiscated.

When Mr. Munroe, had his farewell audience of the executive directory, Barras glanced with contempt at the British treaty, and the British interest by which it had been brought about. Mr. Adams has muſtered up this into an alarming inſult againſt our country, and an attempt to ſow domeſtic diſſenſion. He reprobates ſuch a ſtyle in the bittereſt terms, as " ſtudiouſly marked with indignities towards the government of the United States. It evinces a diſpoſition to ſeparate the people of the United States from the government; to perſuade them that they have different affections, principles, and intereſts, from thoſe of their fellow-citizens, and thus to produce diviſions fatal to our peace."

This ſpeech does not come within the period aſſigned to the preſent volume; but it forms a branch of the plan already explained for provoking a French war. A caſe exactly ſimilar to this of Barras and Munroe happened, ſome years ago, between lord Grenville and Thomas Pinckney. The former mentioned to the latter, in the moſt overbearing manner, the influence of a jacobin faction in America. Choiſeul or Neckar would not have upbraided an Engliſh envoy with the riots excited by John Wilkes or George Gordon. If the American executive of 1793, had felt even the moſt glimmering ſpark of national dignity, the inſult would have been reſented. If Pinckney himſelf had been penetrable by reproach, he would have cut Grenville ſhort. " My lord," he might have ſaid, " England has many jacobins. Scotland has perhaps a ſtill larger proportion, and the number is hourly augmenting. The Iriſh are a jacobin nation. They are as ripe for a revolution, as a peach ever was for dropping. Confine your ſolicitude to them, and leave us to get rid, as quietly as we can, of your correſpondent, Alexander Hamilton, and his funding cancer of ſix per cent."

Mr. Pinckney pocketed the ſtigma. He ſent home the precious notice of a jacobin faction in

America. The executive, proud of such a corroboration to his own doctrine, sent it to Congress; and the letter was read to the House of Representatives without one murmur of disdain. That Pinckney should have endured such mockery was bad. That General Washington should have transferred the indignity to his own shoulders, without any muttering, was a great deal worse. The abject silence of the representatives, when the paper was read, betrayed an equal extinction of any formidable spirit.

Barras could not have wished for a better precedent in his speech to Munroe. The etiquette of federal degradation had been established at London. It had been approved by the President and Congress. Barras, with a thousand reasons for resentment, while Grenville had not one, was highly excusable for giving us a repetition of the dose.

The President affects to bristle up at the mention of American parties. He knows that there are such, and an allusion to them was not *separating the people from the government.* The British treaty was squeezed through the Senate by a party of twenty against a party of ten; and two of the former, on account of their personal characters, would hardly be admitted as evidences in a court of justice*. In the House of Representatives the treaty escaped by a single vote. Every second number of Camillus represents America as full of desperate incendiaries.

---

* Extract from the journals of the Kentucky legislature, November 21, 1795. " On motion, resolved, that a committee ought to " be appointed to draught a memorial to Congress, setting forth " that Humphrey Marshall, one of our Senators from this " state, has been publicly charged with being guilty of *perjury*, and " requesting that an investigation may be made on the subject, and " that, if the fact be sufficiently proved, he ought to be expelled " from the Senate. And a committee was appointed," &c.

Of Mr. Gunn, some notice hath already been taken.

The Gazette of the United States is an egg hatched under the very wing of the Senate. It produces a constant stream of invective against the republic, and against every man in this country who has approved of the French revolution. On the part of Barras the sarcasm was perfectly fair. We had no right or pretence to complain about it.

The House of Representatives have set out with a direct breach of one of their standing rules. This is that "in ALL cases where others than mem-" bers of the house are eligible, there shall be a *previous nomination.*"

The propriety of adopting this rule will be happily illustrated by a recent circumstance, which occurred within the walls of that house. In the second session of the third Congress, Mr. Sedgwick presented a petition from a person who wanted to be appointed as their short hand writer. It was afterwards known that this man* had, sometime before, been publicly tried at Baltimore, and banished, as *a receiver of stolen goods.* Had a stenographer been, at that time, chosen by ballot, Mr. Sedgwick might have probably brought himself into the dilemma of voting for this *honest* candidate. Such an instance has, to be sure, nothing to do with the successful candidate in the election here referred to; but it shews what may fall within the chapter of possibilities.

Mr. Giles urged the justice of naming the candidates beforehand, that gentlemen might have an opportunity of balancing, in their own minds, the merit of each. This looked like fairness. The proposal was resisted by Dr. William Smith of South-Carolina. That state hath, in the fifth Congress, sent two members of the same name and

---

* David Hogan, editor of the State-Trials of Pennsylvania.

surname. The one here meant is the writer of PHOCION's letters. This is the man who dispatched pilot boats, while Congress met at New-York, to Charleston. The object of this maritime embassy was to buy up continental certificates. They were obtained at eighteen pence or half a crown per pound. They were then funded by the doctor at twenty shillings. By a special act of Congress, to which he gave his vote, an hundred and twenty or an hundred and fifty thousand dollars of his precious commodity were transferred from the public stocks into the stock of the bank of the United States. There the Doctor draws eight per cent. of interest for the nominal amount of a sum of which the principal originally cost him but ten per cent. In plainer words, he advanced as it were ten dollars to serve his country, and, by various steps, he now draws an yearly interest for them, at the moderate rate of eight dollars. A nation cannot help flourishing, when under the auspices of such a *disinterested* legislator.

The point in view, by the breach of the above standing rule, was, to remove Mr. John Beckley from his office as Clerk of Congress, an office which he has held ever since the operation of the new government. There was not a member in the house, who could, even in the smallest degree, impeach his official conduct. This made it necessary to exclude him by a *silent* vote. The motion was carried by forty-one voices against forty. Mr. Beckley may now, like Sully, find leisure to write an history of the abominations to which he has been a witness. His talents are equal to the task, and he cannot render America a more important service.

From what has been said about the sale of certificates, it is not inferred that every purchaser of them, at an inferior price, acted dishonestly. No certainty existed of their being funded by the new government, and much less of their being funded at the full nominal value. It was a lottery whereof no one could tell the proportion of prizes. The blame in speculating rested entirely with those members of Congress who bought up the certificates at a cheap rate, with the view of thereafter voting for their being funded at the full price; or who gave such a vote with an eye to subsequent purchases. Among other defects of the new government, one was that the House of Representatives consisted only of sixty-five members. This number was too small, and twenty, joined together, by the sacred bond of paper-jobbing, were next to certain of carrying any point about which they were anxious.

On the 1st of January, 1790, this domestic debt amounted, in principal and interest, to forty millions, two hundred and fifty-six thousand dollars*. A majority of each house voted for funding the whole mass at its nominal value. How many millions belonged to themselves cannot be ascertained until the arrival of that day, which is to disclose all human secrets. Thus did the nation suffer a dozen or perhaps thirty speculators to sit as judges upon their own job.

A member of Congress might, on this occasion, be very fitly compared to an attorney whom you send into court to make the best composition that he can with your just creditors. They had heard of your being partly insolvent, and offer to transfer their claims for an eighth part of their nominal amount. It is the business of your agent to take advantage of this juncture; instead of which he clandestinely buys up all those debts against you, at the reduced price, for which his funds afford

* Gallatin, p. 96.

him ability. To shelter himself in a croud, he encourages other adventurers to buy up all the remaing debts against you in the same way. He then comes forward, in name of himself and his associates, and compels you to give a mortgage for forty millions of dollars, when he could, in reality, have rid you of the whole sum for five millions. You would not think that such an attorney had discharged his trust with fidelity. You never would employ him again. It is even possible that he might be turned out of his profession. Within the last twenty years, Mr. Alexander M'Kenzie, an attorney at Edinburgh, was employed to sell an estate. At the time and place publicly appointed, no purchaser appeared, and Mr. M'Kenzie bought it up in his own name. Several of his brethren, men above being suspected of collusion, attended the whole transaction, and gave evidence that they had no jealousy of unfair dealing. The price itself, though alledged to be somewhat low, was not much under the mark. Yet the Court of Session declared that no factor could buy and sell at the same time. They reversed the bargain, and the house of peers confirmed their decree. But, if Mr. M'Kenzie had been directed to buy an estate at its market price of two thousand five hundred pounds, and if he had first procured it for himself, and thereafter forced his client to pay twenty thousand pounds for it*, his gown would have been torn from his shoulders. The first glance from the bench would have announced the annihilation of his scheme.

Of the above forty millions of dollars, a small part was funded at only three per cent. though with

---

* This proportion of one to eight is laid down by Mr. Gallatin as the medium difference between the market price, and the full amount at which the certificates were funded.

the profpect of certain advantages, needlefs here to be explained, which were fuppofed to place it on a level in value with the remainder of the debt. Another part, though but a fmall one, was funded in name of original creditors, the men with palfies and rheumatifms caught on board of the Old Jerfey, with wooden legs and weather-beaten faces, whofe very looks are difgufting to a *friend of order*. Thefe heroes promoted an American revolution, when we were fifty times lefs heavily taxed than any other fubjects of the Britifh crown. They began a rebellion when its expence, for a fingle week, exceeded the value of all the taxes that England had either got or afked for the preceding twenty years. Hunc *tu Romane caveto*. After fuch doings, they are unfit to be trufted under any government.

For the fake of round numbers, and to be confiderably under the fact, fuppofe that only twenty four millions of dollars, out of the above forty, had been funded in the name of purchafers at half a crown per pound. The intereft, at fix per cent. comes to fourteen hundred and forty thoufand dollars per annum. If this fum had remained in the pockets of thofe who pay it, we fhould have been faved from many of the burdenfome taxes which are fo heavy on the inhabitants of the fea-port towns; and more or lefs fo upon every part of the country. Again, thofe traders or manufacturers, who pay fuch taxes, muft always add more than the net addition, to indemnify themfelves for the trouble which attends it, as well as for the advance of money*. The enormous dearth of labour muft partly be deduced from this caufe, and it produces, in an hundred different ways, inconvenience and

---

* This circumftance has been fully explained, and proved in *The Political Progrefs of Britain*.

backwardness to all sorts of business. The expence of collecting or borrowing the money forms also a serious item; and all these together, make a real loss to the public, by these twenty-four millions of dollars, not merely of fourteen hundred and forty thousand dollars, but of at least three millions. This equals the whole principal sum that the buyers of the twenty-four millions advanced. Thus nominally we pay about fifty per cent. but in reality, at the lowest, an hundred per cent. of interest for the sum truly given before hand.

The common body of creditors must have been very glad to see six millions of dollars This would have doubled their principal and made a very snug adventure. Judging by the statute of limitations, and other desperate leaps of congressional economy, we may be perfectly sure that other creditors would not have got one sixpence more than they really advanced, if it had not been to serve as a screen for the full gratification of Camillus and his myrmidons. They have ever since been constantly haranguing the public about conspiracies. *The greatest rogue always turns king's witness*, says the proverb. Nothing, since the new constitution, has, within an hundred degrees, as much the appearance of a conspiracy as this certificate business, unless, perhaps, the uproar which forced Congress to ratify the British treaty.

This was the dawning scene of that government whose wisdom and virtue have resounded through the four quarters of the globe. The annals of ancient or modern finance record not a more deformed transaction. In the black luxuriance of Roman rapine, a more pregnant field never exercised the ferocious contempt of Claudian, or the majestic severity of Juvenal. If imperial Rome could boast of her Sejanus, and Byzantium of her Rufinus, the

R

the future historian of federal glory, may brighten the tints of his canvas, and refresh the verdure of his laurel, by the congenial names of Hamilton * and of Smith.

CHAPTER IV.

British piracies on American shipping in 1796.—Case of the schooner John.—Of Capt. Samuel Green.—British privateers built in the United States.—Skirmish in Port Jeremie between the Americans and Capt. Reynolds.—Impressments by the Severn, the Hermoine, and the Regulus.—Twelve Americans whipt.—Case of the brig Fanny.—Of the ship Bacchus.—The Swallow.—The Paragon.—The Voluptas.—The Lydia.—The Hannah.—Fray at Liverpool; and rout of a press-gang.—The Friendship.—The Ocean.—Letter from Samuel Bayard.—The brig Polly.—Vigilance of the American tories.—The Hannah of Baltimore.—The ship Diana, of New-York.—The ship Polly, Captain Mayo.

MR. BACHE has compiled two volumes of speeches on Jay's treaty, which were made in the House of Representatives of Congress, in spring, 1796. It would have been a service of still more consequence to this country, if he had reprinted a collection of the various narratives of British piracy on American vessels in the West-Indies. This monument of bucanneering might have served as an useful curb to national vanity, and have taught us, if not quite incurable on that side,

---

* *Excise has gone down in other countries, and it* SHALL *go down in this.* These were the words of Camillus, then Secretary of the Treasury, to Mr. Isaac Jones, of Philadelphia, when consulted about the snuff act.

to apprehend the meanness of our present maritime condition. The devastation has been going on, with different degrees of violence, since the summer of 1793. A complete account of these piracies would very far exceed our present limits. A few examples are here selected from the mass; and beginning with the early part of the year 1796; several miscellaneous anecdotes and observations being occasionally interspersed.

A Salem newspaper, of March 8th, mentions the arrival of the schooner John, captain Philip Saunders, from Jamaica. While he lay there, an English officer and five men, from a sloop of war, came on board to impress his crew. Only one of them happened to be on board, besides the mate and a boy. The rest were on shore on business. The gang took the sailor. On being told that he was an American, they replied that they knew this, but wanted men, and would have them, whatever might be the consequence. Captain Saunders went on board of the sloop of war, to reclaim his seaman. The commander told him to go back to his own vessel, make out his account of the wages due to the hand, and send them and his clothes to the sloop. In case of non-compliance, he was threatened with a flogging. Whether he obeyed this order, we are not told. The rest of the crew were secreted on shore by the captain, for ten days, till the sloop of war sailed, as her declared design was to impress the whole. During this time, the schooner lay exposed to the weather, as well as the insults of the sloop of war, without any person to take care of her, except the captain, his mate, and the boy. The sloop's crew consisted of eighty-seven men. Of these, *thirty-five* were said to be Americans, who had been impressed in the West-Indies. Such, at the distance of twenty months, was the success of Jay's appeal to the *mag-*

nanimity of George Guelph, and of his kissing the hand of " the meat, drink, snuff, and diamond-" loving dame." Captain Saunders further informed, that several vessels belonging to the southern states, were lying at Jamaica, when he left it, without seamen to navigate them home. The crews had been impressed.

The same post brought an article from the Minerva, which is in admirable unison with the preceding narrative. An entertainment had been given, a few months before, at Amsterdam, where, " the " portrait of our beloved Washington, was exhi" ted as the chief decoration of the room." Webster then gives a long rhapsody, pronounced by some Dutchman, on the President, " As a Cato in " council; a Cæsar in the field; a Hercules in the " political tempest; the scourge and admiration of " proud Albion; Columbia's bulwark," &c. &c. Mynheer should rather have said the jossing-block of proud Albion, from which she vaulted into the saddle of sea-robbery; for now, since the mountain of compensation hath been happily brought to bed of its mouse, all parties must, in their hearts, agree, that, from the day when Jefferson left his office*, our British concerns could not have been more wretchedly managed than they actually have been. If Hercules had permitted Cacus to keep his stolen oxen, the insertion of his name would have been more intelligible. As for Cæsar and Cato——but it is needless to tread upon imbecility.

Early, as it seems, in the year 1796, captain Samuel Green made a voyage from Norfolk, in Virginia, to Martinico. He had the command of a fast-sailing schooner, of three hundred barrels burden, and carried a cargo for the British at that island.

---

* The 1st of January, 1794.

On his arrival, the consignee shewed him a bill of sale of the vessel, and told him, that he was no longer master, because the schooner was bought for the *British government*, and to be fitted out as a privateer. If captain Green chose to remain on board, he was told that he might have employment. This offer he refused. Several of the sailors were *impressed by the British*. Others were enticed to enter as volunteers in the different ships. This was the treament which other American crews, in the same trade, met with as well as his. These privateers, when thus fitted out, were to intercept our shipping in their way to the West-Indies. Thus the United States furnished privateers and seamen for the destruction of their own commerce. This is one proof, among many, of the indifference of some American owners to the personal safety of their sailors. Captain Green arrived from Martinico at Baltimore, about the 14th of March, 1796. He related the above particulars to Colonel Lowry of that town, who gave them for publication to the author. Put the case, that a merchant of Liverpool were to freight a vessel for Calais or Petersburg, with the previous but concealed certainty before him, that the ship was to be sold, the captain turned adrift without warning, and the crew to be seduced or pressed into the Russian or the French service. The attested recital of such a fact would make the owner completely odious to the public. But, in this country, a series of such transactions does not excite the smallest emotion, or even attention. About twenty-five years ago, an English sailor at Dantzic, was entrapped by a recruiting party, belonging to the late king of Prussia. The man got a letter conveyed to England, and though Frederic possessed, in all its vigour, the faculty of retention, yet he found it necessary to give Jack his freedom. The ſtory was printed in the Engliſh newſpapers, and became, for a ſhort time, a topic of converſation. Compare this ſenſibility to national rights, with the ſelfiſh American apathy, and ſay which of the two countries has the greateſt appearance of being *enlightened.*

A newſpaper of this city, of the 15th of March, 1796, contained a narrative ſubſcribed by Jacob Peterſon, maſter of the ſloop Polly, of Philadelphia. He ſays that, on the 29th of January, 1796, he arrived at cape Nicola Mole, where he had ſcarcely caſt anchor, when the Syren, a Britiſh ſixty-four, preſſed one of his beſt ſeamen. On the 31ſt, he ſailed for Jeremie. While he remained in that port, about nine o'clock in the evening, of the 9th of February, captain Reynolds, of the Harriot, a Britiſh armed ſhip in government ſervice, manned his boat and preſſed ſeveral American ſeamen from different ſhips in the harbour. He began with the ſhip Carolina, of Baltimore, captain Luſher.

Next day, Reynolds, when on ſhore, ſwore that he would that night make a ſweep among the Americans. The latter, hearing of this threat, aſſembled themſelves into two veſſels that lay in the harbour, one of them the brig Richard and James of Philadelphia, and the other the ſchooner Eliza of Baltimore. About nine o'clock in the evening, a boat full of armed men was obſerved coming from the Harriot towards the Eliza. She was hailed and enjoined to keep her diſtance. Reynolds cauſed his men to fire. This was returned; and, after ſometime, the boat went off. She came back with a freſh ſupply of men, and again found it prudent to retire. The people in the Eliza then went on board of the Richard and James. Reynolds went on ſhore, obtained a reinforcemt, and came back to a third aſſault. Finding the Eliza deſerted he gave up the attempt. In this contest, the British said that they had seventeen men killed or wounded. The Americans had one killed, and one wounded.

The above account, as to what happened at port Jeremie, was almost immediately confirmed by the arrival of captain Webb, of the brig Nymph. Captain Webb added, that the Americans had presented a petition to the commandant at Jeremie, admiral Murray, for the recovery of their impressed men, and satisfaction for the behaviour of Reynolds. Murray answered, that he had given no orders for the impress, and that he would use *his influence* to get the men restored; but, when captain Webb left Jeremie, there was no appearance of that taking place. The answer of Murray was mere mockery. Reynolds durst not have fired a pistol against the real inclination of the admiral. A British officer, in the river Thames, durst no more impress a seaman without orders, than he durst set fire to the city. For the bare loss of so many men, independent of other circumstances, he would have been called to a most severe account, even at Jeremie, unless he had acted by express orders, or connivance.

On this affair, Webster has a curious paragraph*. In spite of his British pension, it was necessary to save appearances, by saying something about it. Accordingly he observes, that, " hereto-
" fore, this villainous business has been justified
" under the pretence, that the men were British
" subjects, and indeed *this has often been the fact;*
" but these lawless fellows *now* openly, and avow-
" edly take Americans." The *heretofore* insinuates an untruth; because, from the beginning, multi-

* Minerva, March 17, 1796.

tudes of Americans were taken without any such pretence. "As the admiral," says Webster, "did not justify him (Reynolds) it is possible the insulted Americans may obtain redress, and we presume [and what is your reason for that *presumption?*], all impressments are made *without orders* from the British government." [The best and only *redress* will be, when the French shall burn Plymouth and Dover.]—" Their conduct is now, if possible, aggravated, as it is a direct violation of the *treaty ;*" which, to England, is of equal concern with the violation of a pancake. As for acting without orders, that is the constant sham. Dorchester was said to act *without orders*, when, on the 10th of February, 1794, he made his famous or infamous speech to the savages. Simcoe, undoubtedly, acted also *without orders*, when he sent a body of British regulars and Detroit militia, to assist the Indians in assaulting fort Recovery. The rank and file, with their faces blacked, and the three British officers dressed in scarlet, who kept at a distance, in the rear, and directed the motions of the Putawatimes, were certainly acting likewise *without orders*. Nay farther, Henry Knox, late Secretary at War, did infallibly act *without orders*, when he refused to give the newsprinters a copy of the long and important letter from Wayne, giving evidence of these facts*.

---

* This is not a hearsay. Not more than a sixth part of the letter could be obtained. The late Mr. Andrew Brown, was in the War-Office, trying to get a full transcript for the Philadelphia Gazette, and both he and others met with a refusal. They received, besides a list of the killed and wounded, only some scraps which make up a paragraph of about thirty lines. Nothing was suffered to transpire in the public prints that could place the behaviour of Simcoe in a proper light.

But, on the 21st of November, 1794, it was thought proper to read this dispatch to Congress, with some depositions that had like-

UNITED STATES.

On the 15th of March, 1796, Mr. Samuel Smith, presented to the House of Representatives a protest taken by captain John Green, of a Baltimore brig, trading to the West-Indies. He deposed that, when he was at cape Nichola Moie, he was on board a schooner from Virginia, where he saw two of the crew, native Americans, impressed by the officers of the British ship Severn. One of the men was afterwards returned as unfit for duty. The commander of the Severn said, that he was authorized, by the late treaty, to take all seamen who had not protections from the United States. In saying this, he paid a compliment to Jay's treaty which it does not merit. All seamen, whether with protections or without them, are alike unnoticed by that paper. On presenting this protest, an insignificant debate ensued in the house. The question was, whether it should be referred to the select committee on American seamen, or to the Secretary at War, that the President might make suitable representations to the British government. It was remitted to the committee. Congress might as well have deliberated, whether the protest should be cast under the table, or into the fire.

wise been kept secret. The latter shewed, in the strongest light, the extreme aversion of the Indians to fight Wayne, and the artifices of the British to make them do so. A person who overheard the papers read, obtained, a considerable time after, permission to copy them from the repositories of Congress. So late as May, 1796, they were successively printed in the Maryland Journal, the Aurora, and the Argus. Mr. M'Henry, now Secretary at War, being greatly surprised at their appearance, wrote a letter to one of these printers, intreating to know which of his clerks in the war-office had betrayed official confidence ; and assuring the printer, that if he would give up the name of this correspondent, *the mode of discovery should be concealed*. Such is the minute vigilance of the American cabinet ! and so culpable it is to let the people become acquainted with their own business! In reply, the Secretary was assured of the entire innocence of all his clerks, and advised to proceed with his inquiries.

S

The Philadelphia newspapers of the 18th of March, related that captain M'Keever, of the brig Amiable Creole, sailed from Port-au-Prince, on the 25th of February, preceding. The captain said that while he lay there, the Hermione frigate pressed, from time to time, a vast number of American seamen out of different vessels. On a moderate calculation, *two-thirds of his crew were Americans.*

The Regulus, another frigate, pressed all hands of all nations indiscriminately, who could not produce protections. Those who refused to do duty were whipt. Four days before capt. M'Keever left Port-au-Prince, twelve American seamen were returned on shore from the Regulus, after receiving several lashes for having utterly refused to do duty on board of her. The rest of the impressed men, in these two frigates, had found it prudent to comply with British orders. This was the treatment of our seamen fifteen months after the signing of Jay's treaty, and *before* Congress began to debate, on the propriety of accepting it.

REMARKS from the brig Fanny's log-book, William Swinburn, master, from the West-Indies, arrived at New-York, on the 21st of March, 1796.

"On Thursday, January 28, 1796, at five P. M. was "boarded off St. George's bay, Grenada, by the Zebra's "boat (a British sloop of war), who impressed one of the peo- "ple, John Burt, being born in the United States, and having "a regular protection. I accordingly made application to the "commanding officer, in expectation of getting him clear, but "to none effect; their answer was, *they wanted men and must* "*have them.*

"On Monday, February 8th, at two P. M. was boarded by "the Mermaid's boat, a British frigate, who impressed one of "the men (he not being a British subject), and overhauled us "very strictly on suspicion of my having sailors stowed away. "That same night I went on board to solicit for my man. "After communicating to the captain my errand, he told me "he was certain I had men stowed away, and he would send "his boat on board, and overhaul us from keel to gunnel; and, after giving me much abusive language, said *he would flog me, and all I had on board.* Accordingly, the Mermaid's boat came on board with a great many hands, hove the long boat out of the chocks, hoisted up twenty-two barrels of beef, moved part of the ballast, and, as the saying is, turned every thing upside down. They went on board, first being convinced I had no people stowed away. I shortly after went on board the Mermaid to see if they would send the boat and crew on board to stow the cargo in its proper place, as I had no people to do it, and put the boat in the chocks, &c. and after distressing me all they could, with respect to my people, I was told they had done with me, and bid me go about my business, and get people where I could.

"Shortly after I had got on board my vessel, the Charlotte, captain Williams, a British sloop of ten guns, sent her boat on board, who overhauled us, &c. On the 9th, at meridian, with much difficulty weighed anchor, and made sail, as I could get no redress, and no probability of getting hands.

"Shortly after was brought too by a shot from the above sloop, and after we hove the sails to the masts, and brought too, she fired no less than half a dozen musket shot, aimed right at us; but providentially we received no hurt from them, though I heard the whistle of several of the balls.

"After we had laid some time, they sent the boat on board, who rummaged and overhauled; but seeing they could find nothing, they returned on board.

"On Thursday, the 11th, at nine A. M. saw a sloop to the leeward, which shortly knew to be the same sloop, that had boarded us two days before, in St. George's bay.

"When she came within a league of us she fired, and continued to do so, as long as the guns would bear, she reaching one way and we the other. When she got into our wake she tacked but did not come up with us until two P. M. when we tacked, and she fetched and brought us too with another shot. I received a great deal of abusive language from the captain without giving any reasons.

"He cursed and damned the Americans and said they were their greatest enemies. He said he had fired twelve shot at us, that I should pay two dollars for the first, and double for every one after: however, I not being willing to comply with this unreasonable request, and seeing he had no business to have fired at us, as he had boarded us the day before, and "as he did not think fit to send his boat on board, he suffered us to set sail.

"This is a short specimen of the usage we meet with from the British cruizers in the West-Indies. All which I can attest to; and much more if required.

WILLIAM SWINBURN."

On the 28th of March, 1796, the ship Bacchus, captain George, arrived at Philadelphia. On the 20th he was boarded by the Thetis, a British frigate. She pressed his mate and cabin boy, on a suspicion of their being British subjects. The boy was an indented apprentice.

As it is proper to do justice to all parties, it may here be noticed that, at this time, captain Burnet, of the Brig George, arrived at Philadelphia from Kingston, and brought a complaint of the French privateers. He said that several of them were cruising off Jamaica, when he left it. They were very troublesome to American vessels, sometimes plundering them of their sea stores, and otherwise behaving with the greatest insolence. No farther particulars are specified; and this is the first complaint against France, or at most the second, which hath as yet occurred in collecting materials for the present summary of piracies. At the same time several articles of British rapine have been omitted for want of room. So contrasted at that period was the conduct of these two nations to this country.

A gentleman at Kingston in Jamaica, in a letter to the printers of the Maryland Journal, dated the 25th of February 1796, gave the following particulars. The Argonaut man of war of sixty-four guns, had, a few days before, sent into Kingston, two American vessels. The one was the schooner Swallow, captain Stubbs, from Cape Francois to Boston. Her cargo consisted of cotton and coffee, with six thousand dollars in specie. The whole property belonged to Mr. Trisdale of Boston. The other vessel was the schooner Paragon of Norfolk, laden with coffee, and owned by Mr. Moses Myers of that town. In June, 1794, coffee cost in retail, at Philadelphia, about a shilling per pound. In June, 1795, it had got up to one shilling and four-pence. By November, 1796, if not sooner, it rose to two shillings and four pence. The piracies just now stated, which are only part of hundreds of the same kind, explain, very fully, the cause of this alteration. The writer of the above letter added that both vessels were libelled, and that indeed *none need expect to escape that fate*, whatever might be the final verdict about them. The very delay, disappointment, and rise of insurance, in consequence of such alarms, impose a ruinous tax on the owners, while, in the mean time, the sailors were frequently pressed. Sometimes they were swept off by the yellow fever; and cargoes of a perishable nature were often destroyed while the ship waited for a decision.

The same letter adds that the schooner Voluptas, Jonathan Hall, master, of Baltimore, had been sent into Kingston, by the Severn of forty-four guns. She had on board a valuable cargo of coffee and cotton, and part of an outward bound freight of provisions, with a large sum of money. The supercargo, Mr. Duncan, was going from Gonaives to the Platform, to purchase coffee to load the sloop for Baltimore. The pretence for sending in the Voluptas was, that she carried provisions for an enemy's port. At this time, the captain of the Severn had kept Mr. Duncan a prisoner for fifty-two days, and threatened to try him, as a British subject, for high treason; although he had with him a certificate of his being an American citizen.

Captain Hall, and Mr. Duncan had been sent prisoners from cape Nichola Mole to Port Royal, on board the Lark man of war. On their passage, they were put upon two-thirds of the British seamen's allowance of salt beef and bread. One of them, the letter does not say which, happening to sleep in the next birth to the lieutenant, had his watch and money stolen out of his pocket. It was their opinion that the Severn had designed to send the schooner to the bottom, for she ran so near as to carry away their bowsprit.

A few days before the writing of this letter, the ship Lydia, Robert Blount, master, from Portsmouth in New-Hampshire, had arrived at Kingston. About four leagues to windward of Port-Royal, he had been boarded by the Regulus. She took away his mate, and four men. They were all natives of Portsmouth, married, and had regular protections. Before taking them on board, the British captain sent his surgeon into the Lydia, to examine the men, and see if they were in good health. The Regulus had pressed above fifty seamen, went to Port-au-Prince, and from thence to England; so that when the Portsmouth sailors were to see their families, or whether they were ever to see them at all, was extremely doubtful.

The same correspondent gives an account of the conduct of a French privateer to an American brig which, on the 14th of February, had come into Kingston. This privateer had taken the British ship Barzillai, captain Blackburn, which left Kingston on the 3d of February, and was taken on the 7th, in sight of Port Royal*. The French put Blackburn, with

---

* "But the misfortune is, that men will oppose imagination to "fact. Though we see Great Britain *predominant* on the ocean, "though we observe her *pertinaciously resisting the idea of pacification*

his whole private property, on board of the brig. In his trunk were two bags of money; the plate of the ship's cabin; and two bills of exchange to the amount in whole of eight hundred pounds. The Frenchman faid that he difdained to take any thing from a prifoner, and wifhed him a good voyage to Kingfton. From the brig this jacobin took a barrel of beef, and paid fifteen dollars for it. Thus far the letter to the printers of the Maryland Journal.

A Philadelphia print of the 26th of March, 1796, contained an extract of a letter dated March 2d, from Bermuda. The writer mentions that the fhip Hannah, captain Hoare, from Philadelphia to France, was, on the 24th of February, taken by the Lynx floop of war. She ftript the Hannah of her whole crew, excepting the mate, the cook, and the cabin boy, and fent her into Bermuda. Moft of the hands impreffed had protections. The captain of the Lynx had fpoke, on the day before, with the Roebuck of Philadelphia, and faid that he was prevented from taking her by a violent gale of wind.

An article dated Salem, the 22d of March, gives what is called *verbal information by captain Blacker*. Part of it is in fubftance as follows:

On the night of the 22d of January, 1796, the prefs gang at Liverpool crimped an American feaman, having previoufly ferved feveral others in the fame way. Two hundred and fifty American failors affembled, went to the houfe of rendezvous of the gang, and refcued their companion. They placed the officers of the imprefs in the centre of the room, obliged them to uncover, and give three cheers to

---

" *with France, &c.*" Camillus, No. v. A valuable predominancy, when her veffels were captured in fight of her own ports, and almoft in fight of her fhips of war!

the United States. On the 27th, another American was impressed. His countrymen again assembled, rescued the man, killed one of the gang, threw another into the dock, where he was drowned, and severely beat the remainder, who fled.

On the 2d of February, the American captains were called before the mayor and magistrates of Liverpool. They were admonished to keep their crews in order. They made an answer which must have occurred to any body excepting a member of Congress vindicating appropriations for the British treaty. The account adds that, from thence forward, the Americans were unmolested.

About the 29th of March, 1796, the ship Friendship, captain Atkins, arrived at Norfolk. The captain said that, within the capes of Chesapeake, he was boarded by a boat from the Thetis, captain Cochran, which pressed a man who had been naturalized for ten years past. As the Chesapeake is within the territory of the United States, the British might as decently have taken him from the streets of Philadelphia. A letter from New-York to a merchant in Philadelphia, dated the 2d of April, informed that his ship, the Ocean, captain Vredenburgh, had been taken on the 31st ult. and sent into Halifax by La-Prevoyance, a British frigate. The whole crew, at the time of writing the letter, were detained on board of the frigate, except the master, the first mate and a boy. The Ocean was from Havre-de-Grace, and the frigate took her, not far from the Highlands, with a pilot on board. The Argus, of April 4th, says, that before she was dismissed for Halifax, " several " passengers were most graciously permitted to jump " into the long boat, and come up to New-York." When captain Vredenburgh remonstrated, the British captain told him that this conduct was justified by Jay's treaty. The Minerva says that the Ocean was taken three days before she made land. But the Conecticut goddess of wisdom is distinguished for want of veracity*. It is at least very uncommon to take in a pilot, at such a distance from shore; and it is agreed that the Ocean had one. While the British were thus plundering American shipping, Mr. Pickering received a letter from Mr. Samuel Bayard, dated London, 29th of December, 1795. The following extract appeared, on the 31st of March, 1796, in the Philadelphia Gazette.

"In the course of this next month, the Judge
" of the Admiralty has authorized us to expect an
" order for the restitution of the vessels and car-
" goes seized and sold by sir J. Jarvis and sir
" Charles Grey, at Martinico, St. Lucia, and Gua-
" daloupe.

"In the court of appeals, also, two illegal sen-
" tences of the Vice-Admiralty Courts, in the West-
" Indies, have lately been annulled, and the con-
" duct of the judges severely censured by the lords
" commissioners of appeals."

This intelligence, as if worth a perusal, was communicated by Mr. Pickering to the committee of merchants in this city, appointed to superintend the business of indemnification. Nothing but the blindness of interested hope, could have drawn any comfort from such an account. The attainment of an object is at a very indefinite distance when the parties are only *authorized to expect*. The annulling of two piracies, out of five or six hundred, was merely casting a tub to the whale. As for the censure bestowed on the West-Indian judges, how much it was in earnest, and how much it was respected, appears from their persisting, at that very moment, to proceed in the same track. There

---

* Webster is a native of that state.

T

could not be a more palpable delusion, though indeed the thinness of the disguise almost precludes it from that name. The British had been plundering American merchantmen for almost three years. A treaty, which was to stop every proceeding of the kind, had been ratified eight months before. Yet still piracy and impressment went on at full vigour. But when we consider the uncommonly petrified ideas of many merchants in the sea-ports of America, nothing but the most snivelling timidity could be looked for. In summer, 1793, British effrontery declared the French republic in *a state of siege;* and, under that pretence, confiscated American vessels freighted for any French port with provsions, as if France and her colonies had only been some fortified town with an area of a square mile. At that crisis, merchants of eminence in this city were to be found who vindicated that enormous robbery. If, in a similar situation, any citizen of London had harboured such feelings, the certainty of public abhorrence would at least have forced him to hold his tongue. When captain Barney, about that time, made a voyage to the West-Indies, and declared his determination, if attacked, of giving battle to the successors of Blackbeard, the tory party in Philadelphia were violent in his condemnation. A report having reached the continent, that the English at Jamaica had resolved to hang him it was solemnly pronounced, in this city, to be perfectly right; and that he was an incendiary who wanted to embroil the two countries. It was to be expected that such people would abominate the American Annual Register as *the veriest catch-penny that ever was published, the mere tittle tattle of jacobinism**. They are welcome to feel no *excitement except that*

* See Gazette of the United States.

of disgust at any thing it contains; for, if it had met with *their* approbation, it would have completely disgusted its author, and that class of people whom he is chiefly desirous of pleasing. It cannot escape observation that the above notice from Bayard contains not one syllable about the impressment of sailors. This blank in Jay's treaty, and Bayard's commission, may be compared to the capitulation of a general, who, without a single stipulation about protecting the sick and wounded men of his army, thinks of nothing but the security and free departure of his baggage.

Captain Paulding, of the brig Polly, in a letter to his owners, at New-York, from Curracoa, dated March 3d, says, that he had been sent into Grenada, by the Favourite sloop of war, after she had taken from him *all his hands*, with sailing orders, letters, invoices, and bills of lading. He was detained for some weeks. At lenth he had orders to depart, but could not recover his papers. His cargo was, he says, considerably damaged by his detention. He does not tell whether he got back any of his men, which is very unlikely, or by what means he worked the vessel to Curracoa.

The Maryland Journal, of the 13th of April, 1797, has an extract of a letter from an American seaman dated Spithead, December 26th, 1795, on board the ship Assistance, in which he had been detained from the 20th of October preceding. The man belonged to the Hannah of Baltimore, Captain Wescott. This vessel, with four other Americans had been carried into St. John's, Newfoundland. He expressed a hope that the Hannah would be liberated. The printers added, that the sticklers for British amity, might, upon calling at their office, see the original letter. This intimation was needful in the case where such an article had not been copied from some other print; for, in Baltimore, Philadelphia, and perhaps in every sea-port-town in the union, a number of people are constantly ready to browbeat and even ruin any printer who publishes articles unfavourable to Britain. Thus, at the death of Dr. Franklin, a newspaper of this city observed, that the flags of the ships in the Delaware were lowered. The printer unthinkingly subjoined that *even the British** did so. Next day several of his subscribers came into his office, and, with many reproaches, threw up his paper. The author had the story from himself. Indeed no better state of society can be expected in our sea-ports, where the whole mass of British tories, who had been doing the utmost mischief in their power to this country, during the revolution, were permitted, almost universally, without distinction, to return and mix upon a level with the republican citizens. In private morals, they were just as good as other people. But, in a political light, they were at best concealed, and often professed enemies. In private life, no man would lodge under his roof an incendiary who, for eight years, had been attempting to burn his house. At the last election for Congress, in the county of Philadelphia, one of the most officious of the *federal* managers had formerly acted as a British guide. He was, for this offence, tried by the state, and very nearly hanged. A shoal of similar examples might be traced.

The next article, in the same Maryland Journal, shews in what subjugation the tories hold the press.

---

* A lady, who is very nearly related to Dr. Franklin, had occasion, since his death, to make a voyage to England. In several fashionable companies she met with the coldest treatment, as being connected with the family of *a rebel!* If George the Third escapes the dagger or the scaffold, his most faithful subjects in Philadelphia, and they are not few in number, will have a notable opportunity for bowing and scraping, on his alighting at Oeller's hotel.

Captain Herring, from Jamaica, had informed the printers that, when the British captured and sent into that island American vessels, the sailors were either turned ashore to starve, or pressed into the British service. He added, that all of them received " the " most indignant treatment from these *tyrannical* " *sea monsters*." For inserting such harsh language, the printers made a long and humble apology. This timidity betrays a feature of degradation unknown in France or England. Was it ever heard of that a British mariner, on returning home from a French jail, durst not publish his complaints in a British newspaper; or that the editor would be forced to apologize for giving him a corner *?

Captain Herring, abovementioned, furnished the printer of the Journal with the following list of vessels left at Kingston, on the 8th of March last, which were all prizes to the Argonaut. Schooners Voluptas, Hall, Baltimore; Active, Compton, do.; Adelaine, Stanley, do.; Fortitude, Rofs, do.; Swallow, Stubbs, Boston; Paragon, ———, Norfolk; and a number of other vessels, belonging to several ports in the United States; in all FIFTY-FIVE.

The infatuation and stupidity of a certain set of people in this country surpasses all description. They embrace every opportunity to revile and exasperate the French, to whom we were at first indepted for independence, and who, at this mo-

---

* Just below, in the same column, there follows a string of resolutions from Cumberland county, in the state of Maryland, in favour of Jay's treaty. They say that " the esteem of his fellow-" citizens is *the only reward*, which he (the President) is willing to " recieve for his *unexampled* services." It signifies nothing to chime over this impertinent fable of the President serving his country for *nothing*. Yet, though he has asked and received the last cent of his two hundred thousand dollars, besides thirteen thousand six hundred to assist him in setting up a house, the friends of *order* will never cease to prate that he would accept of no salary.

ment, are the shield which saves us from the implacable fury of Britain.

On the other hand, though they cannot deny the scandalous conduct of our blessed mother country, they do not wish, if they can help it, to hear a single word upon the subject. Language of this kind, can, they say, be productive of no good; and it may irritate Britain, with whom, you know, we are in *amity*.

A letter from Norfolk, dated 4th, and published in the Philadelphia Gazette on the 11th of April, 1796, has these words.

" A vessel, yesterday, returned from the Mole,
" which carried out some of the horses, and lost
" about one-half of them. Also a sloop from here,
" arrived there with only four horses alive; and a
" brig from here lost about one half of the cargo
" of horses which she carried out, the rest were
" all sickly."

The next paragraph shews the difference of behaviour at this time, between the French and English privateers. A French cruiser fell in with the schooner Little John, sent her into the Havannah, and detained her five days. The French took half a puncheon of rum, a barrel of bread, and a spyglass. The captain gave an order for the amount upon his agent in Philadelphia.

NORFOLK, April 4.

" We stop the press to mention the arrival of
" captain Wanton Steer, of the brig Charlotte, in
" twenty-four days from Port Royal, Martinique;
" from him we have obtained the following:

" That the ship Diana, of New-York, David
" Chadeayne, master, on his passage from the East-
" Indies to New-York, was boarded by his Britan-
" nic majesty's brig Pelican, captain J. C. Searle,
" who sent an officer and crew on board and took

" out the mate, six people, and carried her into
" Port Royal; where, on the 6th of March, while
" in their poffeffion, fhe caught fire and *was burnt
" to the water's edge, with all her cargo, of im-
" menfe value!"*

The following article is here copied from a Bofton newfpaper, of the 7th of April, 1796.

MORE BRITISH AMITY.

" Captain Elkanah Mayo, who arrived in town this week
" from New-York, has favoured us with the following ac-
" count of the cruel treatment he and his men received from
" the officers and men of the Britifh frigate La Pique, at Bar-
" badoes, in December laft, viz. Captain Mayo, in the fhip
" Polly, of Cape Ann, homeward bound, from a whaling voy-
" age, was drove in, by ftrefs of weather, to Barbadoes, where
" he lay near three weeks for the arrival of fome Americans
" to freight his oil home; during which time, the Britifh fri-
" gate La Pique arrived there from a cruife, and in two days
" after, preffed two of his hands. Captain Mayo applied to
" the governor for protection, who caufed the men to be re-
" leafed; three days after, captain Mayo's boat, being afhore,
" with three men waiting for him, the frigate's barge hauled
" in clofe to his boat, and boarded him with cutlaffes to prefs
" the men by force. The men called on captain Mayo, from
" the fhore, who run to the boat for their relief, where he found
" the crew of the Britifh frigate with the tillar of their barge
" beating his men over their heads, with faid tillar, till the blood
" gufhed from their mouths and nofes, and otherwife mangling
" them in a barbarous and fhocking manner. Captain Mayo
" fprung into the boat and cleared it of the Britifh crew. The
" commanding officer, who was then on the wharf, faid he
" would have every man aboard the fhip. Mr. Woodruff,
" with whom captain Mayo did bufinefs, being on the wharf,
" offered his bonds to the captain of the frigate that he would
" bring his protections on fhore. Captain Mayo then went
" on board his fhip to bring his protections. While he was
" on board, the commanding officer of the frigate, and all the
" reft of the officers, got into their barge, waiting for captain
" Mayo, who was returning with all his protections; they
" boarded him; the commanding officer jumped into captain
" Mayo's boat with his drawn cutlafs, and dragged by force all

"his men into their barge, and then presented his cutlass to capt.
"Mayo's breast, and ordered him into the barge, which he refu-
"sed; after which he pricked him several times in the breast, and
"then towed him on board the frigate; he put capt. Mayo's men
"into the hole among his men who were sick with the yellow
"fever; he then ordered a pair of irons to be fixed on captain
"Mayo, which were not, however, fixed; he kept him on the
"quarter-deck until evening, then ordered captain Mayo's boat
"to be hauled up, and ordered him on board alone. Capt. Mayo
"requested him to let him have a man to go with him, which
"the captain of the frigate refused; then said he would cast
"him off, and let him go adrift, he told him he might perish
"at sea, to which he replied he hoped he would. Captain
"Mayo told him he would not go, unless he cast him off, he
"then took his barge, and towed captain Mayo on board his
"own ship; the next morning captain Mayo went to the go-
"vernor, and complained of the officers conduct; the gover-
"nor ordered his men to be immediately released, who were
"accordingly sent on shore. Four days after, three of his men
"were taken with the yellow fever, which they took while on
"board the frigate, and which spread through captain Mayo's
"ship's company: four of his men died of the fever, the rest
"were obliged to leave the ship, and he hired negroes to pump
"her. Captain Mayo then chartered vessels as he could find
"them to take his men and cargo to the United States. This
"base conduct of our new-treaty-allies occasioned the loss of
"eight thousand dollars to his owners.
"I, the subscriber do testify to the above account.
ELKANAH MAYO."

While the British were going on at this rate, a letter, dated January 17th, was received in Philadelphia, from Samuel Bayard agent of the United States, at London, on the business of restitution. Mr. Bayard writes thus:

"As soon as ministry learn the line of conduct,
"which the House of Representatives mean to pur-
"sue, I am persuaded their conduct, as it regards
"us, will be less fluctuating. Should the house co-
"incide with the President and Senate, every thing
"here will go well: should obstacles, on the other

"hand, be thrown in the way by the popular branch
"of the government, I doubt whether the western
"posts will be surrendered, or *restitution made of
"our captured property*. However, I trust that
"every man who has any regard to the *honour*,
"the *faith*, or *interest* of his country, will see the
"necessity of carrying the treaty fully into effect,
"so far as regards the United States."

The scope of the letter is, that, if Congress appropriated for Mr. Jay's treaty, compensation would be made for the piracies in the West-Indies. If they did not, the prizes would be kept. This plainly infers, that the British were acting as consummate bucanneers. For, whether the treaty past or not, they had no title to have taken these vessels. But the superior talents of Mr. Jay had happily interwoven two matters totally distinct. If you sign this treaty of commerce, you shall get compensation for the vessels. If not, we shall have them to ourselves. Before entering upon the old story of debts due to Britain; of the western posts, and of matters relative to the last war; before plunging into treaties of amity, the recent seizure of the vessels should have been fully and separately settled. If that could be done, it was time enough to get into a treaty. If it could not be done, the way for America was to have stood by in wait for contingencies, while an embargo on provisions would have laid the British West-Indies prostrate at her feet. Instead of this obvious policy, matters the most distinct were all jumbled together; and the bait of compensation made America snap at the gilded hook.* Suppose that one of her neighbours

---

* In justice to Mr. Jay, it must be believed that his conduct was affected by some reasons not yet communicated to the public. The

V

hath broke into a widow's wheatfield, nightly, for months together, and carried off or destroyed her crops. An envoy is sent to demand satisfaction. The robber answers that he has old accounts to settle with the landlady, that he wants a wife, and that, if she will agree to a settlement, and at the same time let him have her hand, he will enter into one sweeping treaty for the whole. Any servant girl would see the absurdity of this jumbling application of the following anecdote cannot be mistaken. It shews the frequent appeals that Pitt makes to Macedonian logic.

On the 9th of February, 1794, colonel Whitlock wrote a letter to general Lavaux, who commanded at Port-au-Paix, in St. Domingo. He required Lavaux to deliver up the town, the forts, and shipping. He then, in the name of the British government, adds thus: " The sum of FIVE THOUSAND CROWNS TOURNOIS shall " be paid to you in person, or deposited in the bank of England, " payable to your order."

In his answer, Lavaux says, " permit me now to complain to " yourself, of the indignity you have offered me, in thinking me so " vile, so flagitious, so base, as not to resent," &c. He concludes with sending Whitlock a challenge immediately to meet and fight him. See New Annual Register for 1794, History, p. 338.

But if Port-au-Paix was worth five thousand crowns to England, Jay's treaty was worth fifty millions. The Representatives were in the direct way to the destruction of the British West-Indies. A suspension of commercial intercourse, and an embargo, would have reduced both England and those colonies to the utmost difficulty. These two measures would have broke no treaty, nor afforded any pretence for a quarrel, and they would have humbled England too much to leave her any appetite for the wanton declaration of hostilities. All this was so evident, the track pursued by the Representatives was marked with such luminous circumstances of invitation, that nothing but ignorance, corruption, or the most abject imbecility of understanding, could mistake it.

Like Sennacherib's angel, Camillus interfered to suggest an express libel on Congress, to tarnish the character, to undermine the interest, and to hamstring the vengeance of America. With a message so welcome, so necessary, to the very being of the court of London, Jay must have been a favourite guest. And, after the sacrifices which he made, if he did not pay due attention to the future independence of his family, he is a greater simpleton than the world can possibly think him to be.

proposal. She would reply, that intermarriage might come time enough, when former complaints were cleared up. But the object of Mr. Hamilton and his friends was, right or wrong, to have a *British* treaty; and the present one could not have been got through, but for entwisting it with the prospect of compensation.

On the 8th of April, 1796, a Philadelphia print contained the following extract of a letter from London, dated February 2d.

"I this moment came from the court of admi-
"ralty, where the first case of the captures at Mar-
"tinique, by Grey and Jervis, was tried this mor-
"ning: it was reversed, which will be a precedent
"for all the others, and a point gained for all of
"us that have cases in the courts here. And now
"they say, on Saturday next, the lords will sit,
"and will go on to try the legality of the condem-
"nations in the West-Indies."

As to *the point gained for all of us*, there is yet very little progress made, nor is it of much concern to the claimants whether there is or not. The above, and Mr. Bayard's letter, are quoted chiefly because they contain not even one single, solitary, word, about the relief of the sailors, who had been torn from their families, and their country, starved, hand-cuffed, and flogged, to make them enrol in the British service of assassination. If this book falls into the hands of any of that class of people, they are entreated to reflect for what sort of *owners*, and what sort of a country, they are braving the hardships of a mariner's life. We have seen how tranquilly Camillus gets over their enormous wrongs. Yet, when a British creditor in the American funds was concerned, he could speak about them like a man who was in earnest. "No
"powers of language," says he, "at my command,

"can express the abhorrence I feel at the idea of violating the property of individuals, which, in an authorized intercourse, in time of peace, has been confided to the faith of our government.— In my view, every moral, and every political sentiment, unite to consign it to execration."* Compare this glowing style with the frigid accents in which he observes, that it was impossible to help the impressment of American seamen. They should be at least as near our hearts, as the mere pecuniary interest of an English creditor in the American funds. This will be granted by every friend to the country; and, on this principle, *every moral and political sentiment will consign to execration*, Jay and his treaty, wherein the safety of our mariners has been totally neglected. As for the twenty treaty-making senators, they are neither worse nor better than the numerous bodies of our citizens, who thanked the President for signing this monument of American apathy—an instrument by which thousands and ten thousands of seamen were consigned to British mercy. There is no desertion of fellow-countrymen so thoroughly disgraceful in the annals of any independent people under heaven. A century of heroism could hardly wipe out the stain. Fifty-five American ships are captured by a single British corsair,† more than a twelvemonth after a treaty of amity had been signed, and above six months after it had been fully ratified. With such intelligence staring in their faces, while every newspaper, for eighteen months preceding, had been suffocated with similar information, "the FREEST and most enlightened nation in the world," compelled their representatives, *for fear of a British war!* to appropriate for the treaty.

* Camillus, No. 28. † The Argonaut. See above.

As Mr. Hamilton has betrayed so much concern for British creditors, it may be asked why he does not feel equal interest in the state of Maryland? Before the war that province had vested considerable sums of money in the bank of England. On the 17th of December, 1795, a select committee reported to the legislature of that state, that "they "have no information as to the probability of their "recovering the stocks in the bank of England, to "which they claim a title." When Jay took so much care for the safety of British creditors in American funds, he might likewise have paid some attention to the interest of Maryland in the British funds.

The tenth article of the treaty contains a plain commentary on this stoppage of Maryland property. It says that "neither the debts due from individu- "als of the one nation to individuals of the other, "nor shares nor monies which they may have in the "public funds, or in the public or private banks, "shall ever, in any event of war or national differ- "ence, be sequestered or confiscated, *it being unjust* "*and impolitic*," &c. Why then did England seques- trate, or with what pretence of decency does she continue to keep the funds of Maryland? When the Senate and Executive signed the treaty, they might surely have thought of this important omission. But this article has even a worse fault. The words *unjust and impolitic* contain a direct libel on Mr. Dayton, and that party in the House of Representatives, who, in March, 1794, had proposed to sequestrate British debts, as a security for American compensation. The Senate and President ratified this insult on the Representatives, though, as being a solemn act of government, it contained an attack on the American legislature, a million of times more flagrant than the transitory squib of

Barras. Yet the latter is to be made the handle for a French war, while the former, *because it came from Britain*, was pocketed in silence. If an English minister had subscribed a treaty conveying such a direct reference to, and such an abrupt censure of any previous motion in parliament, the parties aggrieved would have taken the matter up. But indeed no English minister dared to have made such a digression. In discussing the treaty, none of the Representatives adverted to this tacit reproach. The pulse of national dignity seems to beat higher in England than in the United States.

Camillus clamours loudly about the iniquity of America in neglecting the payment of debts due to Britain, before the last war. What here follows, on that head, was related to the author, in January 1796, by Mr. James Madison.

Much noise has been made about the justice of America, in neglecting the payment of debts due to Britain before the last war. In Virginia, it was formerly usual for the planters, in that country, to consign their cargoes of tobacco to a correspondent in Britain, who was vested with a discretionary power of selling them as high as possible. It was often observed, that when two planters had each of them, at the same time, sent cargoes of tobacco of equally good quality to England, the one received perhaps twenty pounds the hogshead, and his neighbour not more than four pounds. There was no regularity or equality in the prices, and this gave rise to complaints and suspicions.

Sometime ago, a gentleman, in Virginia, brought a counter-action against his British creditor, in one of the courts of that state. His plea was, that the creditor and consignee had actually sold his tobacco in Europe at a much higher price than *he had stated in balancing their accounts*. The facts alledged were clearly proved, and the jury gave a verdict for damages to the amount of *thirty thousand dollars*.

CHAPTER V.

Federal plan for a French War.—Specimen of French justice.—The Sea Horse.—The Musquito.—Remarks on the British treaty by Mr. Gallatin.—Reply by Mr. Tracy.—Hints on the Western insurrection.—Case of the brig Maria, captain Wilmans.—The schooner William, captain Scott.—Despotic influence of the tories in American seaports.—Elegant style in some of their publications.—The Polly, captain Wade.—The Edward and William, captain Jones.—The Ariel.—The brig Sisters.—Capture of the brig Jay, by the French, and barbarous treatment of the captain.—Mr. Jay's instructions.—*Extracts from them* never before published.—*Proofs of his* neglect of orders.—*Anecdotes relative to the British treaty.*

THIS chapter begins with a few instances of the maritime conduct of France and England, that occurred about, or previous to, the commencement of the year 1796. They had been omitted for the sake of brevity. But while this work is printing off, President Adams, and a formidable phalanx in the fifth Congress, are driving the federal chariot, at full speed, to the brink of a French war. One great pretence for this measure is the republican robberies on our shipping in the West-Indies. But if it can be proved that our commerce endured greater injury, in 1796, from England, than it hath since done from France, and that the government of laſt year took very ſmall concern about the outrages of the former, while it has conſtantly exaggerated thoſe of the latter, the reader will gradually be convinced of " a conſpiracy perpetually ex-" iſting*" to embroil this country with France, and to entangle her in an alliance with the guinea-note monarchy of Britain†.

A letter from Port-au-Paix, dated the 18th of December, 1795, to a merchant in Philadelphia, has the following particulars. Anthoine Chaplin, captain of the Guillotine, a French privateer, had maltreated captain M'Keever of the American ſhip James. For that and a ſimilar offence againſt the ſhip Molleville, of St. Thomas, Chaplin was fined in two hundred dollars, and all damages that might accrue from the illegal capture of theſe veſſels. His privateer was confiſcated; and the pirate himſelf was condemned to fifteen months of impriſonment in irons. " I this day ſaw him," ſays the letter-writer, " chained with a negro working in the " ſtreet, in the ſame kind of dreſs in which he for-" ced captain M'Keever to leave the privateer and " go on board an American veſſel. So much for " our Laveaux's juſtice."

Anthoine Chaplin was leſs culpable than Reynolds, and other Engliſh kidnappers. His puniſhment was immediate and complete; but we have never

---

* Supra Chap. II.

† Private letters from north Britain give curious details about the decline of paper money. Take a guinea-note to the butcher, and you muſt either lay out the whole with him, or go without your change. He parts with no ſilver. The only place where hard money has a chance to be had is at the ale houſe, where, after you ſpend half a crown, the landlord ſometimes gives twenty ſhillings in caſh for your guinea-note. Theſe traits come exactly to the point. They portend the future peace of Europe. A gentleman who left Dublin on the 2d of March, ſays, that Corke guinea-bank-notes were then at eighteen ſhillings hard money. Other bank paper had alſo fallen.

heard a single instance of a British offender meeting with such a check. At the time here spoke of, the American executive had signed Jay's treaty, to the extreme joy of England, and the utmost provocation of France. Yet the former continued to rob America, and the latter did not*. For what reason was Laveaux able to execute justice, while admiral Murray could only promise to *use his influence?* Thus Pichegru might have promised to use his influence with one of his own corporals. The fact seems to have been this. The Directory still valued federal friendship as something; while Pitt held it as *nothing*.

On the 4th of January, the schooner Hiram, captain Brooks, arrived at Hartford in Connecticut. He related, that the Sea Horse, captain Smith, from Guadaloupe for Boston, had all her crew, excepting the master and first mate, taken out by an English ship. She was sent to Antigua, and released, but her crew were detained on board of the ship that took them.

A more complete account of the sufferings of captain Smith and his people, was given by himself, dated Baltimore, January 5th, 1796. On the

---

* The most solid argument then urged against the French in the West-Indies was, that they had taken many American cargoes upon credit, and either paid an inferior price, or exacted a delay that became equivalent to no payment at all. But we have never been told of their flogging American seamen, to make them enter into the republican service. The convulsive state of the French West-Indies was well known. Anarchy, conflagration, and massacre, strode successively from one island to another. If a merchant in Philadelphia, chose to send his cargo to such a market, he could expect no better reception, nor did he, in all cases, merit much sympathy. These speculators raised the price of flour from seven dollars per barrel, to fifteen, to the utter oppression of the labouring poor in this and other seaport towns. In Britain, neither the laws, nor even the people would have endured such forestalling.

X

13th of November, preceding, he was taken
frigate Refource, captain Watkins. Five
men, two of whom had the fever, were imp
A prize-mafter and four men were put on b
the Sea-Horfe. They confined captain Sm
three days below, under the guard of tw
with drawn cutlaffes, and loaded piftols.
captain Smith was on board of the Refou
was ill treated by a midfhipman; and told h
he would not be infulted by a boy. Captai
kins faid, that, if he had heard the expref
would have tied up and flogged Smith for
to infult his *majefty's officer*. To the feel
an *enlightened federalift*, this language r
acceptable. Watkins offered him two h
pounds, and a fhare of the prize-money, to {
the fhip was French property. At Antigua, t
mate of the Sea Horfe died, and the prefide
fed his body to be thrown into the fea. He a
a pilot and negroes on board to carry the ve
to fea. Captain Smith offered to knock them
The prefident fent for him, and threatened t
the fort to fire into the veffel, if fhe did
out to fea, either with men or without the
Smith's refufal, the prefident faid that he
have him confined. What a fplendid blaze
tifh honour and hofpitality! And how fondly
Noah Webfter have chuckled over it, if th
had only paft in a French port inftead of a
lifh one! Watkins had brought three other
can prizes into Antigua. He cut them out o
in Guadaloupe; and, their regifters being in
fice on fhore, he boafted of them as a fure pre
were, notwithftanding, difcharged. How
Smith got hands to work his veffel to Ba
does not appear. Two leagues from Cape
he was boarded by admiral Murray, who, a

man had not already suffered enough, took
him Wilkinson Gilt, a mate whom he had
:d at Antigua. Somebody called citizen
es, is sincerely thanked for supplying him with
)f a crew. But whether this was Victor Hughes,
here the help was given, we are left in the

the 8th of January, 1796, the brig Experi-
captain Houston, arrived from Port-au-Prince
iladelphia. He informed, that three British
of war, at the former place, pressed every
ican who could not produce a protection.
were chiefly manned with American seamen.
mber of our vessels, lying at Port-au-Prince,
in a most distressed situation for want of hands.
letter from St. Kitts, dated 4th January, 1796,
eceived by a merchant of Philadelphia, says,
he brig Fame, captain Medlin, of this port,
ibout to sail for it. The letter adds, that she
)een plundered by a French privateer, but
no particulars.

the 17th of January, the Musquito, captain
iaw, arrived at Baltimore from Bourdeaux.
ιε voyage, he was met by the Hussar, a British
:e. His keys were taken, his chests broke up,
every thing stolen that the British could lay
hands on. They also drank a case of his wine,
pressed the Musquito's mate, and one of the
s, who was an American.

ius far we have instances of British piracy, for-
y overlooked or omitted, as observed in the
ining of this chapter. The reader must have
me tired with this uniform and disgusting tale
ιr commercial degradation. As a relief to the
ncholy picture, let us turn, for a moment, to
lebates on the British treaty. The enthusiasm
:tachment which it inspired, forms one of the

most singular phenomena in the history of the human mind. Many of its sanguine advocates were men unsuspected of a sinister design.

On the 26th of April, 1796, Mr. Gallatin, in speaking of the British treaty, had these words:

"The fact was uncontroverted, that the British
"still continued to impress our seamen and to cap-
"ture our vessels. If they pretended to justify
"that conduct by the treaty, it became necessary
"to obtain an explanation of the doubtful articles;
"if there was nothing in the treaty to justify it,
"their acts were acts of hostility; were an infrac-
"tion of that treaty; and even, according to the
"doctrine of those gentlemen who thought that,
"in common cases, the house had no discretion;
"the treaty once broken by one party, was no lon-
"ger binding on the other; and it was the right
"as well as the duty of this house, not to proceed
"to pass the laws necessary to carry it into effect,
"until satisfactory assurances were obtained, that
"these acts should cease, and until Great Britain
"had evinced a friendly disposition towards us*."

It was impossible to conceive a plainer, or a more substantial argument. These few lines contain just enough to have convinced an audience of accessible understandings, of the propriety of suspending proceedings toward fulfilling the British treaty, till an effectual check had been given to British piracy. On the 27th of April, Mr. Tracy rose in answer to Mr. Gallatin. Two passages shall be here given from his speech. The first is as follows:

"It had been acknowledged, by Mr. Gallatin,
"that a new negociation, at present, cannot be ex-
"pected. Great Britain possesses the posts, the

* Bache's Debates, vol. iii. p. 266.

" confidence of the Indians, the many millions of
" dollars despoiled from our commerce, the bene-
" fits of our trade, and proceeds to make more in-
" vasions on our property and our rights, and yet
" *the gentleman says we will not go to war!* What
" would be the American conduct under such a state
" of things? Would they tamely see their govern-
" ment strut, attempt to look big, call hard names;
" and the moment they were faced, like an over-
" grown lubberly boy, shrink into a corner? Is this,
" he asked, the American character? He thought him-
" self acquainted with a part of the United States,
" too well, to believe they merited such a cha-
" racter; the people where he was most acquain-
" ted, whatever might be the character in other
" parts of the union, were not of the stamp to
" cry Hosannah to day, and crucify to-morrow;
" they will not dance round a whisky pole one day,
" and curse their government, and, upon *hearing*
" of a military force, sneak into a swamp. No, said
" Mr. Tracy, my immediate constituents, whom I
" very well know, understand their rights, and will
" defend them, and if they find that the govern-
" ment either cannot, or will not protect them,
" they will at least attempt to protect themselves.
" And he could not feel thankful to Mr. Gallatin
" for coming all the way from Geneva, to give Ame-
" ricans a character of pusillanimity*."

This rhapsody makes up with ill-nature what it wants in meaning. From the first part of it, where the gentleman speaks of the injuries committed on this country by England, one would suppose, that he was going to recommend an immediate exertion of American vengeance. But, so far from that, he only recommended that we should kiss the British

* Bache's Debates, vol. ii. p. 295.

rod by instantly appropriating for Jay's treaty. The blustering sound of his words, and the abject prostration of his ideas form a striking contrast. His comparison between Connecticut and the western counties of Pennsylvania is a master-piece of vulgar calumny. That the people of the former state are as brave as any in the union has never been denied; and the convention of Saratoga will, for ages to come, be remembered and cited as a monument of their courage. But this ought not to be converted into a handle for reproach, and much less for slander, against other states. As to the western insurrection, it is time that we should begin to speak truth about it. The way in which that affair was suppressed did, in itself, discredit the government of the country. The late king of Prussia would not have thought all the military conduct displayed about it, worth an ensign's commission. Here are a few specimens of the federal army.

"On Thursday the 13th of November, there were
"about forty persons brought to Parkison's house,
"by order of general White; he directed to put the
"damned rascals in the cellar, to tie them back to
"back, to make a fire for the guard, but to put the
"prisoners back to the father end of the cellar,
"and to give them neither victuals nor drink.
"The cellar was wet and muddy, and the night
"cold; the cellar extended the whole length, un-
"der a log-house, which was neither floored, nor
"the openings between the logs daubed. They
"were kept there until Saturday morning, and then
"marched to the town of Washington. On the
"march, one of the prisoners, who was subject to
"convulsions, fell into a fit: but when some of
"the troop told general White of his situation, he
"ordered them to tie the damned rascal to a horse's
"tail, and drag him along with them, for he had only

" feigned having the fits. Some of his fellow pri-
" foners, however, who had a horfe, difmounted,
" and let the poor man ride: he had another fit
" before he reached Wafhington. This march was
" about twelve miles. The poor man, who had the
" fits, had been in the American fervice, during
" almoft the whole of the war with Great Britain."

General White has not denied this accufation, nor profecuted the hiftorian who records it. Hence we muft admit the ftatement to be true; and New Jerfey may congratulate herfelf on the acquifition or production of a fecond DUKE OF CUMBERLAND. Mr. Findley gives fome farther traits of this federal hero. " Stockdale was forbid, on the peril of
" of his life, to adminifter any comfort to his neigh-
" bours, though they were perifhing with cold, and
" famifhing with hunger. The general treated the
" prifoners, as they arrived, with the moft infulting
" and abufive language, caufing them all to be tied
" back to back, except one man, who held a re-
" fpectable rank, and who, however, was faid to be
" one of the moft guilty in his cuftody. One of the
" neareft neighbours, who had a child at the point
" of dying, and obferving that they were bringing
" in the whole neighbourhood prifoners, without
" regard to guilt or innocence, went and gave him-
" felf up to general White, expecting that, as he was
" confcious there was no charge againft him, he
" would be permitted to return to his family on gi-
" ving bail, but he alfo was inhumanly thrown
" into the cellar, tied with the reft, and re-
" fufed the privilege of feeing his dying child; nor
" was he permitted to attend its funeral, until after
" many entreaties he obtained that liberty, accom-
" panied with the moft horrid oaths and impre-
" cations." Of the fmall honour acquired in

this expedition, a great part falls to the share of captain John Dunlap, of this city. "Captain "Dunlap and his party, while they behaved with "the greatest dexterity in taking the prisoners, trea- "ted them with as much politeness and attention as "their situation would admit of, and engaged their "gratitude by accompanying unavoidable severity "with humanity*." At Carlisle, a part of our army, after a hearty dinner, were on the point of setting fire to the town, and of charging each other with the bayonet. Mr. Tracy is left to judge whether such conduct was not as bad as that of dancing round a whisky pole. But when the member attempts to stigmatize the whole constituents of Mr. Gallatin, as rebels and poltroons, it is hard to find, within the compass of decency, a term suitable to his behaviour.

Mr. Tracy farther complained of Mr. Gallatin for having said that " the negociation with Great " Britain was begun in *fear*, carried on through " *fear*, and the treaty made by the same motive; " when it arrived in this country the Senate sanc- " tioned it, and the President placed his signature " to it from *fear;* and now there was an attempt " to obtain the sanction of the House of Represen- " tatives from *fear*. All these expressions, in an un- " qualified manner, the gentleman had applied to " this country, in its most important transactions, " by its most important characters, and to crown " all, we were to defeat the treaty, and sit down " quietly under injuries the most irritating, and " not attempt a redress, or to do any thing like " going to war. Under impressions made by such " declarations, he had said what he had, and he " now said, he wished to look in the face of Mr.

---
* Findley's History of the Insurrection, p. 202.

" Gallatin, or Mr. Heifter, or any other, who da-
" red fay, the American character was that of cow-
" ardice. He would fay again and again, it was
" madnefs, or worfe, to fuppofe. we could defeat
" this treaty and avoid a war."

What Mr. Gallatin fays about *fear* is perfectly true. Mr. Tracy always takes it for granted, that America had no medium between the acceptance of Mr. Jay's treaty and a Btitifh war. An embargo for four months would have reduced the mother country to our terms, without occafion for the firing of a piftol.

Mr. Tracy next denies the reality of Britifh impreffments. " He took this opportunity to afk for
" *the proofs of fuch tranfactions*, as impreffing our
" feamen, by the Britifh government. He decla-
" red he knew of none; and had never heard one
" inftance of the Britifh government either avowing
" the right, or practifing upon it, of impreffment of
" an American into their fea fervice; many inftan-
" ces had occurred of complaints to the govern-
" ment, and all were immediately redreffed; and,
" although it was become very fafhionable to
" calumniate the Britifh government, he was
" impelled, from his own belief and conviction
" on the fubject, to fay, that no fuch inftance
" had ever taken place or would ever, of the Bri-
" tifh government, juftifying the impreffment of
" natives of the United States, or one who was an
" acknowledged citizen. Is it not unfair, faid Mr.
" Tracy, to attribute to the government unautho-
" rized mifconduct of individuals, far removed
" from the feat and controul of the government?
" It was equally unreafonable to fay, that we were
" not protected by the treaty, and fhould not be,
" when the Britifh government had promifed to pay
" for all former depredations made in that way up-

" on our commerce, was it not reasonable to sup-
" pose, they would prevent or pay for any such depre-
" dation now made? And they certainly would pre-
" vent all such, which were not from the confusion
" of war rendered inevitable."

As for the *proofs* of impressment, the gentleman is referred to the deposition of Cyprian Cook, emitted at Norwich in Connecticut. As for his never hearing of *one* instance, where the British government avowed the right of impressing, or practised upon it, the inference must be, that Mr. Tracy has ears of a particular construction. Whether Mr. Pitt himself asserted the right is of no consequence. The British, in the West-Indies, universally avowed and practised upon it. Mr. Tracy says that all complaints to government were immediately redressed. He should have told us what redress was obtained in the case related by captain Cook. He then mounts upon that favourite topic of the British officers acting without orders. *Compensation* closes the chorus. We now proceed with the list of British piracies, leaving Mr. Tracy to deny their existence, as long as he shall think proper.

A Philadelphia newspaper, of the 8th of April, 1796, informs, that the brig Maria Wilman, of Baltimore, captain Oaks, was taken in Tortola by the Bull Dog sloop, and there sold at auction. She was from Demarara, bound to Baltimore, with a cargo of sugar and coffee. It farther says, that, on Monday, the 11th of April, 1796, the brig Charlotte, of Providence, arrived at Baltimore, in thirteen days from Martinique. Captain Watts, of the schooner Alexandria, of Alexandria, came passenger, along with a number of other Americans. Their vessels had been contracted for, and they were *obliged to leave them.* This corroborates the account already given by captain Samuel Green. In summer, 1793, Gideon Henfield and John Singletary had been arrested on board of the Citizen Genet, a French privateer, lying in the Delaware, and Henfield was tried in this city, soon after, for having enlisted in the French service. In spite of a bustle made by government, he was acquitted. In the eye of reason, it seems equally culpable to have sold privateers to Britain, yet no notice has been taken of that practice.

A paragraph from Fredericsburg, dated April 1st, 1796, says, that, 'last week, arrived in the river, the schooner William, captain John Scott, from Bassaterre, St. Kitts. He said that on the 23d of February, between nine and ten o'clock in the evening, in Bassaterre road, he was boarded by a boat with five men with cutlasses. They belonged to a British armed sloop lying there. They ordered William M'Coy, a native of Fredericsburg, into the boat; but, being prevented from taking him, they went back to the sloop. Immediately after, they returned with their commander, one Williams, and an additional number of men, armed with pistols and cutlasses. They took away from the schooner, John Mansfield, William M'Coy, and two blacks. Next morning, captain Scott went on shore, and proved these people to be citizens of the United States. He could recover only the two blacks. Every American at the port shared a similar fate. A Baltimore schooner was stript of all her hands, excepting the mate and a boy.

A practice had for sometime prevailed at Norfolk, in Virginia, of sending horses to the British West-Indies to mount their cavalry. This, if not a breach of neutrality, was at best a plain enough indication to France that we preferred the most petty self-interest to any success on her side. A Kingston newspaper, of the 23d of February, 1796, has the following article. " Captain Huntington reports, that,

"when he left America, admiral Murray, with
"his squadron, was lying in Hampton road, waiting
"to convoy the horses that were purchased for *the
"dragoons in St. Domingo.*" Two articles, dated
Philadelphia, April 12th, say, that three of these vessels, with their freights of horses, were taken by the French, and sent into Cape Francois. This is the only capture by the French of American shipping that has yet occurred in compiling the last or the present chapter.

The Federal Gazette of Baltimore, of the 15th of April, 1796, contains a letter from Tortola. The writer mentions the irregular proceedings of the British court of admiralty in that island, respecting American captures. The captains of the ships of war were permitted to detain the masters and supercargoes of the prizes as prisoners on board of their vessels, till they were deprived of opportunities for employing proper counsel. Enormous costs were granted, of which the bench received a share. Some particular circumstances of injustice are mentioned in the case of the Maria Wilman, captain Oaks, who, in the same newspaper, is noticed as having, at this time, arrived safe with his vessel at Baltimore. It is likely that he wrote this very letter; but perhaps neither he nor his owners durst avow it, for fear of offending the British party. In an *independent* country, this dread may seem strange, yet nothing is more notoriously true, than that such influence is extremely active and formidable. Every mercantile man, and every newsprinter, who dares to speak, with energy, of the insolence and rapine of the Queen of Isles, runs imminent hazard of persecution. The British tories, in our seaport towns, seconded by the American interest, will spare no toil or expence to make him insolvent and infamous. General description cannot convey a complete picture

oceedings. Their own pencil furnishes
)rtrait. Here follows an extract from a
ftioneering hand-bill. An hundred years
nay be hoped, that Americans will turn
outcasts of typography, with the same
ous pity as an Englishman of the present
back on the sallies of Settle and Tom

To the Citizens of New-York.

n men and jacobin measures are all hol-
·otten. An instructive instance has just
. The bank of Pennsylvania was estab-
opposition to the bank of the United
\ jacobin president, secretary, and a ma-
jacobin directors were appointed. The
disclosed a scene of jacobin villainy. It
t, that the president, secretary, and the
ohn Swanwick, have fraudently, and by
, drawn out of the bank one hundred and
housand dollars more than they had a
John Swanwick, the famous French
1 democrat, whom the good democrats
lelphia have lately made a member of
, in opposition to the prudent and honest
he city, now appears in his true colour,
1cipled swindler. Such is the authentic
ce just received from Philadelphia. And
;e body of citizens, many good but delu-
are straining every nerve to place once
Congress the aristocratic, democratical,
al, Edward Livingston. Pause, fellow-
be assured time will prove to his most in-
followers, that he is as rotten and hollow
m peers."

* See Johnson's Life of Dryden.

Posterity, if this page chances to read them, will naturally ask where lies the propriety of reprinting such rubbish? The answer is, that such writings were, in December, 1796, propagated at New-York, with the approbation of a very numerous party. The design was, to defeat the re-election of Mr. Livingston as representative in Congress for that city; and while any remembrance of this handbill shall remain, its authors and its abettors must be abhorred by every honest man.

The bank of Pennsylvania was not established in opposition to the bank of the United States. The field of competition was alike open to every person. It has never been said that the Pennsylvania bank used an unfair means to rival or injure the bank of the United States. The latter is here referred to, as if it were something sacred; and yet the holders of its stock are ashamed or afraid of telling their names*. Mr. Swanwick did not, in the close of 1796, nor for a long time before it, owe the Pennsylvania bank a dollar. Here he is charged as *an unprincipled swindler*, for having made fraudulent draughts out of it. Those who voted for his election opposed the *honest* part of this city. But even if it had been all as true as it was false, this had nothing to do with the election of Livingston, any more than the idle story of Mr. Gallatin, sleeping under hedges, afforded a reason for rejecting general Dearborne†. The same tissue of defamation, falsehood, and vulgarity, runs through a very large proportion of the writings of the federal party. So many different samples are here given to convince people, at a distance from the scene, that these are not partial specimens. One would think that the friends of *order* have imported a cargo of Cossacks or Hottentots to act as

---

* Supra, chap. ii. † Ibid.

their penmen. Their encomiums are, if poffible, more loathfome than their invective. To cenfure Prefident Wafhington is ranked, by the Columbian Centinel, with "ridiculing ********, or black-"guarding the Bible*."

Recurring again to the cafe of the Baltimore brig, it may well be fuppofed, that captain Oaks was afraid of provoking fuch a fwarm of fcorpions. For the fame obvious and weighty reafon many narratives of Britifh piracy have been fecreted, by the fufferers, from the public prints. Of the fifty-five fhips taken by the Argonaut, perhaps no regular account of the capture of fix has appeared in any newfpaper.

The Maryland Journal, of the 2d of May, 1796, gives the following account as from captain Wade of the fchooner Polly, from Jamacia. He fays, that from the 20th of February to the 1ft of April, thirteen American prizes had been fent into Kingfton. Three of thefe were fchooners, belonging to Oliver and Thomfon, of Baltimore. Another was a new copper-bottomed fhip from Baltimore to Calcutta.

On the 3d of May, the fchooner Edward and William, captain Levin Jones, arrived at Baltimore, in nineteen days from Port-au-Paix. In the paffage, fhe met with a brig from Port-au-Prince bound for New-London. The people told captain Jones, that five of them had been impreffed by a Britifh frigate. On the 28th of April, they were chafed by another, but night coming on they got out of her way.

On the fame day, the Ariel, captain Fifher, arrived at Baltimore from Jacquemel. He had fpoke to the fchooner Elizabeth, of Philadelphia, from Jamaica. The captain gave him an account of *twenty-feven* American veffels carried into that ifland

* Aurora, January 4th, 1797.

for trial, and of *two* carried into the Molly which were to be sent to Jamaica. He adds, that all vessels to or from French islands were seized.

On the 17th of April, the brig Sisters, captain Brent, arrived in Hampton roads from Guernsey. She had, on the 12th of March, been boarded by the Thetis, a Bermudian corsair. These pirates took out the master and crew, rummaged the vessel, broke up all the letters and papers, and, after three hours, permitted her to proceed.

" BOSTON, APRIL 16.

" By an arrival, on Saturday, of a vessel from Curracoa, we
" received the following protest of Hugh Wilson, master of
" American brig called the Jay, belonging to Baltimore; who
" being duly sworn before the notary royal and public of St.
" Bartholomew, declareth :—

" That, having got his vessel captured and condemned,
" as hereafter will appear, and having had his log-book and
" all the papers belonging to the vessel and to himself
" taken from him, all to the shipping articles and a small
" memorandum book of his private disbursements, he is obli-
" ged to give his declaration from memory, and to the best of
" his recollection, viz. that, on the 10th of April last, 1795,
" he sailed in said brig from St. Pierre, in the island of Mar-
" tinique, bound to Antigua : that, on the 12th of said month,
" in the morning, he was boarded by the French armed schoo-
" ner called, (as near as he could recollect) the Alhenienne,
" commanded by one Pascal from Guadaulope, under the lee
" of which island the brig then was, and in the evening was
" carried into Bassaterre road, in said last island. That the
" same deponent and all his crew were immediately put on board
" a French sloop of war, where they were detained about eight
" or ten days, without knowing what was the intention of the
" French to do with the said brig, and without ever having been
" heard or examined. That the deponent and the supercargo, Mr.
" John Starck, were sent on shore and conducted to the interpreter
" or linguister, who told them the brig Jay and her remaining
" cargo, consisting in corn and staves, had already been con-
" demned, and who furnished Mr. Starck with a copy of the

" condemnation. That Mr. Starck was put at liberty; but
" the deponent was, the next day, thrown into Baſſaterre goal,
" where he remained about ten days; after which he was drove
" out of the ſaid gaol and put in chains, on board a ſmall French
" ſchooner bound to Point-a-Petre, the deponent lying all the
" paſſage (about ſixty hours), with eight priſoners more, chained
" to the ſame bar, in the hold of ſaid ſchooner, upon the ſtone bal-
" laſt, with a very ſcanty and indifferent food. That, having
" arrived in ſuch a ſituation at Point-a-Petre, the deponent was
" was immediately put on board one of the priſonſhips in the harbor
" where he was detained for near eight months, that is to ſay,
" until the 1ſt inſtant, (January, 1796,) when captain Whee-
" ler, of the brig Peggy, of New-York, having obtained per-
" miſſion to pick out American ſailors, that might be found on
" board of the different priſonſhips, came along ſide the ſhip
" where the deponent was detained. That having made his
" caſe known to him, he, the ſaid captain Wheeler, took the de-
" ponent along with him, and put him on board the ſaid brig
" Peggy. That, on the 11th inſt. or thereabout, the depon-
" ent went in ſaid brig from Point-a-Petre, and arrived in this
" harbour of Guſtavia yeſterday, the 13th inſt. without yet
" knowing what has become of his veſſel, the brig Jay, her
" cargo, or any thing belonging to her, and without ever hav-
" ing been heard, either in behalf of ſaid property or of himſelf,
" during all the time of near nine months, he was detained in
" Gaudaloupe plundered of every thing belonging to him, and
" not left a ſecond ſhirt to put on; that, during his detention in
" Point-a-Petre, captain Lyle, of Baltimore, as he paſſed by
" the ſaid priſonſhip, having ſeen and recollected the deponent,
" had applied to the commiſſaire de guerre in his behalf, but in
" vain, as ſaid captain Lyle afterwards told the deponent.

" [Here follows the proteſt of the judge and notary public
" declaring the capture and condemnation to be contrary to the
" law of nations, and of humanity; the whole is dated at Guſ-
" tavia, (St. Bartholemew,) the 14th January, 1796.]"

The inſertion of the preceding article, ought to vindicate this work from the ſuſpicion of a deſire to conceal or palliate the injuries committed againſt American commerce by the French republic. Nothing of that nature has been intentionally overlooked; for the only object of the author is the

Z

discovery and publication of truth, without the smallest concern what nation, or what individual may chance to appear in an unfavourable light. From this instance of French piracy, we return to British depredations.

A paragraph, dated Norfolk, April 26th, 1796, mentions the arrival of the schooner Eleanor, captain Jackson. He gave an account of the Hussar, a British frigate, having captured the ship Alexander of Yorktown, captain Orr, from Lisbon to Norfolk. The crew were taken on board of the Hussar, and the ship herself was sent to Halifax. The Maryland Journal, of the 2d of May, gives an account of the schooner Betsey of Boston, captain Philips. She was taken by the British, but re-captured by the crew, who delivered up the British as prisoners to the French, at Jacquemel. The same newspaper tells of the seizure of the ship Alexander, of Baltimore, by the British. She was bound from Demarara for Baltimore. The captors sent her into Grenada, where the cargo was libelled. There is also a statement from captain Wade of the schooner Polly, of thirteen sail of Americans which had been sent into Kingston, Jamaica, between the 20th of February, and the 1st of April, 1796. One of these vessels was bound from Baltimore to Calcutta.

It seems amazing that, in the face of such injuries, any member of Congress could recommend appropriations for the British treaty. Public curiosity has been excited by the concealment of Mr. Jay's instructions. Access has been obtained to this paper, and leave has been given to make an abstract of every material part of it. This, though not in form, yet in substance, will answer the end in view.

Some notice has already been taken of the singular conduct of the executive in refusing to treat with Genet, becaufe the Senate were not then fitting, and thereafter, while they actually were in feffion, of his refolving to enter into a Britifh negociation, and nominating Mr. Jay as envoy, without giving the Senate previous intimation of fuch a defign. The meffage does not afk either advice or confent, but abruptly declares that *he has thought proper.* This is not the conftitutional ftyle of afking advice or confent. The departure from the fpirit of the conftitution is obvious.

The meffage was received by the Senate on the 16th of April, 1794. On the 17th, a motion was made in the following words: "that, previous to " going into the confideration of the nomination of " a fpecial envoy to the court of Great Britain, the " Prefident of the United States be requefted to in- " form the Senate of *the whole bufinefs with which* " *the propofed envoy is to be charged.*" This motion was negatived. Thus the *advice* and *confent* of the Senate, as required by the conftitution, were overlooked. Without confulting them, the Prefident refolved to enter into a negociation, and named an envoy. When he fent down the meffage to the Senate, as to his having done fo, he did not let them know what the negociation was to be about. If the words *advice* and *confent* mean any thing, it muft furely be, that the Senate are to be previoufly acquainted with, and confulted upon, the bufinefs that an ambaffador is going to undertake. There can be no other rational explanation of the phrafe. The Senate could not pretend to give their advice about the expediency of commencing a treaty, when they did not know the terms on which it was to begin. Yet, fuch is the fpirit in a majority of that body, that they refufed, as appears above, to requeft a communication from the Prefident upon this point. They had a title to have *demanded* fuch an ecclairciffement. In private life, it would be mockery to ask a man to consent to any business, without first telling him the scope of it. Without such knowledge it is impossible that he can give any thing deserving the name either of *advice* or *consent*.

On the 19th of April, a motion was made in the Senate of which the following is part. " That to " permit judges of the Supreme Court to hold, at " the same time, any other office or employment, " emanating from, and holden at the pleasure of " the Executive, is contrary to the spirit of the con- " stitution, and, as tending to expose them to the " influence of the Executive, is *mischievous* and *im-* " *politic.*" This motion passed in the negative, ten to seventeen. On the 27th of November, 1794, Dr. William Smith objected in Congress to the democratic society of this city, for the holding of such a doctrine. But its being supported by so large a part of the Senate ought at least to have softened the severity of his censure.

We now come to the instructions of our envoy. Of these an entire copy cannot, as above stated, be obtained; but permission has been procured to make a copious abstract. They set out with directing Mr. Jay to obtain redress for the piracies committed on our commerce by authority of instructions from the king and council. He is next enjoined to draw to a conclusion all points of difference concerning the peace of 1783. The Executive then expresses a wish, that " *the debts, the interest claimed upon* " *them, and all things relating to them, be put out-* " *right in a diplomatic discussion, as being certainly of* " *a judicial nature to be decided by our courts.*" If this point could not be obtained, he was to support the doctrines of government, " with argu- " ments proper for the occasion, and with that at- " tention to his former public opinions, which self- " respect will justify." This phrase, as to former public opinions, does not seem very happy. Mr. Jay, as a judge, had declared, from the bench, that the English were justified in detaining the western posts, on account of the debts due to Britain. Hence attention to his former opinions, would lead him to vindicate the latter, at the expence of America.

The instructions proceed to say, that, "the Bri"tish government, having denied their abetting the "Indians, we must, of course, acquit them. But we "have satisfactory proofs, some of which, howe"ver, cannot, as you will discover, be well used "in public, that British agents are guilty of stir"ring up, and assisting, with arms, ammunition, "and warlike implements, the different tribes of "Indians against us.

"It is incumbent upon that government to re"strain these agents, as a forbearance to restrain "them, cannot be interpreted otherwise than as a "determination to countenance them." Mr. Jay was farther directed to insist, "that the Indians "dwelling in the territories of one, shall not be in"terfered with by the other." He was likewise enjoined, "to explain the pacific wishes of America, "in case that he should find the court of London "equally disposed for amity." Mr. Jay was, besides, instructed to mention the dangerous effect that might be produced upon the minds of the citizens of America, by the continuation of outrages in the West-Indies, while, at the same time, our courts gave entire authority to claims for British debts. Mr. Jay was, in particular, enjoined to consider," *the* "*inexecution and infraction of the treaty, as standing* "*on distinct grounds from the vexations and spolia-* "*tions ; so that no adjustment of the former, is to be* "*influenced by the latter.*" Mr. Jay was, in the next place, instructed, if he should be able, to obtain satisfaction, as to the trespasses on the treaty of 1783, and as to the West-Indian piracies, to found the British ministry on the subject of a commercial treaty. If he found this subject eligible, he was especially directed to insist upon the following points.

" 1. Reciprocity in navigation, and particularly to the West-Indies, and even to the East-Indies.

" 2. The admission of wheat, fish, salt meat, and other great staples, upon the same footing with the admission of the great British staples in American ports.

" 3. FREE SHIPS TO MAKE FREE GOODS.

" 4. Proper security for the safety of neutral commerce in other respects; and particularly by declaring provisions never to be contraband, except in the strongest possible case; as the blockade of a port; or, if attainable, by abolishing contraband, altogether. By defining a blockade, if contraband, must continue, in some degree, as it is defined in the armed neutrality. By restricting the opportunities of vexation, in visiting vessels, and bringing under stricter management privateers, and expediting recoveries against them for misconduct.*

" 5. Exemption of emigrants, particularly manufacturers, from restraint*.

" 6. Free export of arms and military stores.

" 7. The exclusion of the term " the most favoured nation," as being productive of embarrassment.

" 8. The convoy of merchant ships, by the public ships of war, where it shall be necessary, and they be holding the same course.

" 9. It is anxiously to be desired, that the fishing grounds now engrossed by the British should be opened to the citizens of the United States.

---

* Every body knows how admirably this point has been attended to.

"10. The intercourse with England makes it necessary that the disability arising from alienage, in cases of inheritance, should be put on a liberal footing; or rather abolished.

"11. You may discuss the sale of prizes in our ports, while we are neutral; and this, perhaps, may be added to the considerations which we have to give, besides those of reciprocity.

"12. Proper shelter, defence, and succour, against pirates, shipwreck, &c.

"13. Full security for the retiring of the citizens of the United States from the British dominions in case a war should break out.

"14. No privateering commissions to be taken out by the subjects of the one, or the citizens of the other party, against each other*.

"15. Consuls to be admitted in Europe, the West and East-Indies.

"16. In case of an Indian war, none but the usual supplies in peace shall be furnished.

"17. In peace, no troops to be kept within a limited distance from the lakes.

"18. No stipulation whatever is to interfere with our obligations to France.

"19. A treaty is not to be continued beyond fifteen years."

The above enumeration presented, in a general point of view, the objects which our Executive considered as desirable to be comprehended in a commercial treaty. But Mr. Jay was especially cautioned not to expect that a treaty could be positively effected with so great a variety of advantages in fa-

---

* It is hard to guess what our Executive could mean by this injunction. In case of a rupture between this country and England, the chief way in which we can affect her interest, must be by attacking her commerce. Hence a stipulation for restricting our own efforts in that quarter, has not an extreme appearance of perspicuity.

vour of America. Here it is difficult to suppress the feelings of surprise, at so very injudicious a choice of the time for making a commercial treaty with Britain. Something has been said upon that subject already, and to which the reader is referred.

The sixth chapter of an act of parliament, past in the 28th year of the reign of George the third, mentions certain articles which may be carried from the United States to the British West-Indies, in *British* bottoms; and certain others which may be conveyed from the British West-Indies to the United States in *British* bottoms. Mr. Jay was enjoined, if practicable, to obtain the same privilege, in both cases, for *American* bottoms, but such treaty, instead of the usual clause of ratification, was to contain the following. " This treaty shall be ob-
" ligatory and conclusive, when the same shall be
" ratified by his Britannic majesty of the one part,
" and by the President of the United States, by
" and with the advice and consent of the Senate, of
" the other."

But if a treaty of commerce could not be formed upon a basis as advantageous as that above stated, Mr. Jay was prohibited from *concluding or signing any such;* " it being conceived that it would
" not be expedient to do any thing more than to
" digest with the British ministry, the articles of
" such a treaty, as they appeared willing to accede
" to, *referring them here for consideration and fur-
" ther instruction,* previous to a formal conclusion."

From this part of Mr. Jay's instructions, the plain inference seems to be, that he was not at liberty to sign any treaty at all, till it had been previously remitted to this country for examination. Indeed it was plainly enough admitted, in the House of Representatives, that our envoy had exceeded his powers.

After this injunction, the instructions to Mr. Jay proceed immediately in the following words. "Some of the other points which it would be in-"teresting to comprehend in a treaty, may not be "attended with difficulty. Among these, is the "admission of our commodities and manufactures, "generally, in the British European dominions, "upon a footing equally good with those of other "foreign countries. At present, certain enumera-"ted articles only are admitted, and though the "enumeration embraces all the articles which it "is of present consequence to us to be able to export "to those dominions, yet, in process of time, an ex-"tention of the objects may become of moment. The "fixing of the privileges which we now enjoy, in the "British East Indies, by toleration of the company's "government, if any arrangement can be made with "the consent of the company for that purpose, "would also be a valuable ingredient."

As Denmark and Sweden were upon very indifferent terms with the British ministry, and as Russia, the nominal ally of England, had, in the American war, appeared at the head of the famous armed neutrality, it was to be expected, that some co-operation from that quarter would greatly tend to enforce the success of Mr. Jay's errand. Accordingly, some ideas on this subject seem to have occurred to our American cabinet. But the timid and indecessive style in which the instructions, as to that point, are couched, shews how little could be rested upon them. Our envoy was cautioned as to entering into such a negociation, if there was a danger of its being discovered by the British court. Now this notion of our Executive runs expressly counter to the common experience of mankind, For, the very dread of Jay maturing such a treaty, would have been the most likely way to bring Grenville to favourable terms. Nothing was to be depended upon from that quarter, but through the operation of interest or fear; and the shortest way to make this impression, was, by affecting a correspondence with the Danish and Swedish ministers, even though America had previously determined to decline such a conjunction. The former armed neutrality had struck England with unusual alarm, and the very dread of a second combination of that sort would have chilled the warmest drop of blood in the veins of the English nation. In private life, when you want to cheapen a piece of goods, the first argument is, that you can go to the next store. But Jay was expressly directed to conceal any design of such a nature. To give our Executive full justice, the whole passage, as it immediately follows the last quotation, is here inserted *verbatim.*

" You will have no difficulty in gaining access to
" the ministers of Russia, Denmark, and Sweden,
" at the court of London. The principles of the
" armed neutrality would abundantly cover our
" neutral rights. If, therefore, the situation of
" things with respect to Great Britain should dictate
" the necessity of taking the precaution of foreign co-
" operation on this head; *if no prospect of accomoda-*
" *tion should be thwarted by the danger of such a mea-*
" *sure being known to the British court;* and if an en-
" tire view of all our political relations, shall, in your
" judgment, permit the step; you will found those
" ministers upon the probability of an alliance with
" their nations to support those principles. How-
" ever, there can be no risk in examining what can
" be concerted with Denmark and Sweden, or any
" other power, against the Algerines. It may be re-
" presented to the British ministry, how productive
" of perfect conciliation it might be to the people of
" the United States, if Great Britain would use her

" influence with the Dey of Algiers for the libera-
" tion of the American citizens in captivity, and for
" a peace upon reasonable terms. It has been *com-*
" *municated from abroad*, to be the fixed policy of
" Great Britain, to check our trade in grain to the
" Mediterranean. This is too doubtful to be assu-
" med, but fit for enquiry."

As to the restriction in corresponding with the ministers of Sweden and Denmark, with regard to an armed neutrality, the reader can compare the text with the commentary, and decide whether a minister like Jay, who had justified the British in detaining the western posts, was likely to negociate with the northern powers, under such equivocal and tremulous injunctions.

Another part of the above paragraph, refers to getting the British ministry to obtain the liberation of American prisoners in Algiers. Our minister was to tell how productive this step would be of *perfect conciliation.* If the British had desired the latter, American sailors would never have been carried as slaves into Barbary. It was publicly understood in both countries, that the court of London, by patching up the Portuguese truce, were the real authors of the Algerine piracies. *Nostro quoque seculo monstrum.* To such atrocious, such abandoned political bloodhounds, whose guilt rivals the darkest precedent in the records of perdition, the application of this trimming, fawning style, was perfectly useless. It was like telling a highwayman how greatly you would thank him for returning your purse. Jay, if in earnest, ought to have assumed a different tone. " You are not only," he might have said, " corsairs in person, but corsairs by proxy. You
" have not only accumulated upon our commerce
" every wrong that British bucanneers were capable
" of inflicting, but with a meanness and baseness

"which no language can describe, you have sum-
"moned to your aid the dregs of the human race.
"Till you make reparation, common sense loudly
"exclaims that no treaty between us can repay the
"trouble of subscription."

The last sentence of the above extract from Jay's instructions, speaks of something as a secret, which was in reality known to the whole world. England adhered to the policy of checking, not merely *American trade in grain to the Mediterranean*, but American trade in every commodity to every quarter of the world. Lord Sheffield had even wrote a book, extremely popular in England, wherein he recommended that protection from "the powers of Barbary" should not be granted by England to American commerce. This was, in other words, recommending that these robbers should be turned loose upon us, at the first opportunity. When Jay went to England, lord Sheffield, the apostle of this project, was high in the confidence of Mr. Pitt. So that the conduct of the latter was merely an illustration of the principles of the former. Yet our Executive speaks, in the instructions, as if this news had been conveyed by some secret channel, though the doctrine and practice of the British ministry were alike notorious. Nay, Mr. Tench Coxe had wrote an answer to Sheffield, and in particular to this Algerine plan, several years before Mr. Jay went to England. Thus our Executive might have found full evidence as to *the fixed policy of Britain*, in the store of every bookseller in Philadelphia. The next part of the instructions is in these words.

"Such are the outlines of the conduct which the
"President wishes you to pursue. He is aware that
"at this distance, and during the present instabi-
"lity of public events, he cannot undertake to pre-
"scribe rules which shall be irrevocable; you will,

"therefore, consider the ideas herein expressed, as
" amounting to *recommendations only*, which, in your
" discretion you may modify, as seems most benefi-
" cial to the United States, except in the following
" cases, which are *immutable*.

" 1. That, as the British ministry will doubtless
" be solicitous to detach us from France, and may,
" probably, make some overtures of this kind; you
" will inform them that the government of the Uni-
" ted States will not derogate from our treaties and
" engagements with France, and that experience has
" shewn that we can be honest in our duties to the
" British nation, without laying ourselves under any
" particular restraints as to other nations; and,

" 2. That no treaty of commerce be concluded,
" *contrary to the foregoing prohibition.*"

This extract concludes the instructions. A short analysis will evince that they are not remarkable for perspicuity. We shall begin at their outset, and attempt a short sketch of their merits.

The first object stated in the instructions is, to obtain redress for the piracies, or, as the paper terms it, " for the *vexations* and *spoliations* com-
" mitted on our commerce." The most atrocious of these vexations was the impressment of American seamen; yet, in the whole text of the instructions, of which about five-sixths have been exactly cited, nothing distinct or decisive is said on that point. We have inserted above, an entire copy of the whole nineteen articles upon which Mr. Jay was authorised to found a commercial treaty. In these, nothing levels at the practice of impressment, unless it can be implicated under the general phrase, " as to the safety of neutral commerce," and " *restricting* the opportunities of vexations in
" visiting vessels." Restriction is one thing, and prohibition is another; so that even if impressment

had been really implied; the language was too vague and equivocal for the object. The treaty, as it now stands, contains not one single word about the protection of American seamen. After Grenville and Jay had almost finished the articles of this paper, Jay sent a note to the British minister, containing eighteen corrections, or additions, that had occurred to him. Only one of them, viz. the sixteenth, deserves publication here. It is in these words.

" An article ought to be added, to prevent the " impressment of each other's people."

To this clause, the answer was thus.

" Lord Grenville can see no reason whatever, " why such an article should not be added." No farther notice was taken by Mr. Jay of the business. As to the authenticity of this singular correspondence, it has been first had from a member of the House of Representatives of last Congress, who read it when lying on the table of the Senate, and the substance of it was published, last fall, in *British Honour and Humanity*. It was since repeated to the author by a member of the Senate. As for the merit of our envoy, in this case, a thousand volumes of diplomatic history would not furnish such another instance of negligence in the duty of office.

The instructions next observe, that the debts due to England are to be " put *outright** in a diploma-" tic discussion, as being certainly of a judicial na-" ture to be *decided by our courts*." Instead of this, Mr. Jay erected an arbitrary board of five commissioners. Thus American debtors were, with one dash of his pen, deprived of the right of a trial by jury. The President and Senate ratified this breach of justice and of law.

* In passing, one cannot fail to admire the classical style of our cabinet.

The inſtructions likewiſe ſay, that " the Britiſh government, having denied the abetting of the Indians, *we muſt, of courſe, acquit them.*" On the ſame principle, an American debtor, denying his debt before the five commiſſioners, they *muſt, of courſe, acquit him.*

Mr. Jay was alſo to conſider, " the inexecution and infraction of the treaty, as ſtanding on diſtinct grounds from the vexations and ſpoliations; ſo that no adjuſtment of the former, is to be *influenced by the latter.*" The general face of the treaty plainly ſets off the debts due to Britain, againſt the detention of the weſtern poſts, and the piracies in the Weſt-Indies. The public have been ſufficiently tired with harping upon Jay's treaty; but the buſineſs of compenſation ſtands at preſent as follows. Providing that American merchants recover their damages in a Britiſh court of admiralty, they are not to receive immediate payment. The Britiſh claims on American debtors are to be held up as a counterpoiſe; and, when the balance ſhall be ſtruck between the two claſſes of claims, the Britiſh expect and ſay, that ſeveral millions of dollars will be found in their favour. This extraordinary mode of compenſation for piracy, was related by a perſon high in office in the Britiſh ſervice, to a Senator of the preſent Congreſs, from whom the account is here given.

We now come to the queſtion, *whether Mr. Jay broke his inſtructions?* A few literal citations from them will decide this point. On p. 176, there has already been quoted a paragraph beginning thus: " but if a treaty of commerce cannot be formed upon a baſis as advantageous as this, YOU ARE NOT TO CONCLUDE OR SIGN ANY SUCH, it being conceived," &c. The whole paragraph is ſomewhat confused, but it clearly enjoins a prohibition upon Mr. Jay of signing any treaty, unless he could obtain an agreement to the whole of his own terms, which the Executive, as above, says, *could not be expected.* Thus we have one step.

A subsequent passage already quoted, has these words: " you will therefore consider the ideas " herein expressed, as amounting to *recommen-* " *dations only,* which in your discretion you " may modify, as seems most beneficial to the Uni- " ted States, except in the two following cases, " which are IMMUTABLE."

The two cases are above inserted. One of them is, " that no treaty of commerce be concluded or " signed, contrary to the foregoing prohibition." These are the closing words of the instructions; and hence they must be regarded as explanatory of what goes before them. The preceding prohibition can only allude to that passage where Mr. Jay is forbidden from signing a treaty, unless he obtained every thing on his own conditions. The intermediate reference to his *discretion* is instantly checked by the prohibition of signing. The case may then be reduced to three points.

1. Mr. Jay was prohibited from signing a treaty unless *on certain terms,* that were not within the compass of expectation.

2. Mr. Jay signed a treaty.

3. So far from obtaining the terms required, he agreed to a treaty almost entirely the reverse of them. For instance, *Free ships to make free goods* is inverted. The security of emigrant manufacturers is unnoticed. No admission is obtained to British fishing grounds. In the case of an Indian war, we have no restriction of military supplies from Britain to the savages. The free export of arms and military stores is forbidden, in time of

war, for the eighteenth article of the treaty declares them contraband. Thus, out of the eighteen injunctions above quoted, the third, fifth, sixth, ninth, and sixteenth, are either neglected or contradicted; and other infractions, of an inferior nature, may readily be found. But, paſſing by ſuch trite materials, we proceed at once to the two capital points of *ſecurity to American commerce* and of *avoiding all cauſe of offence to France*. As to the firſt, the British continue at this day (June 19th, 1797) to plunder, though two years and ſeven months have paſt over ſince Mr. Jay ſigned his treaty. With regard to the ſecond, the French were, from the firſt, highly and reaſonably exaſperated at the conditions of the treaty, and a war with that republic is likely to be the conſequence.

Thus, in all their material parts, Mr. Jay violated his powers. We aſked for a fiſh, and he gave us a ſerpent. It has been whiſpered that a ſecond ſet of inſtructions were tranſmitted to our envoy. They were never laid before the Senate, and it follows, that, if they really exiſted, which is extremely doubtful, the Senate knew nothing about them. They can form no part of our envoy's vindication, unleſs he ſhall chuſe to produce them.

The tenth article, as to the injuſtice and impolicy of ſequeſtrating Britiſh debts, was written, as it now ſtands, by Mr. Jay. This evinces, if evidence were wanting, that the whole affair was an inſtrument of party.

We have now aſcertained that Mr. Jay treſpaſſed his orders. The next queſtion is, by what motives he could be induced to do ſo? In this country it has been the cuſtom to hold up Americans as a race of ſuperior beings, and from that theory the reſult is, that, for Grenville to purchaſe our federal envoy, was impracticable. But the tenth article of the treaty, by an expreſs implication, arraigns Mr. Dayton and a conſiderable party in Congreſs, as meditating an act of injuſtice. Camillus alſo*, in all the plenitude of his eloquence, can find *no powers of language* equal to the baſeneſs of the Datonian project.

From theſe eſtimates of American purity, every man will make what inference he thinks fit, as to the probable fale of our treaty. Speaking of this country, Thomas Paine has indeed told us that "the *innocence of her character*, that won the hearts of all nations in her favour, may, a thouſand years hence, found like a romance; her *inimitable virtue*, as if it had never been†." At the date of only ten years, from writing of the above ſentence, the tale founds not like a romance, to be ſure, but very like an untruth. It forms a part of that empty blabbing of national vanity, which has been remarked among every race of mankind, from Greenland to Cape Horn. Without launching into the ocean of the revolutionary virtue of the United States, let us hear what the Aſſembly of Georgia have to ſay about its ſituation, in 1796. The picture makes an intereſting part of the hiſtory of that year.

"GEORGIA,

"BURKE COUNTY, 16th of January, 1796.

"Clement Lanier, eſq. one of the Repreſentatives in the legiſlature of this ſtate, who, being duly ſworn, on the holy evangeliſts of the Almighty God, depoſeth and ſays, that, during the laſt ſeſſion of the legiſlature of Auguſta, in the winter of the year 1795, he being a member of the Houſe of Repreſentatives, and ſitting on the ſame ſeat with Henry Grindat, another of the members of that houſe, before the ſpeaker took the chair, the ſaid Grindat recommended to him to be in favour of the ſale of the weſtern lands; for that he,

---

* Supra, chap. IV. † Paine to Waſhington, p. 8.

" the said Grindat, underſtood it was worthy our notice; for
" Mr. Thomas Wylly, a ſenator from Effingham county,
" had told the ſaid Grindat, that he, the ſaid Wylly, could have
" eight or ten negroes for his part: and the deponent further
" ſaith, that, on the ſame day, in the afternoon, the ſaid Thomas
" Wylly, came into the lobby of the houſe, and beckoned to
" the deponent, who followed him out, when the converſation
" commenced about the *Yazoo act*; that, at the ſame time, a
" Mr. Deniſon came by, and aſked what we were upon. The
" ſaid Wylly anſwered, the land buſineſs; the ſaid Deniſon
" then came up, and Wylly withdrew; that Deniſon then told
" the deponent, that he did not pretend to adviſe any member
" to be in favour of ſelling the land, but that thoſe who were
" in favour of ſelling it, were *handſomely provided for*, and that
" if the deponent thought proper to be in favour of ſelling, that
" *he ſhould have part*; and that the ſaid Deniſon ſaid, that he
" was a purchaſer of ſuch of the member's parts, as had a mind
" to ſell, but underſtood that ſome of the members pretended
" to aſk eight and ten negroes for a ſhare, or their ſhares; he ſaid
" he could not give ſo much, but the deponent might depend he
" would purchaſe: the deponent further ſaith, that, previous to
" any of the before recited circumſtances, Mr. William Long-
" ſtreet, one of the members of the ſaid legiſlature, frequently
" called on the deponent, and aſked why he was not in favour
" of ſelling the weſtern lands, who anſwered, he did not think it
" right to ſell to companies of ſpeculators. The deponent at
" this time, wiſhed to make further diſcovery of the conduct of
" the members on that ſale, and therefore affected to be inclined
" to come into the meaſure, and, by that means, kept up a conver-
" ſation about it occaſionally; that on the day the bill received its
" firſt reading, before the houſe convened, ſaid Longſtreet ſpoke
" to the deponent to get his approbation to the ſale. The deponent
" aſked him to ſhew him what ſecurity the members had of
" the purchaſe, when the ſaid Longſtreet preſented a certificate,
" entitling the bearer to two ſhares, of twenty-five thouſand
" acres each, ſigned by *Nathaniel Pendleton, chairman*. The
" deponent then told the ſaid Longſtreet, that that was not
" what he had formerly told him was a member's ſhare; for
" the ſaid Longſtreet had before ſaid, a member's ſhare was
" *ſeventy-five thouſand acres*. That the ſaid Longſtreet, then
" told the deponent, if he would wait a few minutes, or an
" hour, he would bring him another certificate from *Gunn's
" company*, for the ſame number of acres. That the deponent,

"in order to disengage himself from the conversation, then said
"the security was not sufficient to entitle him to the land. That
"the said Longstreet then told the deponent that if he was not
"satisfied with the certificates, he would give him one thousand
"dollars for it, or for them. The deponent then presented the
"certificates to the said Longstreet, and went into the house,
"which was the last interview he had on the subject. The de-
"ponent further saith, that the shares offered him as aforesaid,
"were expressly designed to induce him, the deponent, to vote
"for the bill for disposing of the western territory.
"(Signed,)
"CLEM. LANIER.
"Sworn in the presence of the committee of the House of
"Representatives, before me,
"THOMAS LEWIS, J. P."

The above deposition is one of those published by the legislature of Georgia, respecting the Yazoo business. It was happy for America, that, in June, 1795, the terrestrial speculations of general Gunn did not prevent his attendance at Philadelphia as a senator. An absence so fatal would have deprived this continent of the British treaty, for which he voted; of that maritime security which now constitutes the pride of the seaman, and of that compensation, *in specie*, which now cracks the coffers of the merchant*!

* Even if the British government could preserve its existence, this boasted compensation would be a very remote object. It is amusing to hear people yet say, that, after a peace with the emperor, Britain will still maintain her supremacy at sea. France, in the first place, can exclude her manufactures from every country in Europe, Russia, perhaps, excepted. This cuts off three-fourths, at least, of British commerce, and one-half of her revenue. Second, other objects being out of the way, France will turn her chief attention to her navy, which, in a short time, may rival that of England, as it nearly did in the last war. Third, the explosion of paper money, and the reduction of revenue, will soon disable England from maintaining a navy, equal to what she supports at present. Fourth; France has, in arms, ten or twelve hundred thousand men. A great number of them are proprietors in the national domains. Many may be employed upon canals and other public works. But, for

CHAPTER VI.

British depredations continued.—Mercantile selfishness.—The brig Fame.—The schooner Andrew.—Joshua Whiting.—The brig Columbia.—The sloop Dove.—The May Flower.—The Eliza.—Murder of captain Bosson.—Snuff Excise.—Memoirs of ALEXANDER HAMILTON, *late Secretary of the Treasury.—His singular mode of correspondence with certain persons.—Remarks on his connection with Reynolds.*

TO commence this chapter, a few additional specimens of British amity are inserted. A letter from captain Thorndike Deland, dated Kingston, 1st of April, 1796, to a merchant in Philadelphia, contains, for publication, a list of twelve American vessels taken and carried into that port. Captain Deland farther says, that he had heard of the internal tranquility of the republic, myriads must be discharged upon some foreign enterprise. England will most likely be the scene of action, and a lesser effort than that which conquered Flanders, would convert her into a French province. Though the federal party in Congress cannot see the danger of this event, yet Arthur Young, and Edmund Burke, perceive it very distinctly.

As the friends of *order* are constantly talking of French ambition, and its effects, let them read the following account of the emperor. It is here copied from a London newspaper, of March 23, 1796.

" The Austrian share of the new partition of Poland includes four thousand four hundred and fifteen square miles of territory, two hundred and seven towns, four thousand six hundred and five villages, and one million one hundred and six thousand one hundred and seventy-eight souls." The miles must be of some German standard, otherwise this part of Poland would be twice as populous, to its extent, as Yorkshire. What shall we think of this imperial usurper enslaving, at one stroke, eleven hundred thousand defenceless people? With such facts before us, it is foolery to speak of jacobin depredations. This is one of those crowned robbers, into whose alliance the federal politicians wish to precipitate America.

twenty-seven other ships at Tortola, which were in jeopardy. He informs, that all Americans, when carried into Kingston, were, after examination, turned ashore, without provision for their support. Any one having concern in a house, or having even a factor at St. Domingo, or any French port, was deemed a Frenchman, and his property was, on that account, condemned. On the 21st of April, 1796, the schooner William and Mary, captain Shaw, arrived at Portsmouth, New Hampshire, in thirty-eight days from Kingston. When he left that place, the impressment of American seamen had not subsided. On the 5th of May, the schooner Mermaid, captain Tabet, arrived from the Mole, at New-York. His mate, a native American, was pressed by the Regulus. Several other Americans were, at the same time, pressed from different vessels. The Mermaid had sailed from New-York, with a load of timber, on account of the British government.

The Minerva, of the 13th of April, expresses surprise, that, if all the accounts of impressments were true, they had little or no effect in deterring American seamen from entering into the service. "In a full, public meeting of merchants, in this "city, last week," says Webster, "the question "was asked, whether the British impressments had "operated to discourage seamen from entering in- "to service? The reply was, that no such effect "had been perceived.—If seamen do not com- "plain, how happens it [*that*] printers take up "their cause *with so much zeal?*" Seamen do complain, of which the numerous details in this volume, and which are not, perhaps, a twentieth part of the whole, compose an ample attestation. But a common seaman has more difficulty in changing his profession, than almost any other person.

This explains the general adherence to it, even in spite of British crimping. Webster is angry at printers for taking up the cause of seamen with *so much zeal*. But, if they are not to be defended with ardour, upon what point should zeal be excited? If circumstances require it, the presses of America will continue to remonstrate against such wrongs, when the bones of Webster shall be as rotten as his heart. As to the query started in the mercantile meeting, the members would have gained more credit by subscribing to form a fund for the relief of such seamen, or the families of such seamen, as might be impressed while in their service. This would have been acting like men. It would have been acting like ENGLISHMEN; for, at London or Liverpool, a proposal of that kind would, under a similar situation, have been adopted. But, in the United States, it seems that, if a merchant can only save himself, he is perfectly indifferent, what becomes of the people in his service.

A Charleston newspaper, of the 8th of April, 1796, contains the copy of a sentence passed by judge Green, of Bermuda. It is dated the 6th of January preceding, and respected the brig Fame. In summer, 1795, the Fame sailed from Charleston, for Bourdeaux. On her return she was captured and taken into Bermuda. The vessel and cargo were both American property. But one of the owners, who went along with her, had staid behind in France, to dispose of some remaining part of her cargo. This accident, in the eyes of Green, transformed him into a French citizen, and, on that pretence, both ship and loading were confiscated. Thus the British went on in the West-Indies, while Mr. Bayard was transmitting to Philadelphia his important assurances about indemnification, and the resentment of the London court of Admiralty at the decrees of Green.

Reader! unless you are a British tory, or the British editor of the Columbian Centinel, or Harrison Gray Otis, or Robert Goodloe Harper, or some other curiosity of their cast, who is fitter for a work-house than a state-house*, you must revere the magnanimity of President Washington, who, in his last speech to Congress, disdained all notice of these British pecadiloes.

About the 23d of April, Captain Mercer, of the sloop Ambuscade, arrived in this port from Bermuda. He brought a list of eight American vessels with their cargoes which were condemned at that place; and of seven others which were libelled. One of the latter was a brig from Boston. Captain Mercer had heard that her captain had died of

---

* During the present session the speaker has signified in the house, that Harper spoke like a MADMAN. This justifies the text. The following traits will help to conjecture in what way congressional business hath sometimes been conducted.

Previous to the election of a clerk for the Representatives, in the present Congress, (Supra, chap. 3d,) Dr. Smith convened his party without doors, and they agreed in the nomination of a candidate to oppose Mr. Beckley. Next morning the votes were taken by ballot. The republican members had each to write the name of their candidate; but the friends of *order* pulled theirs ready written out of their pockets. As great part of them could know nothing of Mr. Beckley but by name, this promptitude shews the exactness of their discipline, and what praise is due to the diligence of our legislative Martinet.

In the Senate, matters proceed still more straightly. For instance, a few weeks ago, five resolutions were moved in that body, and it was agreed to ballot, next day, for committees upon each of them. The federal majority consisted of seventeen; and so nicely had matters been ascertained without doors, that the five committees, having each three members, were elected exclusively out of the seventeen. The minority have no share of influence whatever. They are debarred even from the appearance of it.

Compare this plain account with the plaister which Mr. Adams laid upon the Senate in his late farewell address. It might be condensed into a few words. *Gentlemen, you are the greatest legislators in the world.—No sir,* YOU *are the greatest, and we are confident that you will make us all judges or ambassadors, as early as possible.*

abuſe which he received from the prize-maſter. A paragraph of the ſame date ſays, that, at Nevis, the ſchooner Andrew, captain Montayne, of Philadelphia, had her mate and ſeamen preſſed by a Britiſh ſchooner. They were all Americans ; and had protections. The particulars are related in the captain's proteſt, as tranſmitted to his owner.

Theſe maritime anecdotes are valuable, as ſhewing the character of that people, who, in the midſt of ſuch injuries, could wiſh to appropriate for Jay's treaty. It would be vain to look in the hiſtory of England, for any meaſures ſo deplorably deſpicable. To proceed in a regular ſucceſſion, to the end of the year 1796, would occupy a large volume. At preſent, only three or four incidents of this kind ſhall be added, as they come to hand in the order of time.

Joſhua Whiting was a ſeamen on board of the American brig Samuel. At Port-au-Prince, he, and four others of the crew, were preſſed by a Britiſh frigate. Three of them, after eleven days, eſcaped by ſwimming, in the courſe of which, one man had the calf of his leg bitten off by a ſhark. Another of them was retaken, received four dozen of laſhes, and was put in irons. Whiting and the cripple, eſcaped, after loſing their whole adventure, beſides being cruelly treated. In the Boſton Chronicle, of the 18th of April, Whiting publiſhed a narrative, of which the above is the ſubſtance. Inſtead of voting money for the treaty, Congreſs might as well have voted ſome relief to the poor man who loſt the calf of his leg, under that emblem of abaſement, that contempt of nations, that nautical DETERSORIUM, the *American flag!*

The brig Columbia, and the ſchooner Unity, both of Newburyport, ſailed from Port Lewis, on the 7th of March, 1796. Next day, they were brought to by the Ganges, a British seventy-four, and a schooner attendant to the ship. " This " schooner," says the account, " is one of *the fif-* " *teen pilot boats built in Virginia,* not long since, " which are all employed as attendants to the Bri- " tish men of war." They were sent into Mont- ferrat, examined, and on the 14th, dismissed, upon paying forty-four pounds, four shillings, and ten pence, as the expence of their examination.

The sloop Dove, of Newhaven, in Connecti- cut, had gone on a voyage to the West-Indies. While lying at Antigua, she was boarded by a boat's crew from the Narcissus, who took away Benjamin Eastman. He was a native American, and as such, had a protection. On the 3d of April, 1796, the master and mate of the Dove made oath to this fact, at Newhaven. James Smith, master of the May Flower, of Norfolk, published a de- claration, dated the 3d of March, 1796. One of his men, an American, was impressed at Port Je- remie, by the Regulus. Captain Smith, himself, was kept, for three days, a prisoner, on board of the frigate, and half starved. He left about thirty or forty American sailors in her. Almost the whole of them had protections, and he saw some of them severely punished for attempting to escape. The newspapers containing these miserable details, are crammed with exulting encomiums on the number of petitioners to Congress, in favour of the British treaty.

On Tuesday, the 31st of May, 1796, the Spea- ker of the House of Representatives, laid before them, a letter from ten American captains, whose vessels were then lying at Jamaica. Their seamen were on board of British ships of war, where they were treated like slaves. They said that their brethern at Algiers were not greater objects of sympathy. These ten captains might as well have addressed a memorial, on the same subject, to any old woman, in any chimney corner, on the continent. Congress have no fleet, and they can hardly raise money to pay the national debt. 'In this *unparalleled state of prosperity*, what would you have us to do?

The Aurora, of June 2d, 1796, contained a long account of the capture of the Eliza, a vessel, American property, by the British. She sailed from New-York, for St. Thomas's, and had orders to touch at St. Bartholomew's. She was taken by captain Cochran, of the Thetis frigate. The supercargo, a Danish subject, was stripped to the skin. The ship was libelled before the Vice-Admiralty Court at Bermuda, under pretence of being French property. The trunks of the supercargo were sealed up, and he was himself thrown penniless out of the ship, without a second shirt to his back. The captain and crew were put on shore, destitute of subsistence. Six or seven days after the ship and cargo had been libelled, the cattle were sold at half their prime cost, bought in by the agents who sold them, and sold a second time, next day, at a considerable profit.

A Boston newspaper, of the 26th of May, contains a deposition, dated at St. George's, the 27th of April, preceding. It was emitted by the second mate of the brigantine Polly, John Bosson, late master. The vessel was on her way from Demarara, to Boston, when the Cleopatra, a British privateer, took her. Soon after, the prize-master quarrelled with captain Bosson, and wantonly beat him in a most shocking manner. This is the substance of the deposition. Within six days after, captain Bosson died of his bruises. He was only in the twenty-fifth year of his age.

Such was the picture of national independence and dignity that America, during 1796, exhibited by sea. At some future opportunity the narrative will, perhaps, be resumed and completed. In the mean time, these instances may be compared, by an impartial citizen, with the censure bestowed by Barras, on the government of the United States. He can then attempt to decide, wether Mr. Washington had, last year, greater cause to complain of England, or Mr. Adams, in the present year, of France. We shall now proceed to examine some federal transactions by land. In a work embracing such various objects, many points of importance are sure of being omitted. Still, however, even an imperfect history, if candid and accurate, is better than none. The facility acquired by experience, and the resources derived from public patronage, may, hereafter, furnish means for producing a more regular, and less defective, performance.

Among the memorials presented to Congress, in spring, 1796, perhaps none deserved more attention, than that of the snuff-makers of this city, respecting the excise on their manufacture. On the 5th of June, 1794, an act had past in Congress, for levying a duty of six cents per pound, upon all snuff, maufactured in the United States. As this law did not answer the end proposed, it was repealed, and, on the 3d of March, 1795, another was enacted in its room. By the latter, two thousand two hundred and forty dollars were to be paid for every snuff-mill, with stampers and grinders, and sums proportinably less, for those of inferior effect. As a relief to the snuff-maker, he received a drawback of six cents upon every pound of snuff, exported out of the country. The first of these two laws originated with Mr. Alexander

Hamilton, then Secretary of the Treasury. Both of them met with warm opposition in Congress. Both were, in an eminent degree, absurd, oppressive, and impracticable. Both deserve to be held in remembrance, as proofs of what shocking despotism the legislature, even of a free country, may possibly commit. They were said to be laws of experiment, by those who were least eager in their defence. But a government has no right of making experiments, in opposition to probability, on the property of the public. The memorial was presented on the 9th of February, 1796, and is in these words.

" *To the Senate and House of Representatives of the United* " *States in Congress assembled:*

" The memorial of the subscribers, manufacturers of snuff in " the city of Philadelphia,

" *Respectfully represents,*
" THAT whilst the United States exhibit an universal ap-
" pearance of public prosperity, and of private happiness, the
" memorialists feel deep regret and mortification upon their be-
" ing once more compelled to address you in the solitary lan-
" guage of dissatisfaction. They have sometime ago entered
" into a struggle to support a second excise law upon their ma-
" nufacture. Your predecessors, the late Congress, gave a
" fair trial to the first act, which attempted to levy a duty on
" snuff in proportion to the pound weight. This law, as the
" honourable Congress well knows, operated at once like a
" stroke of annihilation. No excise could be paid, at least in
" the state of Pennsylvania; for, out of seven snuff-mills, six
" were instantly shut up, to the infinite injury of the manufac-
" turers. Their stock lay dead on their hands. Their cus-
" tomers dispersed, and in many cases declined to pay the out-
" standing debts, because the subscribers, having no power to
" manufacture snuff, were unable to give them further credit.
" The buildings for carrying on their manufactories, erected
" at an expence of many thousand dollars, were at once conver-
" ted into sepulchres of American industry: and, in the vain at-

"tempt to extract a revenue, where every moral and physical
"circumstance rendered it impossible, six months of business
"and of human life were lost. Even the seventh snuff-mill,
"which actually was entered, never paid any duty.

"Every feature in the history of this first excise upon snuff
"justified the energetic presage of a gentleman, who was a
"member of the last, and is one in the present House of Repre-
"sentatives of Congress. He declared in his place that the act
"would terminate not in revenue, but destruction. The ac-
"curacy of his prediction hath been verified by experience, and
"fully acknowledged and attested on the floor of Congress. The
"effects of that memorable statute were perhaps unrivalled,
"even in the tragical and exterminating annals of excise. Like
"a pestilence, or a tempest, this law blasted and swept before
"it every blossom of industry, and had your memorialists re-
"mained ever since entirely unmolested by excise laws, yet
"some years of good fortune would have been requisite for en-
"abling them to recover the ground which they had lost.

"That, with the deepest astonishment, the memorialists have,
"during the present session, heard of several petitions presented
"to Congress, chiefly as they believe from snuff-makers in
"the eastern states, requesting the repeal of the present excise,
"in order to replace it by the former law for levying the duty
"by the pound weight. These petitioners have indeed honest-
"ly represented many insurmountable objections to the present
"law, and which your memorialists admit, as well as they do.
"But it does not follow, that the present extremely oppressive
"excise on snuff ought to be superceded for the sake of adop-
"ting another statute which is infinitely worse, and which has
"already been tried and cast aside as impracticable. The ruin-
"ous effects of both these laws, have been fully stated in a
"short history of excise laws, drawn up at the desire and un-
"der the inspection of a number of manufacturers in Philadel-
"phia, and of which a printed copy has lately been transmitted
"to each of the members of the two houses of Congress, and
"to the principal officers of the federal government.

"In the last act for an excise upon snuff, a drawback of six
"cents per pound has been allowed upon the exportation. This
"drawback was liable to various abuses. If not granted at all,
"snuff could not be exported after paying an excise, and this
"would tend to depress the American manufacturer. But, in
"order to be entitled to the drawback, it was requisite to ob-
"tain a certificate of the snuff having been duly landed at the

" deſtined port: the chief exportation was to the Britiſh Weſt-
" Indies, were American ſnuff is contraband, and conſequently
" it was quite impoſſible to get the requiſite certificates. But
" farther, nothing could be more eaſy than to make a preten-
" ded exportation of ſnuff to ſome iſland in the Weſt-Indies,
" where it was not prohibited, obtain a regular certificate of
" its being landed, and then ſmuggle it back to this country.
" Thus one barrel of ſnuff, might receive twenty drawbacks.
" Such frauds are practiſed every day in Britain. Many mer-
" chants on the river Thames ſupport their families in ſplendor
" by drawbacks, procured from their government for imagi-
" nary exportations. Your memorialiſts have been aſſured,
" that one bale of muſlin, ſuppoſed to be worth five hundred
" guineas, received in this way a drawback of twelve and an
" half per cent forty times over, ſo that this bale earned two
" thouſand five hundred guineas.

" Traſh of any kind, or even ſand, might be exported from
" the United States, under the name of ſnuff and obtain the ſix
" cents per pound of drawback. Frauds of this kind could
" not be prevented without a multiplicity of inſpectors, whoſe
" ſalaries would ſwallow up the revenue.

" That the eighty-fourth and ninety-third ſections of the
" Britiſh tobacco excise act of 1789, fully ſhew, to what length
" impoſtures of this ſort have been carried in that country.
" The former of theſe two clauſes, inflicts a penalty of two
" hundred pounds, for the mixture of cut walnut leaves, of
" hops, of ſycamore, or any other leaves or herbs, with the
" leaves of tobacco. The injunctions in the ninety-third
" ſection, againſt mixing ſnuff with other materials, are ſtill
" more pointed. The penalty of two hundred pounds is levi-
" ed for mixing with ſnuff, any fuſtic, yellow honey, touch-
" wood, log-wood, red or guinea wood, braziletto or Jamai-
" ca wood, Nicaragua-wood, Saunders-wood or any other
" ſort of wood, or any walnut tree leaves, hops, ſycamore, or
" any other leaves or herbs. This ſingular enumeration aſcer-
" tains how far ſuch practices have gone.

" That there is another material objection to the preſent mode
" of granting a drawback. The price of different kinds of
" ſnuff differs very conſiderably, and yet the ſame drawback
" of ſix cents is granted, without diſtinction, upon all kinds.
" Richard Gernon & Co. in their petition, ſtate, that the ſnuff
" which they have been exporting is worth ten cents per pound,
" beſides the ſix cents of drawback. Thus its value, after pay-

"ing the duty, would be about one shilling and three pence per
"pound. The memorialists are now selling snuff at two shil-
"lings and six pence and three shillings per pound, and were
"they to export it, a drawback of at least twelve cents per
"pound would be necessary to put them on a level with Ger-
"non & Co. who receive six cents per pound drawback on an
"article not half so valuable.

"The memorialists, in their publication already referred to,
"stated the possibility that the drawbacks for a single manufac-
"turer might amount to sixty thousand dollars per annum, and
"if a dozen such manufacturers were to be found in the United
"States, that they would drain the public treasury of seven hun-
"dred and twenty thousand dollars a year, a sum which all the ex-
"cises in the country could not cover. To the great astonishment
"of the memorialists, this prediction received a partial fulfilment
"almost at the instant when it was made. The revenue deri-
"ved from the mills, entered in the state of Pennsylvania comes
"only to eight thousand three hundred and eighty dollars.
"On the 26th January last, the drawbacks at the port of Phi-
"ladelphia, since the new act began to operate, amounted to
"eight thousand five hundred and twenty-three dollars and
"thirty-nine cents, which is already one hundred and forty-
"three dollars, and thirty-nine cents, more than the total re-
"venue for this state. Almost the whole of this drawback
"has been paid to Messrs. Richard Gernon and Co. who have
"been only about four months in business, and within that
"period, have got back above five thousand dollars additional,
"besides the two thousand two hundred and forty dollars,
"which they paid, according to law, for entering their mill.
"It is not the design of your memorialists to cast the slightest
"reflection on the conduct of this manufacturing company.
"On the contrary, if government has laid itself open by a
"law which defeats its own purposes, and sinks a revenue
"where it expected to raise one, the manufacturers are in com-
"mon justice, entitled, to take every legal advantage of such an
"oversight. Nay, they beg leave to state it as a matter of absolute
"certainty, that if this law is not repealed, a number of snuff-
"makers will immediately enter into the business of exportation.
"They only forbear altering their mills, and adapting them for
"the business, till they see whether Congress will adhere to the
"law or not; for the example of Richard Gernon and Co. proves
"how easily a snuff-maker, with the requisite degree of capital
"and enterprise, may take from the public treasury in the shape

"of drawbacks ten times as much as he pays into it. Your
"memorialists cannot believe that Congress, or indeed any le-
"gislative assembly on earth, would suffer the longer existence
"of a law so pregnant with the most preposterous and ruinous
"consequences. A few weeks ago, Messrs. Gernon & Co.
"presented to Congress a memorial, representing the immense
"expence which they have been at in preparing their mill to
"grind snuff for exportation. Among other details, they state
"their having, in the first four months of their copartnery, pur-
"chased four hundred and thirty hogsheads of tobacco, and
"that they are continuing to make large purchases of this kind.
"At that rate, they will, in the course of twelve months, pur-
"chase, altogether, twelve hundred and ninety hogsheads.
"Your memorialists estimate, that, when grinded into snuff,
"the drawback on this quantity will amount to about ninety
"thousand dollars. The company will thus gain, by the pub-
"lic revenue, eighty-eight thousand dollars, the drawback
"exceeding the revenue in the proportion of forty-five to one.
"This is a circumstance perfectly novel in the history of tax-
"ation.

"But further, if this affair is suffered to go on in its pre-
"sent way, Congress may soon expect to see twenty other
"snuff-mills working on the same plan, and to an equal ex-
"tent, with that of Gernon & Co.

"If the government of this country intend, seriously, and
"steadily, to give a drawback of six cents per pound on the
"exportation of American snuff, it is the most acceptable and
"joyful intelligence that your memorialists could ever hear of.
"They will immediately repair their mills, extend their pur-
"chases, and they have not a doubt of clearing, from the draw-
"back, before the end of a year, twenty or thirty times the
"sum which they are to pay into the treasury. Twenty ma-
"nufacturers, like Gernon & Co. would each of them thus
"cost government ninety thousand dollars, or, collectively,
"one million eight hundred thousand dollars per annum. The
"original object of the law was said to be a revenue of forty
"thousand dollars; there is an equal chance, that, in search
"of it, forty-five times that sum will be sunk. It has been
"abovementioned, that the drawbacks, within this state, al-
"ready exceed the revenue. The first year of this law ex-
"pires on the last day of March next, and, before that time,
"there will most likely be a balance of several thousand dollars
"against the revenue, at the port of Philadelphia. But if the

D d

"law stands unrepealed, it is probable that two hundred thou-
"sand dollars will not make up the deficiencies in this state
"alone, for the next succeeding year.

"In their history of excise, the manufacturers stated the prin-
"ciple, that all taxes ought to be levied in proportion to the
"quantum of personal property. Since their publication took
"place, they have seen this doctrine justified by an authority
"of the highest nature. The new constitution of France, in
"the sixteenth article of the first section, lays it down as a fun-
"damental maxim, that, "as all taxes are established for the
"general good, they ought to be apportioned among the taxed
"in the ratio of their means." Under the head of finances, al-
"so, in the same work, it is declared, " that taxes of all kinds
"are assessed among all those liable to contribution according
"to their means,"—Your memorialists cannot deny that the
"word excise is to be found in the letter of the federal con-
"stitution; but they strongly contend, that it is entirely hos-
"tile to the spirit of that instrument. One of the principle fa-
"bricators of that production, was the present judge Wilson.
"When the subject was debated in the convention of Penn-
"sylvania, he argued that it was necessary to give all power
"to government, but he was certain that an excise never would
"be imposed, unless in the last extremity. From the opinion
"which the convention of Pennsylvania expressed of excise, at
"that time, and which the assembly of this state have expressed
"since, it is evident that they never would have consented to
"ratify such a stipulation, if they had conceived that it was to
"become one of the first, and favourite resources of government.

"That your memorialists cannot help considering this excise
"on snuff as coming, exactly, under the description of an *ex
"post facto* law. They had no contemplation of such a bur-
"den, when they built their mills, and gave credit, to so great
"an extent, to their customers. Their mills would not, at
"present, sell for one half of the money which they originally
"cost, and one half of them are, at this hour, standing idle.
"This, of itself, would be sufficient to destroy any set of
"manufacturers. Your memorialists likewise beg leave to
"state, as their opinion, that if the merchants and manufactu-
"rers of Britain had a liberty of petitioning Congress, they
"could not solicit a more favourable mode of conduct for their
"own interest, than persuading you to trammel, and distress,
"the manufacturers of America with excises, which do not
"pay the expence of their collection, which in one state pro-

y, and in a second, rebellion. They humbly
merical to term America independent of Bri-
are forced to send to England for a coat, and
a shirt. It is this commercial chain of de-
hich Britain has entangled so many nations,
the essence and soul of her strength, and that
bully, to combat, and to rob her neighbours.
ority in manufactures, which has enabled this
sidize and embattle pirates and cut-throats,
of the world, while she herself may be termed
Atlantean magnitude, whose grasp embraces
globe, and whose stature reaches from earth

e, your memorialists ardently flatter them-
hope, that Congress will see the expediency,
ositive and inevitable necessity, for an imme-
lete abolition of the excise upon snuff made
'hough some ill-advised manufacturers to the
called for the restoration of the act of 1794,
uff-makers, in that part of the union, regard it
bhorrence, as the memorialists themselves do.
e present excise, and withhold the drawback,
hibit, in a great measure, the manufacture of
ond staple of the continent; and it has alrea-
rated, that, to continue the law, and the draw-
esent shape, is only to squander forty-five dol-
s search after one.
ialists, therefore, earnestly solicit an entire re-
e upon snuff, and they, as in duty bound, will

"THOMAS LEIPER, & Co.
"HAMILTON & SON,
"ISAAC JONES,
"JACOB BENNINGHOVE,
"JACOB BENNINGHOVE, jun.
"PHILIP STIMBLE,
'ebruary 8th, 1796."

hath been since repeatedly suspen-
s, supposed, will never more be put

 may wonder what the House of Representatives were thinking of, when they successively enacted such self-condemned laws. It is likely that, during the discussion, ten or fifteen were employed in reading newspapers, or in writing letters. About as many more might be in private conversation, at the back of the Speaker's chair, or at the windows. General Samuel Smith, who hath saved the house from many woeful mistakes, is the gentleman alluded to, in the second paragraph of the memorial.

We now come to a part of the work, more delicate, perhaps, than any other. The freedoms which the federal party have taken with those who differ from their opinions, are universally known. The most impartial scrutiny would determine, that, in the arts of calumny and detraction, their publications exceed, beyond all proportion, those of their adversaries. In the first session of the fifth Congress, Mr. Harper has publicly declared to the Representatives, that Mr. James Munroe, our late envoy to France, was guilty of corruption by foreign influence. On being questioned by Mr. Giles, he has promised, in due time and place, to bring evidence of his accusation. This example is only one out of hundreds which might be adduced to shew that the friends of *order*, for such they call themselves, are resolved to set no limits to their rage and their vengeance. Of course, they cannot expect to meet with that tenderness which they refuse to grant.

Attacks on Mr. Munroe have been frequently repeated from the stock-holding presses. They are cowardly, because he is absent. They are unjust, because his conduct will bear the strictest enquiry. They are ungrateful, because he displayed, on an occasion that will be mentioned immediately, the greatest lenity to Mr. Alexander Hamilton, the prime mover of the federal party. When some of the papers which are now to be laid before the world, were submitted to the secretary; when he was informed that they were to be communicated to President Washington, he entreated, in the most anxious tone of deprecation, that this measure might be suspended. Mr. Munroe was one of the three gentlemen who agreed to a delay. They gave their consent to it, on his express promise of a guarded behaviour in future, and because he attached to the suppression of these papers, a mysterious degree of solicitude, which they, feeling no personal resentment against the individual, were unwilling to augment.

The unfounded reproaches heaped on Mr. Munroe, form the immediate motive to the publication of these papers. They are here printed from an attested copy, exactly conformable to that, which, at his own desire, was delivered to Mr. Hamilton himself. Not a word has been added or altered, and the period of four years may, surely, have been enough to furnish the ex-secretary with materials for his defence. In the letters of Camillus, the most sublime principles of action are every where inculcated. But we shall presently see this great master of morality, though himself the father of a family, confessing that he had an illicit correspondence with another man's wife. If any thing can be yet less reputable, it is, that the gentlemen to whom he made that acknowledgement held it as an imposition, and found various reasons for believing that Mrs. Reynolds was, in reality, guiltless. An attentive critic will be led to enquire what has become of her husband, and why the indignant innocence of Mr. Hamilton, did not promote the completion of public justice against a person, who had treated his name with such gross disrespect? What a scandalous imputation was it for this culprit to cast upon our secretary, that he had gained thirty thousand dollars by the purchase of army certificates, that this fellow could bring him to capital punishment, &c. &c. ? It is to be wished that Reynolds may still be found, and that, to borrow the words of his friend, Dr. William Smith, the Secretary may come out of this matter, " as fair as the purest *angel in heaven!*"

Before committing the following papers to the world, their editor must again beg leave to remark, that they are nothing more nor less than exact copies, from attested originals, of which Mr. Hamilton, as hereafter specified, has been, at his own desire, supplied with an accurate transcript. Some expressions used by the culprit, Reynolds, are harsh, and convey disgust, without adding to conviction. The editor, from aversion to invective, had, on this account, resolved to leave them out, as well as several other passages, which are of little importance to the main point. But on due reflection, it has been found safer, and more adviseable, to publish the whole, even at the hazard of being tedious. This precludes all pretence of mutilation for unfair purposes.

As to the asperity of style in some parts of the *precious confessions* of Reynolds, the painful reluctance of the editor, to the printing of them, has been somewhat lessened, from the volunteer acknowledgment of seduction, emitted by the ex-secretary himself. This appears to be about as bad, as any thing which his wretched understrapper either said against him, or could imaginably have to say. A procurer has always been regarded as in the lowest scale of human character. *Mutatis mutandis*, the patron of such an agent can have no scruple to become one.

Again, the intemperate style of the convivial, and confidential communications of our ex-secretary, prohibits him from being regarded as any peculiar object of indulgence. For instance, he has often boasted of receiving letters from President Washington, with the word *private* wrote on the back of them, and a cross drawn over the seal. "After opening such a parcel," said Mr. Hamilton, "what do you think were the contents? DEAR HAMILTON, *put this into style for me.* Some speech or letter has been inclosed, which I wrote over again, sent it back, and then the OLD DAMNED FOOL gave it away as *his own.*" Mr. Hamilton is not singular in using this style to general Washington. After the squabble between citizen Genet, John Jay, and Rufus King, the two latter sent a most insulting letter to the President. Randolph advised him to resent it. He had once resolved to do so; but altered his intention, from a jealousy that the writers were in concert with Hamilton, from whom he could not determine to disjoin himself. Jay and King wanted to obtain a certificate, which Mr. Jefferson had drawn up, relating to the behaviour of citizen Genet. The President actually gave them the certificate, but it is thought that they found it not to their purpose; for it was suppressed. Jay and King also got back from the President their impertinent letter; of which, after cooling, they began to be ashamed. But a copy of it is in existence, and some hopes remain of its being obtained for publication. These particulars are derived from undoubted authority. They prove what was so fully stated in the American Annual Register, that the federal party despised the late President; that they took frequent opportunities of insulting him; and that they assumed the popularity of his name with no view but to serve their own ends.

To be the prompter and *primum mobile* of the greatest man in the world, might have flattered the vanity of a more discreet favourite than Mr. Hamilton. To hear the Representatives, as in November, 1794, dispute for three weeks upon the wording of an answer to a speech of his own composition, must have been highly soothing to the self-importance of the ex-secretary. But, as general Washington had been, in the highest sense of the word, his benefactor, he ought to have concealed the imperfections of his friend. He has often compared his influence over the President to that of the wind upon a weather cock, or of that over an automaton, moved only by the hand which directs it. This style was both imprudent and ungrateful. His power was very great, but not entirely unbounded. He wanted to be sent to England as envoy to negociate the treaty. The arguments of Randolph hindered the President from giving his consent. That the pen of Mr. Hamilton has long assisted the President is a story current in Europe as well as in America; and that the speeches and letters of general Washington are extremely different from his more early productions is very well known.

We shall conclude these prefatory observations with an anecdote. During the late canvass for the election of a President, Webster, in his Minerva, gave a hint, that Mr. Hamilton would be an advisable candidate. A person in this city, who chanced to see this newspaper, wrote immediately to a correspondent in New-York. The letter desired him to put himself in Mr. Hamilton's way, and inform him that if Webster should, in future, print a single paragraph on that head, the following papers were instantly to be laid before the world. It is believed the message was delivered to Mr. Hamilton, for the Minerva became silent.

(No. I.)

JACOB CLINGMAN, being a clerk in my employment, (F. A. Muhlenberg) and becoming involved in a prosecution commenced against JAMES REYNOLDS, by the Comptroller of the Treasury, on a charge or information exhibited before Hilary Baker, esq. one of the aldermen of this city, for subornation of perjury, whereby they had obtained money from the treasury of the United States, he (Clingman) applied to me, for my aid and friendship, on behalf of himself and Reynolds, to get them released or discharged from the prosecution. I promised, so far as respected Clingman; but, not being particularly acquainted with Reynolds, in a great measure, declined so far as respected him. In company with colonel Burr, I waited on colonel Hamilton for the purpose, and particularly recommended Clingman, who had hitherto sustained a good character. Colonel Hamilton signified a wish to do all that was consistent. Shortly after, I waited on the Comptroller for the same purpose, who seemed to have difficulties on the subject; and, from some information I had, in the mean time, received, I could not undertake to recommend Reynolds, as I verily believed him to be a rascal, which words I made use of to the Comptroller. On a second interview with the Comptroller, on the same subject, the latter urged the propriety of Clingman's delivering up a certain list of money due to individuals, which Reynolds and Clingman were said to have in their possession, and of his informing him, of whom, and through whom, the same was obtained from the public offices; on doing which, Clingman's request might, perhaps, be granted with greater propriety. This, Clingman, I am informed, complied with, and also refunded the money or certificates, which they had improperly obtained from the treasury. After which, I understand the action against both was withdrawn, and Reynolds discharged from imprisonment, without any farther interference of mine whatever.

During the time this business was thus depending, and which lasted upwards of three weeks, Clingman, *unasked*, frequently dropped hints to me, that Reynolds had it in his power, *very materially to injure the Secretary of the Treasury*; and that Reynolds knew several very improper transactions of his. I paid little or no attention to those hints; but, when they were frequently repeated, and it was even added, that Reynolds said, he had it in his power to hang the Secretary of the *Treasury*; that he was *deeply concerned in speculation*; that he had frequently advanced money to him, (Reynolds); and other insinuations of an improper nature, it created considerable uneasiness in my mind, and I conceived it my duty to consult with some friends on the subject.—Mr. Monroe and Mr. Venable were informed of it yesterday morning.

  (Signed,) F. A. MUHLENBERG.

(No. II.)

 BEING informed yesterday, in the morning, that a person of the name of Reynolds, from Virginia, Richmond, was confined in the jail, upon some criminal prosecution relative to certificates, and that he had intimated, he would give some intelligence of speculations by Mr. Hamilton, which should be known, WE immediately called on him, as well to be informed of the situation of the man, as of those other matters, in which the public might be interested. We found it was not the person, we had been taught to believe, but a man of that name from New-York, and who had, for some time past, resided in this city. Being there, however, we questioned him respecting the other particular; he informed us, that he could give information of the misconduct, in that respect, of a person high in office, but must decline it, for the present, and until relieved, which was promised him that evening: that at ten to-day, he would give us a detail of whatever he knew on the subject. He affirmed, he had a person, high in office, in his power, and had had, a long time past. That he had written to him, in terms so abusive, that no person should have submitted to it, but that *he dared not to resent it*. That Mr. Wolcot was in the same department, and, he supposed, under his influence or controul; and, in fact, expressed himself in such a manner, as to leave no doubt, he meant Mr. Hamilton. That he expected to be released by Mr. Wolcot, at the instance of that person, although he believed, that Mr. Wolcot, in instituting the prosecution, had no improper design; that he was satisfied, the prosecution was set on foot, only to keep him low, and oppress him, and ultimately *drive him away*; that he had had, since his residence here, for eighteen months, many private meetings with that person, who had often promised to put him into employment, but had disappointed him; that on hearing the profecution was commenced againſt him, he applied to this perſon for counſel, who adviſed him to keep out of the way, for a few days; that a merchant came to him, and offered, as a volunteer, to be his bail, who, he ſuſpected, had been inſtigated by this perſon; and, after being decoyed to the place, the merchant wiſhed to carry him [*to*], he refuſed being his bail, unleſs he would depoſit a ſum of money, to ſome conſiderable amount, which he could not do, and was, in conſequence, committed to priſon. As well as we remember, he gave, as a reaſon, why he could not communicate to us, what he knew of the facts alluded to, that he was apprehenſive, it might prevent his diſcharge; but that he would certainly communicate the whole to us, at ten this morning: at which time, we were informed, he had abſconded, or concealed himſelf.

  (Signed,) JAMES MONROE,
        ABRAHAM VENABLE.

(*No. III.*)

BEING deſirous, on account of their equivocal complexion, to examine into the ſuggeſtions which had been made us, reſpecting the motive for the confinement and propoſed enlargement of James Reynolds, from the jail of this city, and inclined to ſuſpect, for the ſame reaſon, that, unleſs'it were immediately done, the opportunity would be loſt, as we were taught to ſuſpect he would leave the place, immediately after his diſcharge, we called at his houſe, laſt night, for that purpoſe; we found Mrs. Reynolds alone. It was, with difficulty, we obtained from her, any information on the ſubject; but at length ſhe communicated to us the following particulars.

That ſince colonel Hamilton was Secretary of the Treaſury, and at his requeſt, *ſhe had burned a conſiderable number of letters from him to her huſband*, and in the abſence of the latter, touching buſineſs between them, to prevent their being made public. She alſo mentioned, that Mr. Clingman had ſeveral anonymous notes addreſſed to her huſband, which, ſhe believed, were from Mr. Hamilton (which we have) with an endorſement " from ſecretary Hamilton, eſq." in Mr. Reynolds's hand, writing; that Mr. Hamilton offered her his aſſiſtance to go to her friends, which he adviſed; that he alſo adviſed, that her huſband ſhould leave the parts, not to be ſeen here again; and in which caſe, he would *give ſomething clever*. That ſhe was satisfied, this wish for his departure did not proceed from friendship to him, but on account of his threat, that he could tell something that would make some of the heads of departments tremble. That Mr. Wadsworth had been active in her behalf; first at her request, but, in her opinion, with the knowledge and communication of Mr. Hamilton, whose friend he professed to be; that he had been at her house yesterday, and mentioned to her, that two gentlemen of Congress had been at the jail, to confer with her husband; enquired, if she knew what they went for; observed, he knew Mr. Hamilton had enemies, who would try to prove some speculations on him, but when enquired into, he would be found immaculate; to which she replied, she rather *doubted it.*

We saw, in her possession, two notes; one in the name of Alexander Hamilton, of the 6th of December; and the other, signed "J. W." purporting to have been written yesterday; both expressing a desire to relieve her.

She denied any recent communication with Mr. Hamilton, or that she had received any money from him to-day.

  (Signed,) F. A. MUHLENBERG.
         JAMES MONROE.
         ABRAHAM VENABLE.

(No. IV.)

Philadelphia, 13th *December,* 1792.

JACOB CLINGMAN has been engaged in some negociations with Mr. James Reynolds, the person, who has lately been discharged from a prosecution instituted against him, by the Comptroller of the Treasury.

That his acquaintance commenced in September, 1791; that a mutual confidence and intimacy existed between them; that in January or February last, he saw colonel Hamilton at the house of Reynolds. Immediately on his going into the house, colonel Hamilton retired. That in a few days after, he (Clingman) was at Mr. Reynolds's house, with Mrs. Reynolds, her husband being then out; some person knocked at the door; he arose and opened it, and saw that it was colonel Hamilton. Mrs. Reynolds went to the door; he delivered a paper to her, and said, he was ordered to give Mr. Reynolds that. He asked Mrs. Reynolds who could order the Secretary of the Treasury of the United States to give that? She replied, that she supposed, he did not want to be known. This happened in the night. He afked her, how long Mr. Reynolds had been acquainted with colonel Hamilton? She replied, fome months; that colonel Hamilton had affifted her hufband; that fometime before that, he had received upwards of eleven hundred dollars, of colonel Hamilton. Sometime after this, Clingman was at the houfe of Reynolds, and faw colonel Hamilton; he retired and left him there.

A little after Duer's failure, Reynolds told Clingman, in confidence, that if Duer had held up, three days longer, he fhould have made fifteen hundred pounds, by the affiftance of colonel Hamilton; that colonel Hamilton had informed him, *that he was connected with Duer.* Mr. Reynolds alfo faid, that colonel Hamilton had made *thirty thoufand dollars* by fpeculation; that colonel Hamilton had fupplied him with money to fpeculate. That, about June laft, Reynolds told Clingman, that he had applied to colonel Hamilton for money to fubfcribe to the turnpike-road at Lancafter, and had received a note from him, in thefe words, "It is utterly out of my pow-"er, I affure you, upon my honour, to comply with your re-"queft. Your note is returned;" which original note, accompanying this, has been in Clingman's poffeffion ever fince. Mr. Reynolds has once or twice mentioned to Clingman, that he had it in his power *to hang colonel Hamilton*; that if he wanted money, he was *obliged to let him have it.* That he (Clingman) has occafionally lent money to Reynolds who always told him, that he could always get it from colonel Hamilton, to repay it; that, on one occafion, Clingman lent him two hundred dollars; that Reynolds promifed to pay him, through the means of colonel Hamilton; that he went with him, faw him go into colonel Hamilton's; that, after he came out, he paid him one hundred dollars, which, he faid, was part of the fum, he had got; and paid the balance, in a few days; the latter fum paid was faid to have been received from colonel Hamilton, after his return from Jerfey, having made a vifit to the manufacturing fociety there.

After a warrant was iffued againft Reynolds, upon a late profecution, which was inftituted againft him, Clingman, feeing Reynolds, afked him, why he did not apply to his friend colonel Hamilton? He faid, he would go immediately, and went accordingly. He faid afterwards, that colonel Hamilton advifed him to keep out of the way, a few days, and the matter would be fettled. That after this time, Henry Seckel, went to Reynolds, and offered to be his bail, if he would go with him to Mr. Baker's office, where he had left the officer, who had the warrant in writing; that he prevailed on Reynolds to go with him. That after Reynolds was taken into custody; Seckel refused to become his bail, unless he would deposit, in his possession, property to the value of four hundred pounds; upon which, Reynolds wrote to colonel Hamilton, and Mr. Seckel carried the note. After two or three times going, he saw colonel Hamilton. Colonel Hamilton said, he knew Reynolds and his father; that his father was a good whig in the late war; that was all he could say; that it was not in his power to assist him; in consequence of which, Seckel refused to be his bail, and Reynolds was imprisoned. Mr. Reynolds also applied to Mr. Francis, who is one of the clerks in the treasury department; he said, he could not do any thing, without the consent of colonel Hamilton; that he would apply to him. He applied to Mr. Hamilton, who told him, that it would not be prudent; if he did, he must leave the department.

After Reynolds was confined, Clingman asked Mrs. Reynolds, why she did not apply to colonel Hamilton to dismiss him, as the money was ready to be refunded, that was received. She replied, that she had applied to him, and he had sent her to Mr. Wolcot; but directed her not to let Mr. Wolcot know, that he had sent her there. Notwithstanding this injunction, she did let Mr. Wolcot know, by whom she had been sent, who appeared to be surprised at the information, but said, he would do what he could for her, and would consult colonel Hamilton on the occasion. Colonel Hamilton advised her, to get some persons of respectability, to intercede for her husband, and mentioned Mr. Muhlenberg.

Reynolds continued to be kept in custody, for some time, during which time, Clingman had conversation with Mr. Wolcot, who said, if he would give up a list of soldier's claims, which he had, he should be released. After this, Mrs. Reynolds informed Clingman, that colonel Hamilton had told her, that Clingman should write a letter to Mr. Wolcot, and a duplicate of the same to himself, promising to give up the list, and refund the money which had been obtained on a certificate, which had been said to have been improperly obtained. Clingman asked Mrs. Reynolds, for *the letters* that her husband had received from colonel Hamilton, from time to time, as he might probably use them to obtain her husband's liberty. She replied, that colonel Hamilton had requested her *to burn all the letters, that were in his hand-writing, or that had his name to them*; which she had done. He pressed her to examine again, as she might not have destroyed the whole, and they would be useful. She examined, and found two or three notes, without any name, which *are herewith submitted*, and which, she said, were notes from colonel Hamilton.

Mrs. Reynolds told Clingman, that having heard, that her husband's father was, in the late war, a commissary under the direction of colonel Wadsworth, she waited on him, to get him to intercede for her husband's discharge. He told her, he would give her his assistance, and said, "now you have made me your "friend, you must apply to no person else." That on Sunday evening, Clingman went to the house of Reynolds, and found colonel Wadsworth there. He was introduced to colonel Wadsworth, by Mrs. Reynolds. Colonel Wadsworth told him, he had seen Mr. Wolcot; that Mr. Wolcot would do any thing for him, (Clingman), and Reynolds's family, that he could; that he had called on colonel Hamilton, but had not seen him; that he might tell him, Mr. Muhlenberg, that a friend of his (Clingman's) had told him, that colonel Wadsworth was a countryman and schoolmate of Mr. Ingersoll, and that colonel Wadsworth was also intimate with the governor, and that the governor would do almost any thing, to oblige him; that his name must not be mentioned to Mr. Muhlenberg, as telling him this; but that, if Mr. Muhlenberg could be brought to speak to him first, on the subject, he would then do any thing in his power, for them; and told him not to speak to him, if he should meet him in the street; and said, if his name was mentioned, that he would do nothing. That on Wednesday, Clingman saw colonel Wadsworth, at Reynolds's house; he did not find her at home, but left a note; but, on going out, he met her, and said, he had seen every body, and done every thing.

Mrs. Reynolds told Clingman, that she had received money from colonel Hamilton, since her husband's confinement, enclosed in a note, which note she had burned.

After Reynolds was discharged, (which was eight or nine o'clock on Wednesday evening); about twelve o'clock at night, Mr. Reynolds sent a letter to colonel Hamilton by a girl; which letter, Clingman saw delivered to the girl.

Reynolds followed the girl, and Clingman followed him. He saw the girl go into colonel Hamilton's house. Clingman then joined Reynolds, and they walked back and forward in the street, until the girl returned, and informed Reynolds, that he *need not go out of town that night,* but call on him early in the morning. In the morning, between seven and eight o'clock, he saw Reynolds go to colonel Hamilton's house, and go in. He has not seen him since, and supposes, he is gone out of town.

Mr. Clingman further adds, that sometime ago he was informed by Mr. and Mrs. Reynolds, that *he had books containing the amount of the cash due to the Virginia line at his own house at New-York, with liberty to copy,* and were obtained through Mr. Duer.

The above contains the truth, to the best of my knowledge and recollection, and to which I am ready to make oath.

Given under my hand this 13th December, 1792.

  (Signed,) JACOB CLINGMAN.

(No. V.)

Philadelphia, 15th *December,* 1792.

Mr. Clingman informs us, that Mr. Reynolds returned to town, on Thursday night, and told him, he had written him a letter which he then had; not having had an opportunity to send it to him, and which he then tore; part of which was thrown into the fire. Other parts he presented to us, and which we now have.

That Reynolds, at the same time, told him, he had been received by Mr. Hamilton, the morning of that day, when they parted, about sunrise. That he was extremely agitated, *walking backward and forward the room, and striking, alternately, his forehead and his thigh; observing to him, that he had enemies at work, but was willing to meet them, on fair ground, and requested him not to stay long, lest it might be noticed.*

Mr. Clingman also informs us, that he received a note from Mr. Wolcot, to meet him, on Friday morning, at half past nine (which note we have). That he attended, and had an interview with him, in presence of Mr. Hamilton; when he was strictly examined by both, respecting the persons, who were enquiring into the matter, and their object; that he told Mr. Hamilton, he had been possessed of his notes to Reynolds, and had given them up to these gentlemen: and to which, he replied, he had done very wrong. That he also told Mr. Hamilton of the letter he had received from Reynolds, since his enlargement, mentioning that he (Mr. Hamilton) would make Francis swear back what he had said; and to which Mr. Hamilton replied, he would make him unsay any falsity he had declared.

Mr. Hamilton said, Reynolds was a villain, a rascal, and he supposed, would swear to any thing.

Mr. Wolcot said, that unless Clingman used the same candour to him, that he had done to Clingman, he should not consider himself bound.

Mr. Hamilton wanted to know, what members of Congress were concerned in the enquiry, and desired him to go into the gallery, where he would see them, and enquire their names of the bystanders.

Mr. Hamilton observed, he had had some transaction with Reynolds, which he had before mentioned, as well as Clingman remembers, to Mr. Wolcot, and need not go into detail.

Clingman also informs us, that Reynolds told him, since his enlargement, that when he was about to set out to Virginia, on his last trip to buy up cash-claims of the Virginia line, he told Mr. Hamilton, that Hopkins would not pay upon those powers of attorney; and to which he, (Mr. Hamilton) replied, he would write to Hopkins, on the subject.

16th. Last night we waited on colonel Hamilton, when he informed us of *a particular connection with Mrs. Reynolds:* the period of its commencement, and circumstances attending it; his visiting her at Inskeep's; the frequent supplies of money to her and her husband, on that account; his duress by them from the fear ... it and them ... letters from ... He acknow[ledged] ... *possession, to* ... suspicions w[ere] ... ward him h[e] ... it. We br[ought] ... did he ask t[he] ... He said, ... Reynolds a[nd] ... der of a list ...

> We read in a good many newspapers that "recent historical delvers have discovered that Hamilton had an affair with a woman which troubled him a good deal and injured him politically." It was hardly necessary to delve very deep to find out this. Hamilton himself printed a pamphlet on the subject, which has now become scarce, but which most persons interested in such curious matters have seen. There is a copy in Boston, in the possession of Mr. Charles Sprague, and one in the library of Mr. Wallace, Reporter of the U. S. Supreme Court, and we think that the New-York Historical Society has one. In this pamphlet Hamilton makes that full and free confession which is good for the soul. It's a curious story, but hardly worth repeating here. The gist of it is, that while Hamilton admits the sin frankly, he vehemently asserts that it had not, as his defamers charged, influenced his bestowal of the patronage of his office. The passage in which Hamilton owns and laments his fault is admirably written.

Reynolds followed the girl, and Clingman followed him. He saw the girl go into colonel Hamilton's house. Clingman then joined Reynolds, and they walked back and forward in the street, until the girl returned, and informed Reynolds, that he *need not go out of town that night*, but call on him early in the morning. In the morning, between seven and eight o'clock, he saw Reynolds go to colonel Hamilton's house, and go in. He has not seen him since, and supposes, he is gone out of town.

Mr. Clingman further adds, that sometime ago he was informed by Mr. and Mrs. Reynolds, that *he had books containing the amount of the cash due to the Virginia line at his own house at New-York, with liberty to copy*, and were obtained through Mr. Duer.

The above contains the truth, to the best of my knowledge and recollection, and to which I am ready to make oath.

Given under my hand this 13th December, 1792.

(Signed,)   JACOB CLINGMAN.

(No. V.)

Philadelphia, 15*th December,* 1792.

Mr. Clingman informs us, that Mr. Reynolds returned to town, on Thursday night, and told him, he had written him a letter which he then had; not having had an opportunity to send it to him, and which he then tore; part of which was thrown into the fire. Other parts he presented to us, and which we now have.

That Reynolds, at the same time, told him, he had been received by Mr. Hamilton, the morning of that day, when they parted, about sunrise. That he was extremely agitated, *walking backward and forward the room, and striking, alternately, his forehead and his thigh; observing to him, that he had enemies at work, but was willing to meet them, on fair ground, and requested him not to stay long, lest it might be noticed.*

Mr. Clingman also informs us, that he received a note from Mr. Wolcot, to meet him, on Friday morning, at half past nine (which note we have). That he attended, and had an interview with him, in presence of Mr. Hamilton; when he was strictly examined by both, respecting the persons, who were enquiring into the matter, and their object; that he told Mr. Hamilton, he had been possessed of his notes to Reynolds, and had given them up to thefe gentlemen: and to which, he replied, he had done very wrong. That he alfo told Mr. Hamilton of the letter he had received from Reynolds, fince his enlargement, mentioning that he (Mr. Hamilton) would make Francis fwear back what he had faid; and to which Mr. Hamilton replied, he would make him unfay any falfity he had declared.

Mr. Hamilton faid, Reynolds was a villain, a rafcal, and he fuppofed, would fwear to any thing.

Mr. Wolcot faid, that unlefs Clingman ufed the fame candour to him, that he had done to Clingman, he fhould not confider himfelf bound.

Mr. Hamilton wanted to know, what members of Congrefs were concerned in the enquiry, and defired him to go into the gallery, where he would fee them, and enquire their names of the byftanders.

Mr. Hamilton obferved, he had had fome transaction with Reynolds, which he had before mentioned, as well as Clingman remembers, to Mr. Wolcot, and need not go into detail.

Clingman alfo informs us, that Reynolds told him, fince his enlargement, that when he was about to fet out to Virginia, on his laft trip to buy up cafh-claims of the Virginia line, he told Mr. Hamilton, that Hopkins would not pay upon thofe powers of attorney; and to which he, (Mr. Hamilton) replied, he would write to Hopkins, on the fubject.

16*th.* Laft night we waited on colonel Hamilton, when he informed us of *a particular connection with Mrs. Reynolds:* the period of its commencement, and circumftances attending it; his vifiting her at Infkeep's; the frequent fupplies of money to her and her hufband, on that account; his durefs by them from the fear of a difclofure, and *his anxiety to be relieved from it and them.* To fupport this, he fhewed a great number of letters from Reynolds and herfelf, commencing early in 1791. He acknowledged *all the letters in a difguifed hand, in our poffeffion, to be his.* We left him under an impreffion, our fufpicions were removed. He acknowledged our conduct toward him had been fair and liberal: he could not complain of it. We brought back all the papers, even his own notes, nor did he afk their deftruction.

He faid, the difmiffion of the profecution againft the parties, Reynolds and Clingman, had been in confideration of a furrender of a lift of pay improperly obtained from his office, and by means of a perfon, who had it not in his power now to injure the department, intimating he meant Duer: that he obtained this information from Reynolds; owned that he had received a note from Reynolds in the night, at the time ſtated in Mr. Clingman's paper, and that he had likewiſe ſeen him in the morning following: ſaid, he never had ſeen Reynolds before he came to this place; and that the ſtatement in Mr. Clingman's paper, in that reſpect, was correct.

  (Signed,)   JAMES MONROE.
          ABRAHAM VENABLE.
          F. A. MUHLENBERG.

January 2d, 1793. Mr. Clingman called on me, this evening, and mentioned, that he had been appriſed of Mr. Hamilton's vindication, by Mr. Wolcott, a day or two after our interview with him. He farther obſerved to me, that he communicated the ſame to Mrs. Reynolds, who *appeared much ſhocked at it*, and *wept immoderately.* That ſhe denied the imputation, and declared, that it had been a fabrication of colonel Hamilton, and that her huſband had joined in it, *who had told her ſo*, and that he had given him receipts for money and written letters, ſo *as to give countenance to the pretence.* That he was with colonel Hamilton, the day after he left the jail, when we ſuppoſed he was in Jerſey. He was of opinion ſhe was innocent, and that the defence was an impoſition.

  (Signed,)   JAMES MONROE.

(No. VI.)

LETTERS FROM COLONEL HAMILTON TO JAMES REYNOLDS, REFERRED TO IN No. III.

Endorſement on the parcel, in the hand-writing of Reynolds. " From *Secortary* Hamilton, eſq.*"

To-morrow what is requeſted will be done. T'will hardly be poſſible to day.

[This card has neither date nor addreſs. It is in a kind of character, half print, half manuſcript. It was admitted as *his own* by the ſecretary.]

* The looſe paper on which theſe words are written, is itſelf part of *ſome deſtroyed letter* from Mr. Hamilton, for it has on the op-

It is utterly out of my power I assure you, PON *my honour, to comply with your request.* Your note *is returned.*

[This is the card referred to in No. IV. being the answer to a request from Reynolds, of money to subscribe for the Lancaster turnpike. It has neither date nor address; but must have been written about the month of June, 1792. On what ground could Reynolds pretend to make such applications to a person so far above his rank? The gentle tone of the refusal, also, deserves notice. It expressly implies a high degree of previous intimacy. The simple assurance of inability was not enough. Mr. Hamilton declares PON HIS HONOUR, that it is not merely *out of his power*, but UTTERLY, &c. How generous! How magnanimous this language of the ex-secretary! especially when he wrote to a being who was in the habit of threatening to bring him to disgrace. If the statement of Mr. Hamilton, as to Mrs. Reynolds, had been true, she must have cost him, in whole, a smart sum. In No. IV. she says, that her husband had, sometime before, " received " upwards of eleven hundred dollars of colonel " Hamilton." A share in the Lancaster turnpike cost three hundred dollars; and though, in this request, Reynolds did not succeed, yet so extensive a scale of application shews, that he had been in the habit of receiving, or at least of expecting, to a considerable amount. In the same number it appears, that Clingman was almost an eye witness to the receipt, by Reynolds, of a large sum from Mr. Hamilton. No. IV. also, shews, that Mrs. Reynolds, during the confinement of her husband, received money from our secretary; and in No. III. when Mr.

posite side, in his *undisguised* hand-writing, this address, as the back of a letter: " Mr. James Reynolds."

Hamilton wanted to get rid of these people, he offered, if they would *leave these parts, not to be seen here again, to give* SOMETHING CLEVER. By the way, this was not the language of a lover. If the colonel was tired he might have quitted the lady with less ceremony. We proceed to the third card.]

Inclosed are FIFTY DOLLARS. *They could not be sent sooner.*

Addressed on the back, *Mr. James Reynolds.*

[This letter has neither date, nor subscription; and is in the feigned hand of the two former. The address is in a counterfeit hand, of a different kind; but resembling that of *the secretary.*]

My Dear Sir,
I expected to have heared the day after I had the pleasure of seeing you.

[This is in Mr. Hamilton's common hand. It has no date or signature. The address, if it had any, has been torn away.]

The person Mr. Reynolds enquired for on Friday, WAITED FOR HIM ALL THE EVENING, *at his house, from a little after seven—Mr. R. may see him at any time to-day, or to-morrow, between the hours of two and three.*

Mr. Reynolds.   Monday.

[The above, and its address, are in the feigned hand. So much correspondence could not refer exclusively to wenching. No man of common sense will believe that it did. Hence it must have implicated some connection still more dishonourable, in Mr. Hamilton's eyes, than that of incontinency. Reynolds and his wife affirm that it respected certificate speculations. The solicitude of Mr. Hamilton to get these people out of the way, is quite contradictory to an amorous attachment for Mrs. Reynolds, and bespeaks her innocence in the clearest stile. The following is the torn letter referred to, in the beginning of No. V. It is in the same hand writing with the indorsement above quoted on the parcel of letters, and merits particular attention.]

Thursday, one o'clock, 13th December, 1792*.
My dear M. Clingman,

I hope I have not forfeited your friendship, the last night's conversation, dont think any thing of it, for I was not myself. I know I have treated ******** friend ill, and too well I am convinsed [Here about three lines are torn out.] to have satisfaction from HIM at all events, and you onely I trust too. I will SEE YOU THIS EVENING. HE HAS OFFERED TO FURNISH ME AND MRS. REYNOLDS WITH MONEY TO CARRY US OFF. If I will go, he will see that Mrs. Reynolds has money to follow me, and as for Mr. Francis, he sas he will make him swear back what he has said, and will turn him out of office†. This is all I can say till I see you.

I am, dear Clingman, believe me, forever your sincere friend,

JAMES REYNOLDS.

Mr. Jacob Clingman.

Here the story comes to a crisis. Reynolds, a man of a bad character, and dependent circumstances, had been cast into jail for an offence of a very deep dye, and which, as it appears, could have been fixed upon him. Instead of comporting himself with

---

* Reynolds got out of prison, on Wednesday evening, the 12th of December. See No. iv.

† The Secretary kept his word. The person here meant was discharged from the treasury office.

that humility suitable to a situation apparently so desperate, he speaks of nothing else but ruining and hanging Mr. Hamilton, who, the President excepted, was the most powerful and dangerous enemy that he could have met with on the whole continent. This was not, certainly, an obvious way to get out of prison. He had been prosecuted by the Comptroller, Mr. Wolcot, with whom he found no blame; but he affirmed, that it was a scheme of the secretary to keep him *low*, and *drive him away*. Even admitting that his wife was the favourite of Mr. Hamilton, for which there appears no evidence but the word of the secretary, this conduct would have been eminently foolish. Mr. Hamilton had only to say, that he was sick of his amour, and the influence and hopes of Reynolds at once vanished. Our secretary was far above the reach of his revenge. The accusation of an illicit amour, though founded in notes louder than the last trumpet, could not have defamed the conjugal fidelity of Mr. Hamilton. It would only have been holding *a farthing candle to the sun*. On that point, the world had previously fixed its opinion. In the secretary's bucket of chastity, a drop more or less was not to be perceived. If Reynolds had no claim to regard but in one of the capacities of Mercury, his accusations and his threats were more than folly. They were synonimous to lunacy.

Grounding merely on the procuring system, the forbearance of Mr. Hamilton is equally inexplicable. The natural temper of our secretary, where he ventures to exert it, is vindictive and furious[*], combining " that unusual mixture of quick ferocity and unrelenting vengeance," which Mr. Hume has marked out as a peculiarity in the character of

---

[*] See Findley and Brackenridge, *passim*.

Charles the ninth*. That such a man, or indeed that any man should tamely endure this treatment is in itself highly incredible. No transient attachment, such as that which the secretary alledged that he had, could have been put in the balance against his official character; and from the time that Mr. Monroe and the other gentlemen saw Reynolds, his reputation was evidently at stake.

In No. V. Clingman says, that he received a note from Mr. Wolcot to call on him. It is in these words.

Mr. Wolcott will be glad to see Mr. Clingman tomorrow, at half after nine o'clock.
Thursday.

At this meeting, Clingman says that he was strictly examined by Messrs. Wolcot and Hamilton, respecting the persons who were enquiring into the matter, and their object. If every thing was found at bottom Mr. Hamilton, might have held such persons

---

* The feelings of Mr. Hamilton may be estimated by the tone of the hireling writers of his party; and shew how little quarter he or they are entitled to. William Cobbett, in his Censor for March 1797, describes Mr. Monroe as " a traitor, who has bartered the ho-" nour and interest of his country, to a perfidious and savage enemy." Messrs. Muhlenberg, Jefferson, Swanwick, Giles, Madison, Gallatin, Mr. Tench Coxe, and others, are all spoken of in the same scurrilous way, without the least regard to truth or decency. What could ail this writer at Dr. Rush? That gentleman has long since quitted politics, and his philosophical works are better known and more highly respected in Europe, than those of any writer whom the new world has produced, Franklin or Jefferson's notes excepted.

This man does not write at random. His enemies laughed at him for boasting of intimacy with some of the first characters in this country. He spoke only truth. Not long since, Mr. Liston, the British ambassador, came down North Second-street, past by the door of his store, looked carefully around him, as if to see whether he was observed, then turned back and went in. Two days after he was in the same store: and, no doubt his excellency derives much improvement from this elegant and dignified connection.

and such enquiries in defiance. The following letter, the last in the order of these pieces, is from Mr. Hamilton himself.

Philadelphia, December, 1792.

Gentlemen,

ON reflection, I deem it adviseable for me to have copies of the several papers which you communicated to me in our interview on Saturday evening, including the notes, and the fragment of Mr. Reynold's letter to Mr. Clingman. I therefore request that you will either cause copies of these papers to be furnished to me, taken by the person in whose hand writing the declarations which you shewed to me were, or will let me have the papers themselves to be copied. It is also my wish, that all such papers as are original, may be detained from the parties of whom they were had, to put it out of their power to repeat the abuse of them in situations which may deprive me of the advantage of explanation. Considering of how abominable an attempt they have been the instruments, I trust you will feel no scruples about this detention.

With consideration,
I have the honour to be, gentlemen,
Your obedient servant,
ALEXANDER HAMILTON.

F. Augustus Mughlenbergh,
James Monroe, and } Esquires,
Abraham Venable,

Addressed on the back thus. " *Frederick A. Mughlenbergh, esquire.*"

The above letter, closes the collection of papers regarding this affair of Reynolds. It only remains to make some observations; and these demand a retrospect.

If we consider the magnitude of the object before them, it was highly commendable in the gentlemen concerned in these enquiries to trace the matter as closely as they did. The funding of certificates to the extent of perhaps thirty, or thirty-five millions of dollars, at eight times the price which the holders had actually paid for them, presents; in itself, one of the most egregious, the most impudent, the most oppressive, and the most provoking bubbles that ever burlesqued the legislative proceedings of any nation. The debt that could have been discharged for ten or fifteen millions of dollars, was funded at forty millions.

But as the universal suspicion and hatred which the formation of this mass had excited, might, at some future period, endanger its existence; the assumption act, was brought forward. This law incorporated into the former stock those debts contracted by individual states during the war. Hence each of them became, for its own sake, interested in the support of public credit which implicated a riddance of the debt especially due by itself. Thus the certificate funds were inseparably embodied with a powerful and popular ally, under the shelter of whose reputation they might hope for some degree of longevity. This artful measure was pushed through Congress by the same party, who funded the half-crown certificates at twenty shillings. But, even in this project, it is entertaining to notice the blindness and precipitation of conscious guilt. The paper-jobbing junto were in such a hurry to shelter their speculations under the wings of the above assumption law, that they acted the measure in the most profligate or bungling manner which can be imagined. Take notice! They pledged the public faith for *twenty-two* millions of dollars, instead of *eleven* millions*; for, the latter sum

" * The accounts of the union with the individual states might
" have been placed in the same relative situation in which they now
" stand, by assuming eleven millions, instead of twenty-two. The
" *additional* and *unnecessary* debt, created by that fatal measure,
" amounts, therefore, to *ten millions eight hundred and eighty-three*
" *thousand, six hundred and twenty-eight dollars, and fifty-eight cents.*"
Gallatin, p. 107.

would have settled the claims, if a reasonable degree of time, of judgment, or of method had been employed upon it. This work was the very pinnacle of stupidity, or knavery, or probably of both. Suppose that you see a man go into a store, and buy ten shillings worth of linen. He receives the cloth, flings down a guinea, and runs away without waiting for his change. You will infer that he is either circulcating false money, or has deserted from bedlam. Yet such is precisely the *profile* view of this assumption act. It is natural that Dr. Smith should be fond of calling Americans the most intelligent of mankind, when his party have made them such egregious dupes. Thus, the founder of some new sect in religion, while cramming the ears of his disciples with visions and miracles, assures them that they are the chosen people. In both instances the encomiast holds in his eye the very same object. As for the state of public information, it is likely that not more than one-tenth part of our citizens recollect or have heard any thing of the assumption act. Not one out of five thousand people is acquainted with this blasting blunder, about the eleven millions being funded at twenty-two.

This is a profile view of the assumption act. But when we look straight into its face, fraud, anarchy, and rebellion, are seen indelibly engraved on its forehead. Witness the debates of last winter in Congress, about the balance due from New-York to the union! A spark a thousand times smaller, has, before now, involved half the world in conflagration. This act is like an ulcer in the midriff of American tranquillity. To paint its possible effects would require the eloquence of Milton describing the *congress* of *Death* and *Sin*.

The bank of the United States was another buttress raised to prop the rampart of corruption.

UNITED STATES. 227

on, and the irresistible influence which
it, afford a striking evidence of the da-
ound genius of its author. By what
constitution Congress thought them-
ised to turn bankers, they have not
l the public. From any thing which
the face of that instrument, they
warrant for erecting banks than
pyramids. Their plea, that the
is to be of national benefit, does not
r apology. It would have been bet-
real motive, which was, that the lea-
ority in Congress expected the scheme
ional advantage to themselves. The
Hamilton to Congress, on this bank,
ghty matters which have never come
the grand point, the bracing of the
n, has been completely secured. The
ington shall be just mentioned, as a
e honest credulity of the President.
been worse than idly sunk upon that
if government removes to it, may be
ed as the tomb of the federal consti-

of all these measures hath been a pub-
ghty millions; instead of thirty; a re-
rnment harnassed in a monarchical fac-
nent overwhelmed with paper money,
I bankruptcies, of a nature and species
most unknown in Europe*; the price
ery article of living; a commerce in-

ple, the polite correspondence between Mr. James
r. John Nicholson, that hath so long blockaded
Sometime ago, bills of a merchant in this city
or sale, by auction, to the amount of about four
dollars. These things make a person from the old
t Americans, perhaps, know better.

sulted and within sight of ruin; a public treasury without money, and without credit; and last and worst, a squadron of legislative conspirators, in the fifth Congress, who, by every insidious artifice, and every unblushing effort, pant and toil to bury their country in a British alliance and a French war.

CHAPTER VII.

Farther observations on the correspondence between Messrs. Hamilton and Reynolds.—Singular mode of secrecy in framing the federal constitution, and of discussing Jay's treaty.—Defence of General Mason.—Report to President Adams, by Mr. Pickering, on French captures.—Singular style of that paper.—Defamatory charge by Judge Iredell to a grand jury in Virginia.—Their pitiful presentment.—Defence of Mr. Cabell.—Curious letter to Mr. John Beckley.—Observations on the PURITY *of the federal government.—Specimens of the mode of travelling in America.—A trip to New-York.*

IN his letter last copied, Mr. Hamilton speaks of an *explanation*. He gave nothing meriting that name. The short way to exculpate himself was, by confronting Reynolds and his wife, who accused him of fraud, with the gentlemen who undertook the enquiry. Instead of that, he sent Reynolds and his wife out of the way, to prevent any such personal exculpation. That *he* packed them off, there can be little doubt, since the suddeness of the disappearance of Reynolds can be accounted for upon no other ground. The letter from Reynolds to Clingman mentions a promise of that kind, and Mrs. Reynolds had previously declared, that this was a scheme in contemplation. Reynolds could not fly from fear. The prosecution against him was closed, and his chief resource for subsistence had been by applying to Mr. Hamilton. That he was removed, to keep him from a meeting with Mr. Monroe and his friends, bears the strongest marks of probability. It may be said, that the infamous character of Reynolds made him unworthy of credit. Taken by itself, his testimony was, indeed, worth little; but, when supported by various circumstances, it might merit more attention. The profligate manners of the accuser afforded an additional reason why Mr. Hamilton, if innocent, should have brought him forward, since it would have been proportionably a more easy task to convince Mr. Monroe of his falsehood. But the secretary sealed the importance of the accuser's testimony, by forbearing to produce him to the gentlemen enquiring after him. When persons of so much weight and respectability had entered upon this business, every principle of common sense called for the clearest explanation. In place of that the chief evidence was concealed, and sent off, while the mass of his correspondence with Mr. Hamilton was, by desire of the latter, abruptly committed to the flames. You will determine whether these fugitive measures look most like innocence, or like something else.

Mr. Hamilton, referring to Reynolds and his wife, calls this an *abominable* attempt. Granted. But, since the measures of himself and his party, on the affair of certificates, had excited a very general and violent suspicion, and since he well knew that the gentlemen who came forward, were supposed to be in the number of those who entertained it, every motive of self-love, and of zeal for the honour of his partizans, should have prompted Mr. Hamilton to tear up the laſt twig of jealouſy. In place of, ſmothering teſtimony, he ſhould have courted it. In place of burning letters, he ſhould have *printed* them. Publicity was the only baſis by which he could maintain the ground that he was in danger of loſing. Yet this was the very mode of defence which he choſe to avoid. When Randolph was arraigned of miſconduct not more culpable than that imputed by Reynolds to Hamilton, he purſued the accuſer to Rhode-Iſland, and obtained a certificate of his innocence, couched in the ſtrongeſt terms. Yet the federal party, with their uſual fortitude of aſſertion, and infelicity of demonſtration, have loaded him with reproaches, and the bare ſuppoſition of the poſſibility of his innocence, has been ſcouted as the height of effrontery. Put the caſe that Fauchet, when his apocrypha was intercepted, had been in jail, that Randolph, inſtead of bringing him forward had paid his debts, burnt all his remaining papers, and hurried him out of the country. Every friend to *order*, would have been convinced that Randolph was guilty, and had removed Fauchet, that " the pool of corruption might " putrify in peace*." The force of moral or preſumptive teſtimony does not augment or diminiſh, becauſe the party accuſed happens to be for or againſt the American funding ſyſtem.

Some years ago, the late Preſident was attacked in the newſpapers for conſtantly uplifting his ſalary, before it became due. Mr. Hamilton immediately printed a reply that filled nine columns of the Philadelphia Gazette. Even the very worſt which could be alledged of Mr. Waſhington amounted only to this practice being irregular, improper, and ſuper-eminently ridiculous from a man who pretended to do the buſineſs of his country for his mere houſhold

---

* Robert Hall, on the liberty of the preſs.

expences. The charge of Reynolds wears a more serious aspect. If he was *one* agent for the purchase of certificates, it may well be conceived, though it cannot *yet* be proved, that our secretary had twenty others. Physician! heal thyself. Before Mr. Hamilton prints any farther defences of other people, before he again arraigns one-half of his fellow citizens as cut-throats*, let him tell us what has become of Reynolds. Let him observe that this narrative is explicit; and that, under all the circumstances of the affair, silence will be more fatal to his character, than the most feeble vindication.

It is easy to see why Mr. Hamilton, and his party, have been permitted to reduce America to its present disagreeable condition. When a merchant refuses not only to balance his books, but vilifies those who advise him to do so, it requires no ghost from the dead, to foretell for what port he is bound. In private life, it is hardly possible to find such a fool; but nations are sometimes actuated by a degree of madness to which, in their individual concerns, it would be impracticable to drive them. Of this remark, America, during the short period of her political career, has afforded various examples. The people of other countries are ignorant against their will. The citizens of the United States appear often averse, and even hostile to information. Thus, the federal constition, highly respectable and valuable as truth must acknowledge it to be, was yet an instrument *framed in darkness*. When the convention who made it met at Philadelphia, they began by shutting their doors. This clandestine appearance exhibited the worst auguries imaginable of what they were going to do. Though they had to frame a constitution, yet, before it could take effect,

---

* See American Annual Register, chap. x.

it was to be submitted, seperately, to each of the thirteen states. To assist the citizens at large in forming their opinions, the safest and fairest method was to have debated with open galleries. If the arguments that swayed the decision of the delegates were well-founded, they might have had the same effect on their constituents*. But, to immure themselves in the way in which they did, looked more like a Venetian senate, a gang of smugglers or coiners, than the Representatives of a free people. The long parliament of England would never have obtained the confidence of their party, they could never have overturned royal despotism, if they had kept their proceedings and debates a secret from the world. In England, a state-trial must be carried on in public. The spirit of the country would not endure the concealment of such a transaction. In the course of ordinary affairs, the present House of Commons do not shut their doors above once in several years. But the framing of a constitution is of infinitely more importance than the usual routine of business; the English people would not, on such an emergency, submit to exclusion. The Scots union was previously known to be detested by all ranks of people; and brought the country to the brink of a revolution. Yet the Scots parliament debated

---

* We have not entirely forgot the mode in which the federal constitution was crammed down the gullet of Pennsylvania. When it first appeared, the assembly were in session. A minority declined acceptance, because they had no special powers to that purpose from their electors; and, to prevent its passing, they seceded from the house. The remaining members did not form a quorum. Here they would have stuck, but the friends of *order*, alias, a troop of ruffians, with the captain of a very modern frigate at their head, broke into the lodgings of some seceding members, seized them, dragged them through the streets, with one-half of Philadelphia at their heels, and, by main force, projected them into the assembly. Thus a quorum was formed, and the constitution accepted, in a way which would have disgraced a gang of gipsies.

with open doors. The acquiefcence of our citizens in the Tiberian privacy of their delegates, has marked a peculiarity in the American character.

The arrival of Jay's treaty afforded another inftance of the fame kind. In London, public impatience would, by fuch a circumftance, have been wounded up to the higheft degree; and the proudeft minifter muft have found his popularity interefted in an early communication. But at Philadelphia, there was even a parade of fecrecy. The treaty reached the Prefident on the 7th of March, 1795. Inftead of laying it before the public, who were ultimately to bear its confequences, and who could have made light break in upon every quarter, he fuppreffed its contents from mankind, till the meeting of the Senate. Thirty gentlemen then fhut themfelves up, like the tranflators of the Septuagint, as if they had been to act by infpiration. Without rafhnefs it may be faid, that this *fuperior* branch of government, as Mr. Fenno calls it, did not collectively know as much about commerce, and its foreign relations, as general Smith and John Swanwick. The refolution of the Senate to ratify, tranfpired on the 24th of June 1795, three months and an half after the Prefident had got the treaty. This long fuppreffion did not excite an audible murmur. Nay, after the ratification, the federal party difplayed ftill more ftrongly their manly notions of government. The Senate had juft one member, general Mafon, of fufficient civility towards the public, to fend a copy of the treaty to the newfpapers. This violated an injunction of fecrefy paft by the Senate. The federal catcalls began inftantly to fqueak; and, if the general had been forging bank notes, they could hardly have made much more noife. Thus the Plymouth refolutions of the 30th of October, 1795, charged him with "a notorious breach of official confidence*." Instead of this language, they should have thanked him for his intelligence. If it had been communicated three months more early, much of the subsequent bad consequences might have been prevented. He should, also, have printed Jay's instructions, with minutes of the notable harangues about the *partition* of the United States†. With open doors, no senator durst have broached a doctrine of such enormous attrocity. *The master's eye makes a fat horse*, says the proverb. In public affairs, the same case holds good. The more that a nation knows about the mode of conducting its business, the better chance has that business of being properly conducted. This maxim appears very plain; and, in his domestic concerns, every man approves of it. On a great national scale, we are the first free people who have rejected it, and that is one of the principal reasons why some parts of our federal administration have succeeded so very ill. Secrecy is a favourite doctrine with our financial Mahomet; and its triumph hath ensured his own.

In the close of the last chapter, the word *conspirator* has been employed. It sounds harshly, but it has been inserted on the clearest evidence, and after the strictest consideration. To be convinced of an executive plot, for involving America in a French war, we have only to look at a report from secretary Pickering to President Adams, and which, on the 22d of June, 1797, was sent by the latter to Congress. The title page professes to state "*the* " depredations committed on the commerce of the " United States since the 1st of October, 1796." Consistency with this profession required, that, as

---

* Carey's Remembrancer, vol. iii. p. 311.
† American Annual Register, chap. v.

much time should have been bestowed on the recital of British captures, as on that of French ones. Apparently grounding on this idea, Mr. Adams, in his message accompanying the papers, hath these words: "I directed a collection to be made of ALL "such information as should be found in the pos- "session of the government."

The report and documents fill about an hundred and sixty pages. The list of French captures is taken from the Philadelphia and United States gazettes. Of the British, Mr. Pickering writes thus:

"Captures and losses by *British* cruisers, the se- "cretary presumes, have not been *numerous*; for, "citizens of the United States having, these three "years past, been accustomed to look up to the go- "vernment for aid in prosecuting their claims, it "is not to be doubted, that generally these cases "have been reported to the department of state. "An abstract of such as have been communicated, "is annexed." Report, p. 5. This list amounts only to *ten* vessels. They are dispatched in *two* pages. That of captures by the republic occupies about *an hundred and forty*. As an apology for this disproportion of bulk, Mr. Pickering, on p. 9, gives a most curious reason. "This examination "was chiefly made *prior* to the call of the house of "Representatives for a report on this subject, with "a view to ascertain the number of French cap- "tures, and the circumstances attending them; and "the result of the whole is annexed. It is regretted, "that the time did not permit a re-examination of "those papers to ascertain likewise the captures "made by the British cruisers." The call of the house was dated the 10th of June. The papers were laid before the house on the 22d, being at an interval of *twelve* days. As the French list had been made out beforehand, the secretary had the more time to compile the British list. Six active clerks, like those in his own office, could, with great ease, have completed the business in forty-eight hours at farthest. Where was the mighty affair of turning over two files of newspapers for the last eight months? With some diligence, the whole might have been finished in a single afternoon. In a city like Philadelphia, full of public offices, and able transcribers, the secretary, if he had been in earnest, could have collected forty proper assistants, on an hour's warning; and even admitting the British list to be as bulky as the French one, each of these auxiliaries would hardly have found an hour's employment. But the secretary himself says, that British captures were not *numerous*. Be it so. Then it would have taken the less time to make them out. Yet it seems that, with a space of ten or twelve days before him, the secretary could not accomplish this Lilliputian task.

Thus does our secretary trifle with the orders of the legislature; and Mr. Adams, by the acceptance of so absurd an excuse, exemplifies the proverb, *like master, like man*. But, to be plain with Mr. Pickering, such palpable sophistication will not go down. All people know very well why the British list of captures was not made out. It would have counteracted his plan of inflaming us against the republic. He proceeds thus.

" The editors of those two gazettes agree in
" saying, that no great attention was paid to the
" subject, for the purpose of inserting accounts of
" all the captures which were published in the va-
" rious other newspapers; yet the number collec-
" ted exceeds three hundred, of which but few es-
" cape condemnation." The Gazette of the United States is, and long has been, as much an engine of the American executive, as that of London is to

an English premier*. Mr. Fenno, beyond all question, inserted every French capture that he could find. As to the Philadelphia Gazette, the present editor has only held it since last February; and, previous to that time, he knows not how it was conducted. When Congress wanted information, it was the duty of Mr. Pickering to have looked at a wide variety of newspapers. But he was well aware, that Mr. Fenno had collected about every thing of the kind. The object of Mr. Pickering is, to insinuate that many French captures have escaped notice. *Yet the number collected exceeds* THREE HUNDRED. So long ago as September, 1794, a list was published, *by authority*, of *British* captures. They were about three hundred and sixty.

" The conduct of the public agents," says Mr. Pickering, " and of the commissioned cruisers there, " has surpassed *all former examples*†." They cannot be worse than the confiscation of the Two Friends, and the murder of captain Bosson. We might add an hundred British piracies recited in this volume, all as atrocious as any possible case of French piracy.

" The persons also of our citizens have been. " beaten, insulted, and cruelly imprisoned; and, in " the forms used towards prisoners of war, they " have been exchanged with the British for French- " men." This is very bad, but the French are only following the example that England, for above two years, had set before them, and at this moment continues to give them. When complaints of im-

---

* * Instead of trying to turn the speech of Barras into an instrument for a French war, Mr. Adams might have bought a set of this *executive newspaper*, and sent it over as a present to the Directory at Paris. For every syllable in the whole speech of Barras, they would have found themselves paid beforehand with a column of invective.

† Pickering's report, p. 8.

preffment were made againſt England, the federal party did their utmoſt to quell the ſtory. In Congreſs, Mr. Tracy, and others, would gladly have denied that Britiſh impreſſments had taken place, and Webſter wondered why American printers ſhould trouble themſelves about the matter*. This was the uniform language of the whole party.

"There have been frequent accounts of attempts to effect condemnations by bribing the officers and ſeamen of our veſſels to ſwear falſely; but it was reſerved to theſe times, when offered bribes were refuſed, and threats deſpiſed, to endeavour to accompliſh the object by *torture*." Report p. 10. American ſeamen have been flogged by dozens at a Britiſh gangway. This alſo was torture. Captain Reynolds, under the very noſe of admiral Murray, attacked American veſſels. Several men were killed and wounded. This was torture. There is not the ſmalleſt deſign to extenuate French outrages, but merely to prove the groſs partiality of our executive in ſhewing only the robberies perpetrated upon one ſide.

Paulo majora canamus. If Mr. Pickering has diſplayed groſs partiality, Preſident Adams has not acted, in the ſmalleſt degree, better. On the 23d of June, 1797, general Smith was reciting in Congreſs the ſteps purſued by the friends of order, for bringing about a French war. He ſaid, that the executive had called Congreſs, and had complained of the French; for the ſpeech did not contain a ſingle word of reference to any other nation. He next recommended the fitting out of frigates, with which he propoſed to convoy American commerce. Our merchant ſhips are to be armed, and, on arriving in a French port, the queſtion is put, *againſt whom are*

---

* Supra, chapters v. and vi.

you armed? The French would say, *we have read your President's speech. By these preparations, he can only mean to fight us.* Your envoys, arriving in France at the same time, are sure of being turned back again. General Smith farther observed, that Dr. Smith and Mr. Harper had avowed the design of employing the frigates to force a trade into ports of the West-Indies which the French have justly declared to be in a state of rebellion. Such was port Jeremie. General Smith affirmed, that these measures led directly to war. He believed that gentlemen *wanted to lead us into war*. The member was right; there can be no doubt of it. This astonishing session of Congress hath afforded a whole dictionary of evidence. Sir John Brute says, " every " thing I see, every thing I hear, every thing I feel, " and every thing I taste, methinks, has *wife* in " it." So at present with the federal party, every thing has *war* in it. A combination more culpable, more hateful, hath not occurred since the age of Cataline or Fiesco.

Mr. Pickering complains of the French maltreating American seamen. His party have encouraged the British to impress them. In proof of this, attend to general Smith, who is no violent democrat, for he professed in Congress great concern, when Mr. Hamilton retired from office. On the 27th of May, 1797, this gentleman said, in the house, that members had affected to treat the law for the protection of our seamen with lightness. It conferred the highest honour on Mr. Livingston, who introduced it. It was opposed in both houses by those who are always combating for an increase of power and influence in the executive government. The Senate mutilated that law, so as to deprive it of its most salutary provisions. After all, *the Senate refused their assent to a law for protecting*

American seamen from impressment, and from being whipped on the bare back at the gang-way of a British man of war. They refused to adopt it, until it was so much mutilated, that the executive, to render it in any shape effectual, was obliged to enforce it with a supplementary part. Thus far general Smith.

If this majority in the Senate had been selected from the Divan of Algiers, they could not have more completely disgraced their station. At the same time, Messrs. Tracy and Harper, below stairs, were attempting to deny the reality of British impressments; and Webster and Russel inveighed against every one who mentioned their existence. These things are part of a system for degrading America into a British footstool. *What kind of an* AMERICAN *Senate is that which refuses its consent to a law for the protection of* AMERICAN *seamen?* The very idea looks so monstrous that one is apt to think himself in a dream when he endeavours to revolve it. The circumstances of their refusal to concur in the bill, stand recorded on the journals of both houses. The full detail shall soon be given to the world. The journals of the British house of peers afford no precedent for such horrible depravity. England has hitherto stood upon her own legs. Her representatives and legislators, though often extremely corrupted, have never been suspected of servility to a foreign nation; and, a trivial instance excepted*, they have not put themselves up to auction for foreign gold. Their opponents, at least, have not alledged that they ever did so; and this forms a strong presumption of their innocence.

In the mean time, Harrison Otis cants about French impressments, and Mr. Harper on the cor-

* In the reign of Charles the second. See Sir John Dalrymple's Memoirs, and Hume's History of England, in the latest editions.

ruption of Mr. Monroe, by French gold. For conceit and ignorance, Otis may be looked upon as the lineal fucceffor of Samuel Dexter. As for Harper, he is faid to be in embarraffed circumftances; and, while he prattles about foreign gold, one might afk him, who pays for the printing of his eternal pamphlets*? By land, our intereft has been as grofsly betrayed as by fea. This appears from the difcouragement conftantly given to the defence of the Indian frontier. On that head, the following narrative will repay a perufal.

On the 19th of November, 1794, Prefident Wafhington, in his fpeech to Congrefs, has thefe words. " Towards none of the Indian tribes have " overtures of friendfhip been fpared. The Creeks, " in particular, are *covered from encroachment* by " the interpofition of the general government, and " that of Georgia." It would have been fortunate for the people of Tenneffee, if the general government had covered them from the encroachments of the Creeks. Refpecting the behaviour of the Creeks, previous to the delivery of that fpeech, information for the prefent work has been derived from two fources, the public newfpapers, and a pri-

---

* During the two laft feffions, it is computed that this gentleman coft the country at leaft ten thoufand dollars worth of time, by making fuperfluous motions, for the fake of making ufelefs fpeeches about them. In the feffion of December, 1796, he repeated one fpeech, about augmenting the duties on imports, at four different times, in the courfe of little more than a month.

He has a very pretty delivery, if any obliging friend would fupply him with a fuitable ftock of ideas. If he could be contented with repeating the fame thoughts not oftener than five times in the courfe of fifteen minutes, he would not fo barbaroufly drive the members from their feats, nor run himfelf into fo many fcrapes with the fpeaker, as to wandering from the queftion. In an antediluvian Congrefs, when people lived to the age of a thoufand years, one might have found leifure for hearing him to an end. Our fpan of threefcore and ten is too narrow for the torrent of his eloquence.

vate manuscript communicated by Mr. Andrew Jackson, Representative from the state of Tennessee in the fourth Congress. An examination of these details will assist in ascertaining what sort of friendship the Creeks deserved, and to what side the balance of protection ought to have leaned.

The account given in the newspapers amounts in substance to what follows. Continual skirmishes had been taking place for a long time. In one of these, on the 13th of August, 1794, lieutenant M'Clellan, with thirty-seven men, had been attacked on the Cumberland path, eighteen miles from South-West-Point, by above an hundred Creeks. He had four men killed, and four missing. He likewise lost thirty-one horses, with several other articles. A multitude of murders by the Indians are mentioned. Of these, it would be needless here to attempt a catalogue. A letter from Knoxville, dated 22d of September, 1794, says, that the general assembly of Tennessee had then been in session for several weeks. They had prepared another memorial to Congress with a list of the citizens killed, wounded, or taken prisoners by the Creeks and Cherokees, since the 1st of March last, the date of a former statement to Congress. The number of citizens was an hundred and twenty-seven, besides which the Indians had stolen four hundred and seventy-four horses. These thefts and murders had been chiefly committed while a party of the Lower Cherokees were at Philadelphia, giving the strongest promises of peace, and while major Seagrove, an agent for Indian affairs, was making assurances of the friendship of the Creeks. The letter concludes with an account of some fresh murders which had, at that moment, been received. They were said to have been committed on the 16th of September current. Nickajack and Running Water were two of the most populous of the Lower Cherokee towns. They were situated close on the south bank of the Tennessee, below a place called the Suck. They were principal crossing-places for the Creeks over the Tennessee, when they wanted to make war on Cumberland and Kentucky. They had co-operated with the warriors of Look-out Mountain, and Will's towns for several years past. They boasted of perfect security from their situation. They were surrounded on three sides by mountains, and protected on the north by the south branch of the Tennessee. They were also formidable by their numbers.

On the 7th of September, major Ore marched from Nashville to attack the savages. He had with him five hundred and fifty militia, of whom an hundred and fifty were from Kentucky. They arrived on the bank of the Tennessee, opposite to Nickajack, and undiscovered, in the dusk of the evening. About eleven o'clock at night, a part of them crossed the river on rafts, and surrounded the town, while another party lay in ambush on the opposite side of the river. The attack began about day break. Many of the savages plunged, according to their custom, into the water, and having got almost to the opposite shore, the militia in reserve rose from their covert, and discharged a volley at the fugitives in the river. The victory was compleat. Nine squaws and children were taken. About forty or forty-five warriors were killed. Accounts differ about their exact numbers. As no particular detail is offered about Running Water, but barely that it was destroyed at the same time with Nickajack, it seems probable that they stood very near to each other. In these towns two fresh scalps were found; and several others dry, that had been hung up as trophies. Many articles of property were recovered which the militia knew to have been taken from their owners.

when killed by the Indians, in the courſe of the preceding twelve months. Among theſe were found a number of letters. They had been carried off when the Kentucky mail was robbed and the poſt murdered. In Nickajack was found a quantity of powder and lead, that had juſt been received from the Spaniſh government, as alſo a commiſſion to Braeth, chief of the town, who was among the ſlain.

The priſoners confeſſed that ſixty Creek and Cherokee warriors had paſſed through Nickajack, only nine days before, on their way to make war againſt the United States. Two nights previous to the deſtruction of Running Water, a ſcalp dance was held in it. Among others, John Watts was preſent; and it was there reſolved to carry on the war with additional vigour. This the white people learned from the priſoners. The towns were burnt, and every thing deſtroyed. Such is the ſubſtance of the newſpaper account. That received from Mr. Jackſon is to the following effect.

Major James Ore was, in the cloſe of Auguſt, 1794, ordered by governor Blount to march to the diſtrict of Mero, to defend its frontier; and, on the 6th of September, was ordered, by general Robertſon to march to the Lower Cherokee towns, and deſtroy them.

" It is proper for me here to obſerve," ſays Mr. Jackſon, " that the Indians inhabiting thoſe towns
" were daily killing our citizens, and our officers,
" tranſmitting a *Roſtrum* of the captured, killed,
" and wounded to the ſecretary at war*; and the
" anſwers returned were, *not to purſue on any ac-*
" *count acroſs the Indian boundary,* or carry on any
" offenſive meaſures againſt the Indians; *conſtruing*
" the word offenſive to be an act of croſſing the

---

* Mr. Henry Knox.

"Indian boundary in the purfuit of depredating
"parties."

Major Ore obeyed the orders of general Robertfon. He marched to Nickajack and Running Water, fwept them with the befom of deftruction, and killed about thirty warriors. It is neceffary here to ftate fome facts. The night before major Ore made the attack on Nickajack, the Indians held the fcalp dance over two frefh fcalps, which they had taken on the frontier. Ore had purfued the track of this party. On the very day that he made the attack twenty-two Indians fell upon the ftation of the widow Hays, killed one man, and wounded three; and the evening before, they had burnt captain John Donelfon's ftation. At the time that general Robertfon iffued the order to Ore, he had information of an intended *general* attack, contemplated on that frontier. This was well fubftantiated, and the expedition of Ore was the only circumftance which prevented it, and eftablifhed peace on the frontier.

The pay of thefe troops hath been fufpended, becaufe they croffed the Indian boundary, although they precifely purfued the orders given by general Robertfon. The mufter and pay roll's were, in the latter end of the year 1794, depofited with colonel David Henly, agent of the war department at Knoxville. Governor Blount, in 1794, tranfmitted to Mr. Knox general Robertfon's order, authorizing and commanding the expedition, and on the 19th of December of that year this communication was laid before Congrefs. Yet though frequent applications have been made at the office of the fecretary at war for payment, they have conftantly been refufed. After a delay of more than two years, Mr. Jackfon, in the laft feffion of the fourth Congrefs, has applied to Mr Pickering to recover the neceſſary papers, that he might lay the ſubject before the Houſe of Repreſentatives. " I " am informed by him," ſays Mr. Jackſon, " that " he knows *nothing of the buſineſs.*" Here the matter ſtood, on the 22d of February, 1797.

Mr. Jackſon further adds that this is not a ſingle inſtance. In 1794, major Thomas Johnſton commanded a party of Tenneſſee militia who were ordered to purſue a gang of Indians. The latter had murdered colonel John Montgomery, and the Titſworth family. In the purſuit, they croſſed into the Kentucky territory. Colonel Henly gave that reaſon for ſuſpending their pay. Theſe were the only two parties of Tenneſſee militia, whoſe arrears have not been paid up, excepting thoſe comprehended in the appropriation act for 1797.

Many parts of the union lie beyond the reach of public information. The country newſpapers are commonly very barren. To remedy this inconvenience, ſome members of Congreſs ſend printed circular letters to their conſtituents on the exiſting condition of the political world. Mr. Samuel J. Cabell, of Virginia, tranſmitted two of ſuch letters. One of them was dated the 11th, and the other the 23d of January, 1797. They contained nothing uncommon. They mentioned the brilliant and irreſiſtible progreſs of the French arms, the unfortunate chagrin which had taken place between France and the United States, and the deplorable conſequences that would enſue to this country from an actual rupture. Mr. Pickering's letter to Pinckney was referred to as more likely to promote than prevent a French quarrel. Mr. Cabell expreſſed his regret at the election of Mr. Adams as Preſident, and added, as a conſolation, that of Mr. Jefferſon.

On the 22d of May, 1797, judge Iredell, of the federal court, delivered a charge at Richmond to the grand jury, for the diſtrict of Virginia. It conveyed encomiums on the government, and a ſtrong recommendation of confidence in it. The jury immediately gave in the following preſentment.

"We, of the grand jury of the United States for the diſtrict of Virginia, preſent, as a real evil, the circular letters of ſeveral members of the late Congreſs, and particularly letters with the ſignature of Samuel J. Cabell, endeavouring, at a time of real public danger, to diſſeminate unfounded calumnies againſt the happy government of the United States, and thereby to ſeparate the people therefrom; and to increaſe or produce a foreign influence, ruinous to the peace, happineſs, and independence of theſe United States."

The jurors themſelves were evidently committing calumny. The phraſe of *ſeveral members* was caſting their ſtink-pot in the dark. As to Mr. Cabell, they ſhould have ſpecified the calumnies. When the grand jury of Chatham county, Georgia, arraigned judge Wilſon as a land-jobber, they condeſcended on matters notoriouſly true*. When a citizen of Maryland cenſures judge Chaſe, he begins with a hiſtory of the bankrupt law. If Mr. Cabell declared his diſſatisfaction at the election of Mr. Adams, one half of the American citizens were doing the ſame. This did not produce the ſmalleſt confuſion or embarraſſment on the ſide of government. It is unfortunate for the union, that Mr. Cabell had ſo much foundation for regret. The outſet of the new Preſident has been marked by an endeavour to hurry his conſtituents into an unneceſſary war, while ſecretary Pickering has been writing, and ſecretary Wolcot has been encouraging

---

* It was upon the queſtionable evidence of this judge, that the preſident declared the four weſtern counties of Pennſylvania to be in a ſtate of inſurrection.

others to write invectives against the French nation*. America needs not to hope for a sincere peace with France, while either Mr. Adams or his present ministers remain in office. She cannot forget nor will she forgive the many volumes of ribbaldry, which, under their countenance, have been printed against her. Besides, upon a British spy, upon an associate with the attorney general of England for the ruin of Thomas Paine†, every honest Frenchman, every true republican, of every country, must look with horror.

> " For never can true reconcilement grow,
> " Where wounds of deadly hate have pierc'd so deep‡."

On the 31st of May, 1797, Mr. Cabell sent a third letter to his constituents. "It has," says he, "been a regular practice of the federal judges, to "make political discourses to the grand jurors.— "They have become a band of political preachers." This is true, and their sermons are often very dull. In Britain, judges have generally been foremost to undermine the liberties of the people, and encourage the encroachments of the crown. There is a country where speculators occupy, in part, the supreme bench of justice. There, the assertion of a public officer, whose want of probity is proverbial, has been taken as complete evidence, that four counties were in a state of rebellion. It would certainly be very wrong in a private citizen to contest the

---

* British Honour and Humanity, p. 55.

† Mr. Adams has acted in both of these HONOURABLE capacities. See American Annual Register, chap. vi.

‡ The following anecdote ought to be known, and it is here given on the best evidence. A few weeks ago, the first person in America gave a dinner to a party of the Senate. They were all from the eastward excepting two southern members. The whole conversation turned on ridiculing *the southern states*.

purity of such legislators. In a subsequent letter of June 5th, Mr. Cabell says, upon an assurance of the fact from general Smith, that the just claims of America, for French depredations, do not exceed a million of dollars, and that the accuracy of his statement is confirmed by the president of the American Insurance Company. In the Congress debates on Jay's treaty, dr. Ames computed British depredations at *five* millions, and the account hath since been augmented.

The federal party naturally wish to drive out of their way every man who dares to think for himself. Thus Monroe was recalled from France because, without orders from Mr. Washington, he had obtained the releasement of Thomas Paine from the Luxembourg; and because he had retained with the directory a degree of that confidence which Mr. Washington had lost. Thus captain Montgomery, of one of the revenue cutters of this port, hath been dismissed from his office because he voted for the Jefferson ticket. Mr. Beckley hath not only been discharged and attacked from the press, but even from the post-office. An elegant and polite letter came to him a few days after his dismission. It is printed here for an odd enough reason. The character is feigned, but still, on a careful comparison, it has a strong likeness to the hand writing of Mr. Oliver Wolcot, as the Saracen's head, in spite of disguise, resembled sir Roger de Coverly*.

Dear Sir

You will now Experance the frut of your fooly in being so great a Demicrate & bitter Enemay to that Goverment whose Bread you have Eaten which has now cast you out of hir service & is certainly nothing less than you could have expede considering your conduct for a number of years past I can feal for your situation as I Understood all your Land speculation

* See the Spectator.

has turned out but little to fuport a family in that Dignefied Way you have keept up However this I hope will turn for your Good to make you Humble & know a little more of the Deficulties attending thofe whofe Cup has not ruin over with that fullnefs & fweet you have long injoyed [plafe turn over] Let me give you an advife as a friend Not to let your former ftation Hinder you from Acepteing of a lefs & not fo hounorable a place as that you have loft to enable you to fuport your family You now ftand Yet a Refpectable Character for if your Pride & Haughtenefs keeps you out of Employ becaufe you are not in fo honourable a ftation as before till your finances get lower & Lower you find that it will be tenfold more dificult then to get into a place then at prefent & Endeavour to lay afide your politicts leave that to thofe whofe Country have called them to the Important afairs of there Country by giveing them all the Aid & not throwing Impedements in there way by fuch a prudent Conduct youll Only deferve Well your Country and in time come forward again and *get a good place* take thefe hints from a friend who Wifhes the Happeinefs your family Belive me to be with much refpect

Your Moft Obt fervant,
JONATHAN WOTHERSPOON.

Nine years ago, the fuppofed writer of this piece was copying in the office of the treafurer of Connecticut, at feventy-five cents per day. The grovelling infolence which marks his elegant epiftle has been too frequent with men unexpectedly raifed from mediocrity to fomething above it. The letter affords a fine fpecimen of the fpirit of the party. *Your fooly in being fo great a demicrate;* that is to fay, in being fo great a friend to the political rights and importance of the people. Frederick of Pruffia once wrote a letter to this effect: " If my fub-" jects of Neufchatel chufe to be eternally dam-" ned, I can fay nothing againft it." In like manner, if the citizens of America chufe to be trode down by an ariftocracy, no third party fhould interfere.

Your conduct for a number of years paft. The official conduct of Mr. Beckley was unexceptionable. Indeed no audible complaint has been made about it. Dr. William Smith, at the head of his regiment of forty, declined argument, and obtained a silent vote. Where any thing can be said, the doctor is not a niggard of accusation. *That government whose bread you have eaten,* which has *now cast you off.* The bread was not eaten for nothing. The salary was moderate, and the duties laborious. As to the *casting off,* it was by the odd vote of Dr. Smith, who is, it seems, *government.* As for *giving them all the aid, and not throwing impediments in their way,* they cannot surely have apprehensions from a discarded clerk, who has to provide for his family by the toilsome profession of the law? If government fear impediments from Mr. Beckley, their situation must be very frail. That something is wrong will appear from what follows.

Alexander Hamilton calls it an *abominable* attempt in Reynolds to charge him with dealing in the purchase of certificates. Thus, by his own admission, the fact, if proved upon him, would be abominable. Colonel Wadsworth spoke of it, as above quoted, exactly in the same way. But if this practice was indefensible in a secretary of the treasury, it was just as criminal in a member of Congress. There is no difference, or, if there be, the case of the member differs for the worse. The secretary could only make a *report* in favour of funding the half-crown certificates at twenty shillings. But the member *voted* for it. The one drew the sword; the other drove it up to the hilt. Hence, by a very short and plain process of reasoning, if one of our legislators was concerned in these speculations, he committed an abominable crime. The heroes of the piece are sensible of this fact. Their concealment of transfers at the treasury, and the bank of the United States of the names and amount of stock holders, proves an irresistible and disgraceful evidence of their internal condemnation. What are you to think of a person who calls himself your creditor, but refuses to tell his name, or the amount of his debt? Such was the plan of the renowned leeches of the Nabob of Arcot. Bonds to an immense sum were constantly produced, yet the catalogues of creditors constantly varied. This rule at the treasury is like the crape over a highwayman's face, or the dark lanthorn of a house-breaker. The public creditors of England wear no such mask. Mr. Rayment printed their names to the number of an hundred and twenty-seven thousand. When Americans begin to think upon this subject, they will refuse to pay one cent more of interest upon the public funds, till they shall have torn asunder the veil that shrouds the system. To the great mass of the present holders the discovery would be indifferent or welcome. It is only the patriarchal, the congressional sharks of stockholding, who can wish for mountains to cover them, the men whose actions Messrs. Wadsworth and Hamilton, have, by the clearest implication, declared to be *abominable*. Mr. Adams, by the way, holds the funding system in abhorrence*, and he will put an end to it, if he can get into his French war. While Americans entrust and admire such leaders, they display a *temporal* likeness to the inhabitants of Neufchatel. These are the paper currency politicians, who rail at jacobin rapacity, and at Jefferson for want of religion†.

* See particulars in the American Annual Register, chap. 6.
† Phocion accuses him, 1. Of trying to *filch a little popularity from a few free negroes.* An important acquisition! The charge is eked through several pages. 2. With impaling butterflies. 3. With disbelieving the story of Noah's flood. 4. With the construction of sideboards and easy chairs. 5. Of resigning his office as governor of Virginia, during a British invasion. Smith himself was in England through the whole war. He chose to let his estate be double taxed rather

In March, 1793, some debate ensued in Congress on the motion of Mr. Giles for examining the conduct of Mr. Hamilton. "The free latitude of dis-
"cussion, practised upon other occasions, was refu-
"sed; the smallest departure was censured; and
"whenever, in particular, an approach was made
"toward the bank, the whole party tumultuously
"crying to order, and *with the directors at their
"head*, rose in arms to defend it. The character
"of the vote itself, which constituted the majority
"is easily given.———Of the thirty-five, twenty-one
"were stockholders, or dealers in the funds, and
"three of these latter bank directors*."

The great cry of the party is about *the sacred nature of public faith*, which they alledge to have consummated by funding the domestic debt. This consisted of arrears of pay due to the army, to contractors for supplies, of loans made to government, and of the remnant of old paper money then in circulation. Now, we must recollect, that, during the revolution, this country had been covered with emissions of paper. When the old Congress borrowed money, they took part of this paper back *in loan*, but not at the value for which they themselves had issued it out. They allowed credit only for what was its current price in the market. The difference was frequently as forty to one. Thus a farmer got four

---

than return to defend his country 6. "Whoever saw him (Jefferson)
"in a *place of worship*?" The doctor has been fully described in a line of Plautus: *Impurus, impudens, inverecundissimus*.

* *An Examination of the late Proceedings in Congress, &c.* p. 25. It was in this struggle that dr. Smith pledged himself for the *angelic* purity of Mr. Hamilton. Supra, chap. 6. Though the number of stockholding members is specified in the text, it appears, afterwards, to have been but a conjecture. The writer gives a list of thirty-four members of the two houses, who were *believed* to be stockholders; but their names are carefully blanked, as if he had thought himself liable to prosecution. With such unexampled ostentation of secrecy, there must be some dirty system that needs concealment.

thousand dollars worth of government paper for his wheat. After the value of paper fell, he came to lend it to them, and they would only give him credit for the fortieth part of its nominal value, being one hundred dollars. This shocking fraud could be excused only by the omnipotence of necessity. But farther, " a part of the paper remained unre-
" deemed at the close of the war, and has been fun-
" ded at the rate of *one hundred* for *one* under the
" present government*."

Thus taking America for a merchant who has three creditors, one of them is paid with a fortieth, and a second with a hundredth part of the sum that he lent. A third receives full payment. But a debt contracted ten years ago, and still unpaid, is as fairly due as if it had been incurred but yesterday. The creditor of 1776, who was paid with one-tenth, twentieth, fortieth, or hundredth part of his just claim, was quite as meritorious as the other of 1781, whose debt has been bought up and funded, in the name of Theodore Sedgwick, at twenty shillings in the pound. A brief consideration will convince you, that this position agrees with the essence of justice.

If the continent had been sold by an hour glass, its utmost value would perhaps have fallen short of satisfaction to the honest demands of public creditors. The greater part of the United States had been swindled or plundered to a degree that exceeds the descriptive talents of the most powerful mind. Funds could not be had to satisfy all the creditors, or even a twentieth part of them. It remains, therefore, to be proved what was the *superior* merit of that class of creditors, whose claims were ultimately admitted, at their full value, as a debt on the public. The common saying is, that they were *old sol-*

---

* Gallatin, p. 89.

diers. A great number of them were so, and possessed the highest merit. A large portion of certificates was also held by contractors, and persons who had furnished various kinds of supplies, but who were not in the army. The country was full of widows and orphans, whose fathers and husbands had been killed in the war, and who, to this day, have received no compensation. Multitudes of soldiers had been also discharged from want of health, or from wounds, and who in equity, though not perhaps in name, were creditors to the public. Hence, if it had been possible to clear off all the last class of creditors, they were not more deserving than a still greater proportion of military sufferers who got nothing. The whole history of American public credit, during the war, holds up a picture of inevitable but enormous iniquity. Three-fourths of the citizens of the United States were, in real truth, creditors to government. The loss by depreciated paper was prodigious and next to universal. If it could have been possible to pick out all the soldiers or their families, and give them a higher proportion of payment than others, it would have been well. But to give one part of them their whole demand, and nothing to the rest, was not strict justice. The widow and orphan of one old soldier were actually taxed to pay the wages of another. When the federal party clamour so loudly on public faith, let them revolve these particulars. Let them look at the annual bundles of petitions referred to the committee of claims, and then they may blush at the very mention of American *public faith*.

Some perhaps think that the friends of order have been treated with too little ceremony in point of of stile. Observe a few specimens of their own. Mr. Fenno's gazette, of the 26th of April, 1796, contains a piece wherein the members of Congress who opposed the treaty, are termed the *war-whoop party*. If they carry their point, "it will *murder all your li-* "*berties, privileges and properties.*" Again, referring to Mr. Albert Gallatin, "*Let the mighty Ita-* "*lian, with his stilletto and bowl of poison come on.*" This piece concludes with saying that the Americans despise all *incendiaries ;* and it is subscribed ORDER.

An extract of a letter in the same newspaper has the following words. "I want to know how Madi- " son has accounted for his *inconsistency* and *dupli-* " *city* of conduct. How long will the people of " America be *duped* by this man."

The first question to be here asked is, whether such *inconsistency* and *duplicity* exist ? No details are attempted, and no evidences are offered. There never was an active and distinguished member in any legislative assembly, farther above impeachment than Mr. Madison. The marked attention which this gentleman obtained in Congress, is a tribute of esteem which all parties pay not more to his abilities than his virtues, to the irreproachable tenor of a life, that, since his first entrance on the political career, has remained without a stain, and which is far above the ordure of Mr. Fenno's correspondents.

As for the destruction of privileges and properties, no party ever displayed greater tameness on that head than the Hamiltonians. After the British had, for, many months, been capturing American vessels without provocation, and almost without pretence, the Representatives, on the 21st of April, 1795, past a resolution prohibiting, from and after the 1st of November then next, " all commercial " intercourse between the United States and the sub- " jects of Britain, or the citizens or subjects of any " other nation, so far as respects articles of *the* " *growth or manufacture of Britain or Ireland.*"

This would have been a most effectual blow to British commerce; and, as six months were to intervene before the commencement of its operation, full time would have been given for a mutual explanation and compromise. The British majority in the Senate of Congress rejected this proposal, so cheap, so simple, and so decisive. Jay, that executioner of his country, was, at the same time, dispatched to Britain. He there, by a clause of the treaty, tied up the hands of America, and destroyed all chance of adopting such a resource in future. The fifteenth article has these words. " Nor shall any prohibition " be imposed on the exportation or importation of " any articles to or from the territories of the two " nations respectively, which shall not *equally* extend " to all other nations." Thus we cannot prohibit the importation of English manufactures, without also prohibiting those of *all other nations*; and that is impracticable.

This article has the appearance of reciprocity, but not the substance. Supposing that England should entirely prohibit all intercourse with this country, her loss would be an hundred times greater than ours. The desolation of her West-Indies would be the first consequence, and a general bankruptcy among her West-Indian merchants, and her manufacturers for the American market, would be the second. On the contrary, the inconvenience and loss to the United States would be very supportable. We should begin to manufacture more among ourselves. American produce would soon find other markets. Other nations would learn to supply our wants, while the artists of England would croud over to this country in quest of employment. More commmanding ground could not be desired. Yet Jay jumped from his eminence to waddle in the slough of pretended reciprocity, to betray every principle of official trust, and to trample on every atom of his inftructions. The reader will infallibly abhor fuch ignorance or treachery, unlefs he has been a Britifh commiffary during the laft war, or a certificate correfpondent with James Reynolds fince it, unlefs he has a fuit of compenfation depending at London, unlefs he expects to be made an officer in the cuftoms, a director of the mint, a chaplain to Congrefs, a printer to the Senate, or an ambaffador to Berlin; or, unlefs he has twenty bills lying protefted at the bank of the United States, and his credit fticking together by the nod of Mr. Thomas Willing.

While the refolution of the 21ft of April, 1794, was under debate, and frequently before that time, in the fame feffion, the gentlemen on the oppofite fide of the queftion, faid that the Britifh would not feel the want of our commerce, becaufe the three millions fterling of exports from Britain to North-America, formed only one-fixth part of her total exports. This reafoning refembled that of fuppofing, that a perfon worth fix thoufand dollars, will not regret the lofs of one thoufand, becaufe he has five times that number behind; or, if you will, that a man would not feel the amputation of one of his fingers, if the other feven are fafe and found. Another circumftance muft be attended to. One-half of the commerce of Britain had been deftroyed by the ravages of the French war, fo that the lofs of American commerce would then have been equal to the annihilation of one third or fourth part of her whole foreign trade.

What effect thefe refolutions, if adopted, were likely to produce in Britain, may be perfectly afcertained upon the authority of Dr. Adam Smith, who was, on a point of this kind, a judge above exception. The paffage now to be quoted, is of confiderable length; but it ferves to illuftrate the prefent fubject so completely, that an apology would be unnecessary for its insertion. After describing some of the numerous inconveniences which Britain met with, in attempting to monopolize the commerce of her North-American colonies, the doctor proceeds thus:

"Her commerce, instead of running in a great number of small channels, has been taught to run principally in one great channel. But the whole system of her industry and commerce has thereby been rendered less secure; the whole state of her body politic less healthful, than it otherwise would have been. In her present condition, Britain resembles one of those unwholesome bodies, in which some of the vital parts are overgrown, and which, upon that account, are liable to many dangerous disorders, scarce incident to those in which all the parts are more properly proportioned. A small stop in that great blood-vessel which has been artificially swelled beyond its natural dimensions, and through which an unnatural proportion of the industry and commerce of the country has been forced to circulate, is very likely to bring on the most dangerous disorders upon the whole body politic. The expectation of *a rupture with the colonies*, accordingly, has struck the people of Britain with more terror than they ever felt *for a Spanish armada, or a French invasion*. It was this terror, whether well or ill-grounded, which rendered *the repeal of the stamp act*, among the merchants, at least, a popular measure. In a total exclusion from the colony market, was it to last only for a few years, the greater part of our merchants used to fancy that they foresaw *an entire stop to their trade*; the greater part of our master manufacturers, *the entire ruin of their business*; and the greater part of our workmen, *an end of their employment*. A rupture with any of our neighbours upon the continent, though likely too to occasion some stop or interruption in the employment of some of all these different orders of people, is foreseen, however, without any such general emotion. The blood, of which the circulation is stopt in some of the smaller vessels, easily disgorges itself into the greater, without occasioning any dangerous disorder; but, when it is stopt in any of the greater vessels, convulsions, apoplexy, or death are the immediate and unavoidable consequences. If but one of these overgrown manufactures, which by means either of bounties or of the monopoly of the home and colo-

"ny markets, have been artificially raised up to an unnatural height, finds some small stop or interruption in its employment, it frequently occasions a mutiny and disorder *alarming to government*, and embarrassing even *to the deliberations of the legislature*. How great, therefore, would be the disorder and confusion, it was thought, which must necessarily be occasioned by a sudden and entire stop in the employment of so great a proportion of our principal manufacturers!"

In despite of this overwhelming narrative, members of Congress could stand up and make speeches, by the hour, to prove, that an interruption of her commerce with America would not be seriously regarded by Britain. If she was so deeply afraid of America in 1766, when victorious, and at peace with all the world, her alarm would, of course, be vastly greater in 1794, when her public debt had doubled since the former time; when her armies on the continent were extirpated; when her manufacturing classes were already starving by thousands*; and when her trade to the United States was computed to be at twice the amount of what it had been twenty years before. This turn of circumstances went directly in favour of America. In 1766, England was more deeply alarmed than she had been by the Spanish armada. In 1794, her tremor would have been ten times greater, as a man dipt up to the chin, stands in more hazard of drowning, than when the stream only wets his ancle.

The exports from Britain to America, were, in 1794, about three millions sterling†; being, as above stated, equal to about a sixth part of her exported manufactures. Let us suppose that every

---

* A letter from a merchant in Manchester to his friend in this city, written about that time, observed, that, *if it was not for America, they would have wanted* BREAD TO THEIR MOUTHS.

† On the 18th of April, 1796, Pitt said, in the House of Commons, that the total exports of Britain, amounted to twenty-four millions sterling; and in 1795, to twenty-seven millions, two hundred and seventy thousand pounds sterling.

manufacturer in Britain requires fifteen pounds sterling per annum to support him; and that one-half of the price of the commodities exported from Britain to America consists in the wages of their labour. Here then we have abstracted from the fund of subsistence for the labouring part of the people of Britain, ONE MILLION AND FIVE HUNDRED THOUSAND POUNDS STERLING. Of these manufacturers, a considerable number must be married, and have families of children. It may seem strange in America, but it is absolutely true, that in Britain, or at least in Scotland, a journeyman manufacturer has raised his family on six shillings sterling a week, which is only fifteen pounds twelve shillings per annum. Let us compute then that one-fourth part of the hundred thousand manufacturers above stated, are married, and that each has three children. This estimate gives us two hundred thousand people reduced to beggary at a single stroke. We must likewise take into the account, that many thousands of British tradesmen depend entirely for their subsistence upon the custom of these two hundred thousand people; so that the whole number deprived of employment may be conjectured at two hundred and fifty thousand. To this we must add the destruction of revenue, the confusion, alarm, and bankruptcy of merchants, and the fall of the stocks, which must be the necessary consequence, and then let any body say, whether the loss of the commerce of America must not be a very serious object to Britain.

This act, prohibiting the importation of British goods, was lost in the Senate, by the casting vote of Mr. John Adams. All the advantages that it would have produced, have been thrown away, and all the mischiefs attending Jay's treaty have been originally caused by the fatal rejection of the vice-president. The advocates against the prohibition discovered a great want of information, of integrity, or of judgment. There cannot be a plainer position than that now before us. Adam Smith was, perhaps, the best informed political writer that Britain ever had. He affirmed, that an exclusion from the United States would affright her more effectually than a Spanish armada, or a French invasion. The Adamites denied all this; and their ignorance, their factious spirit, or their treachery, has cost American trade at least seven or eight millions of dollars. The constant cry was, that the British would declare war. Some weeks before that time, when Madison's resolutions were debated, general Smith asked one of these bawlers, what made him apprehensive that England would attack us? He replied, that he had no apprehensions of such a thing, but some of his neighbours were afraid of it, and he *wanted to please them*. General Smith told this in Congress, on the 27th of May, 1797. This would be one of those impostors who went home and told their constituents, that Madison wanted to destroy the government.

Among the ridiculous arguments advanced in Congress for accepting the British treaty, one was, that it would prevent the renewal of an Indian war. On the 29th of April, 1796, Mr. Dayton said, that, by rejecting Jay's treaty, it "might be calculated "upon as *inevitable*, and the consequent expendi- "ture of fourteen hundred thousand dollars annu- "ally; but in carrying the treaty into effect, and "possessing the (Western) posts with the troops, "they should be free from any danger of a serious "rupture with the savages*." That the Western

---

* Bache's Debates, vol. ii. p. 347.

posts would firmly bridle the Indians, was, at that time, a received opinion.

Dr. Ames took up the subject in a higher strain. The tories were ready to spit in any man's face who did not admire his speech on that occasion. On the Indian war, he sets out as follows:

" On this theme, my emotions are unutterable:
" if I could find words for them, if my powers bore
" any proportion to my zeal, I would swell my voice
" to such a note of remonstrance, it should reach
" every log-house beyond the mountains. I would
" say to the inhabitants, wake you from your false
" security. Your cruel dangers, your more cru-
" el apprehensions are soon to be renewed: the
" wounds, yet unhealed, are to be torn open again.
" In the day time, your path through the woods
" will be ambushed. The darkness of midnight
" will glitter with the blaze of your dwellings.
" —You are a father—the blood of your sons
" shall fatten your cornfield.—You are a mother—
" the war-whoop shall wake the sleep of the cradle.
" On this subject, you need not suspect any decep-
" tion on your feelings. It is a spectacle of horror
" which cannot be overdrawn. If you have nature
" in your hearts, it will speak a language compa-
" red with which all I have said or can say, will be
" poor and frigid.

" Will it be whispered that the treaty has made
" me a new champion for the protection of the fron-
" tiers? It is known that my voice as well as vote
" have been uniformly given in conformity with
" the ideas I have expressed. Protection is the
" right of the frontiers; it is our duty to give it."

All this is very fine. The conclusion implies an internal doubt in the mind of the orator that he was liable to the charge of inconsistency. Indeed, on the 6th of June, 1794, Dr. Ames spoke thus, in

Congress: " I am not one of those who think that " there are too many Indians, any more than too " many wild beasts. The one may, by skilful ma- " nagement, be rendered as harmless as the other." In 1794, when the doctor used this language, he thought only of injuries that Indians have suffered from white people. In April, 1796, he thought only of injuries that white people suffer from Indians. In the latter instance, Dr. Ames proved more than he foresaw. A refusal to appropriate would not have justified England in breaking the peace of 1783; and hence her stimulating the savages to murder, would have been an act of the blackest perfidy. The doctor looked upon this consequence as certain. Jacobinism can do nothing worse. This proves the folly of thinking Frenchmen more barbarous than Britons. The doctor says, that "his voice as well as vote has " been *uniform*." NO. He was an advocate for that system, which ended with refusing payment to the militia of Tennessee, for having done their duty. Yet the capture of Nickajack was nearly as important as Wayne's victory on the banks of the Miamis. Of the former, nobody speaks. For the latter, America has rung with exultation.

Again, if the Indians are ready to break a treaty, when a governor of Canada *shall bid them* do so, we have certainly *too many* of such neighbours, and systematic treachery makes it hardly worth while to negociate with them. This picture of perfidy does not agree with what Dr. Ames had said only a few minutes before. " I see no excep- " tion to the respect that is paid among nations to " the law of *good faith*. If there are cases in this " *enlightened* period when it is violated, there are " none where it is decried. It is the philosophy " of politics, the religion of governments. It is

"observed by barbarians. A whiff of tobacco-
"smoke, or a string of beads, gives not merely
"binding force, but *sanctity* to treaties."

By the subsequent account of the gentleman himself, the beads and tobacco were both to be forgotten at the nod of England. *No exception to the respect to the law of good faith!* Modern history is as full as it can be of the violation of good faith. The British orders of the 8th of June, and 6th of November, 1793, and 8th of January, 1794, were all breaches of treaty. The extravagance of the orator's style is too evident for detection. He then puts the supposition that England "refuses to ex-
"ecute the treaty, after we have done every thing
"to carry it into effect.—What would you say, or
"rather what would you not say?" He then, in a strain of lofty declamation, tells what might be said! The only remark worth making would be that *a blackamoor cannot easily wash himself white;* and that no man versant in history would feel surprize at such national baseness. Dr. Ames makes repeated reference to the states of Barbary, as *unsuspected* of breaking treaties. *A short history of Algiers,* printed some years ago by Mr. Mathew Carey, will give him a precious catalogue of such matters. Jay's treaty itself is regarded by the French as a violation of our treaty with them. The remarks on this speech may be shortened, for the treaty has *de facto* died. This can be proved in a few words.

"There is no position better settled, than that
"the breach of *any* article of a treaty by one par-
"ty, gives the other an option to consider the *whole*
"treaty as annulled*." Now, as England is on the verge of a general bankruptcy, our merchants

---

* Camillus, No. viii.

have no chance to recover their five millions of dollars. This was the temptation for accepting the treaty; and, when that vision has vanished, Congress, by the admission of Camillus himself, are at liberty to declare it void. They could do nothing better.

His majesty's most faithful subjects in Philadelphia toil hard to prove that England will recover her credit. The present distress hath not come of a sudden. In April, 1796, a committee of merchants waited on Mr. Pitt. At this interview it came out that the bank of England had advanced fourteen millions sterling for government. Sixteen millions sterling of cash and bullion had, within three years, been exported from the kingdom. Gambling in the funds had been excited by Pitt's exorbitant premiums to such a pitch, that twenty, thirty, and forty per cent were given for money to carry it on. Manufacturers or merchants could no longer borrow money at five per cent, so that sober trade was not to be supported. All these were the strongest causes and symptoms which could be conceived of approaching ruin. France hath only to rest on her arms, to exclude, as she hath done, English commerce from almost every port in Europe, and then to permit England to proceed with an annual loan of twenty millions sterling. Hence it is of little concern whether Britain professedly stops payment in this year or the next. The event is certain. The delay is but like a fortnight's respite from the gibbet. The predictions of Gerald and Palmer have not been long unfulfilled; nor have their wrongs been long unavenged.

Recurring to Dr. Ames, we can now answer one of his queries. "The articles stipulating the " redress of our injuries by captures, are said to be " delusive. *By whom is this said?*" By every body.

Dr. Ames has been succeded in the fifth Congress by a diligent imitator. Of all that might have been spared in the representative of Boston we find a faithful copy. But from his comprehensive knowledge, his pathetic vivacity, his acuteness of remark, his chaste, yet luxuriant elegance of expression, the honourable Harrison Gray Otis of Massachusetts keeps, and forever will keep, at an immeasurable distance.

On the 1st of July, 1797, an amendment was proposed in Congress to the stamp-duty bill. Twenty dollars were to be charged for a certificate of citizenship to an emigrant. On this occasion, Mr. Otis made, as usual, a speech of considerable length. Mr. Loyd took an extensive sketch of it. But a the commodities of this orator are not much in d mand, Mr. Loyd has not yet presumed to incumb his newspaper with the copy. Mr. Bache gave short account of it, and as Mr. Otis has compla ed bitterly of the negligence of reporters, the lowing extract of the most shining passages has b here inserted, *cum notis variorum*.

"Mr Otis defended the stamp duty. "We di "want population now." [The United state tain above a million of square miles, and abou millions of people. Making large allowanc water, and for useless land, their territory with much ease accommodate twenty time present number of people. An immense ness beyond the Mississippi remains also to b up. We need an increase of numbers mo any other nation. It is momentous to our safety. In the A. B. C. of American polit Otis might have learned this lesson.] " "some observations on the relative m "Europe and this country. He coul

"that there was this *similarity**, at least in the p-
"sent distracted state of Europe; when moral,
"and religion, and every vestige of what was great
"and amiable, was endeavoured to be swept from
"the surface of the earth." [In some parts of Europe, in Portugal and Russia, for example, the human character is degraded by despotism. But in every country where any degree of freedom can be found, the people of Europe will bear, in all respects, a comparison with those of America. How should it be otherwise? The United States have become inhabited by a succession of chips from the old block of European population. They have not been long enough in the New world to attain any important distinction of character. During this debate, an Irish representative remarked to a stranger in the lobby, that nearly one fourth part of the members then present were natives of Europe. To the south of New-England, at least one half of the citizens are either emigrants from thence, or the sons or grandsons of such emigrants. As for the attempt to sweep *morality* and *religion*, every vestige of all that is *great* and *amiable* from the surface of the earth, this is only a round-about way of professing that Mr. Otis is an enemy to the French revolution. Had he been born in due time, he would surely have resisted that of America; for the French had received at least five millions of provocations, where the Americans could produce one. It to be inferred that Mr. Otis laments the destruction of the Bastile, the abolition of the Gabelle, the ack, the wheel, monarchy, nobility, and that utmost of abominations—an episcopal *establishment by v.* He thinks that to let every man believe what

---

* Mr. Gallatin had said that we were in fact an European nation, the manners of the people, on both sides of the water, were ially the same.

creed, and employ what prieſt he pleaſes, is the way to ſweep *religion* from the earth. To deſtroy ariſtocracy is to deſtroy *morality*. This muſt be his meaning.] " He wiſhed to place a bar in the way
" of the admiſſion of thoſe reſtleſs people who could
" not be tranquil and happy in their own country;
" thoſe who had unfurled the ſtandard of rebellion
" at home. He profeſſed an eſteem for ſome emi-
" grants to this country; but he did not wiſh *a horde*
" *of wild Iriſhmen to be let looſe upon us ;* who were
" now endeavouring to effect a revolution in their
" own country. He did not wiſh the introduction
" here of their revolutionary principles. He was
" *willing to fraternize with thoſe emigrants who*
" *might be admitted among us now*, but he wiſhed
" a bar placed to further migrations, and he did not
" think twenty dollars too much.

The term of *wild*, as here applied excluſively to Iriſhmen, is highly impertinent. In thoſe parts of Ireland where the peace and property of the ſubjects have formerly been protected, the general caſt of manners was fully as good as that in New-England. A great body of the people were however kept in a ſtate of inceſſant irritation by the preſſure of their landed ariſtocracy, and their blood-ſucking church of England hierarchy. Of theſe unfortunate victims it would be unfair to eſtimate the morals, till they ſhall enjoy a political ſyſtem, whereby induſtry is encouraged, and property ſecured. Fortune has never ſported more cruelly, than by ſubjecting that hoſpitable and generous nation to the monopolizing jealouſy, and the ſyſtematic barbarity of an Engliſh parliament. An Iriſh revolution is now expected, and in its triumphant iſſue, Ireland, ſpurning the yoke of hereditary tyrants, will aſſume her proper rank and dignity among the powers of Europe.

"Those," says Mr. Otis, "who have unfurled "the standard of rebellion AT HOME." A gang of banditti from the town of Boston began the American revolution, by unfurling the standard of villainy. They wantonly destroyed three hundred and forty-two chests of tea, in presence, and with the approbation of an immense crowd of spectators. The act of parliament for shutting up the port of Boston, was the natural and suitable consequence of that shameful transaction. The burning of the Gaspee schooner, at Providence, in Rhode-Island, because it obstructed smuggling, was another wanton outrage, that must be reprobated by every man who is fit for living under a civilized government. The whole continent was dragged prematurely into war, to save the factious townsmen of Boston from a chastisement that some of them very highly deserved. The friends of America in England, could no longer defend their proceedings. The cause of liberty was disgraced and injured by the unbecoming insolence of its advocates. The townsmen of Belfast have invaded no man's property. The burden of actual oppression crushes them to the earth. The wrongs of America were chiefly in imagination. She was more lightly taxed than any other country in the world. If the people of New-England had behaved with equal moderation and dignity as those of Virginia, it is likely enough that we might still have been British colonies, and in a happy situation, without any revolution at all. When once the contest had begun, there could be no medium between independence and slavery, but that does not lessen the extreme want of sense and honesty in burning the tea. It very ill becomes such people to rail at reformers in Europe. The whole speech proves that Mr. Otis is unworthy even to reside in a free country, and infinitely more so to represent it. Nature intended him for a keeper of the Conciergerie, or a led captain to some prince of Wales. After all, Otis only betrayed the real sentiments of his whole party; and under such leaders, we cannot wonder at the contemptible and pitiable figure which the United States do at present make.

The unexpected length to which some articles in this volume are found to extend, has of necessity prevented the publication of others. This deviation from the first design is more fully explained in the preface. The following miscellaneous remarks have, however, been inserted, as a relief to the reader from the sameness of political details. They refer to subjects of universal interest, and which, in the most expressive manner, demand reformation.

On Saturday, the 12th of March, 1796, two stage coaches, set out at six o'clock in the morning, from Frenchtown for Newcastle. The distance is only seventeen miles; and yet the drivers did not reach the latter place till twelve o'clock. They took six hours to travel a space, which a healthy, active man would have walked over with ease, in four and an half. The road through which the coaches had to go, was very tolerable. One of the drivers, when near Newcastle, attempted a kind of quicker pace than usual. The wretched harnessing instantly gave way; the two foremost horses broke loose, and set off at full gallop: one of them was near breaking his neck.

When the passengers arrived at Newcastle, the wind was fair, the tide was making, and the boat for Philadelphia was ready and waiting; yet they were detained an hour and an half. The only conceivable reason for this delay was, that *the innkeeper might scrub the passengers out of the price of a dinner*.

At last the boat got off, and with a fair wind came up within less than two miles of Gloucester point; but the wind and tide failing, the vessel was obliged to come to anchor. If she had left Newcastle but an hour more early, she might have come with ease to the wharf at Chesnut-street, by six o'clock in the evening.

Seven or eight of the passengers, who were anxious to get forward, were obliged to pay half-a-dollar each to the sailors, to row them ashore. If the owners of these boats are capable of shame, which is extremely doubtful, they must blush at such multiplied instances of negligence, insolence and extortion.

Another tide was expected to begin about one o'clock in the morning. The master, whose name is Mitchell, sate up, drinking grog, playing at cards with some passengers, and making an intolerable noise, till the hour above-mentioned: he then went to bed. About four in the morning, some of his men came down to tell him that the tide was ebbing, and that the boat was run aground. It was a long time before they could make him understand them.

Finally, the boat came up to Arch-street wharf on Sunday evening, with the tide, having performed a passage in *twenty-eight* hours, which, with the utmost ease, might have been executed in *six*.

The above appeared in a Baltimore newspaper. Some of the parties felt themselves angry, and said so; but they did not attempt to contradict the statement, for it was only a specimen of their daily practice.

Extract of a letter from a gentleman in Philadelphia, to his friend in Baltimore, dated 25th of April, 1796.

In the Maryland Journal of the 28th of March last, I observe an account of an expedition from Frenchtown to Newcastle in the stage coach, and from the latter place to Philadelphia by the stage boat. The writer complains that the coach took six hours to drive seventeen miles over a tolerable road; that the boat spent *twenty-eight* hours on a voyage up the Delaware, which might have been ended in *six* hours; that Mitchell, the master of the boat, got drunk; that his sailors fleeced some of the passengers, &c. &c.

This malcontent must undoubtedly be a foreigner, otherwise he never would have attempted to grumble, for two solid reasons. First, because, with a few exceptions, brutality, negligence and filching, are as naturally expected by people accustomed to travelling in America, as a mouth, a nose, and two eyes, are looked for in a man's face. Secondly, because legal redress, and individual reformation, are equally hopeless. The ormer would require such a waste of time and money, with so extreme an uncertainty of the issue, that no person of common prudence ever thinks of it. As for the second, there are exceptions, both as to landlords and drivers, between this place and Baltimore; and others may be found in different parts of the country. But the blanks in this lottery are more numerous than the prizes; and to hope reformation or amendment of character, among the worthless, would be the most visionary of all visions.

Thus standing the case, this gentleman, instead of grumbling, should rather be very thankful to have rode from Frenchtown to Newcastle, without getting his limbs broke, and his trunk, if he had one with him, shattered to pieces, or pitched a yard deep into the mire. Mitchell, the boatman from Newcastle to Philadelphia, did not endanger the lives of his passengers. He only kept them about five times longer than was necessary on the water. If his sailors took half-a-dollar a piece for rowing some of the passengers on shore, they should have been very grateful that the boat was not overset. Permit me to relate some of my own trials and troubles of this nature.

In June 1794, I had occasion to go to New-York. Two rival coaches came near the town of Brunswick, at the same time. The one in which I was, got the start of the other by a few yards; and entered the town at full gallop. I expected every moment when the coach would break down, or some of the horses fall dead under the fatigue. Most of our passengers were as fond of this triumph as the driver himself, and did every thing in their power to encourage him to break their necks. At Elizabeth-town, a young lady, well mounted, came up behind us, and attempted to ride by. Six or eight of us instantly raised a halloo, frightened her horse, and almost unseated her. On attempting to expostulate, I soon found that I might presently be treated still worse than she was. The whole cargo roared out, *What? Suffer any body to take the road of us?* They reviled the lady in the most shameful stile. One of them I learned to be a merchant in New-York, and a man not of an obscure situation. A second was a quaker. I tried to argue with him on the principles of his society, on the vileness and cowardice of hazarding the life or limbs of a fellow creature for such a jockey piece of etiquette. I had a surly answer, and was at the same time, taken up short by a clergyman from the north of Ireland, who constantly kept himself in a state of elevation during the last sixty miles of our journey.

At New-York, I was lodged with two others, in a back room, on the ground floor. This was a dirty hole about three yards and an half square.—What can be the reason for that vulgar hoggish custom, common in America, of squeezing three, six, or eight beds into one room? No such thing is seen in the British islands. Among genteel or decent people, every person has not only a bed, but even a room to himself, and very frequently locks the door.

The back yard, into which the window of our cell opened, was about six yards wide every way. Within this space, and just opposite to our window stood a little brick kitchen, and cheek by jowl, an edifice of the most *necessary* nature. They were separated by a brick partition about six or nine inches thick. The delicacy of this arrangement must strike every person of superior taste. Having occasion to visit the temple, I found that the roof had tumbled in. It was about noon, and a very sultry day, and before I could get out again, I had well nigh fainted with the most horrible stench that ever assailed my nostrils.

If the continent of America were only ten miles broad, there might be some excuse for jamming buildings together in such a disgusting, aukward and dangerous way. 'I call it disgusting,' as the scene just described might turn the stomach of a Hottentot. It is aukward, for when these receptacles of filth come to be emptied, matters are often so badly laid out, that the only passage to get the nastiness away, is through the very middle of the house itself. Such is not universally the mode of purgation, but it occurs, in too many instances. Now it is surely aukward to be thus, almost in a literal sense, entrenched up to the teeth in human excrement; and it is the more extraordinary, as the Americans are highly and justly commended for the general cleanliness of their domestic economy. Can any body wonder that a city, under the fortieth degree of latitude, should be visited by the yellow fever, when a part of its inhabitants are permitted to render it a centre of putrefaction? The *danger* of squeezing houses together like herrings in a barrel, is readily seen in cases of fire. A house burnt down last winter in Philadelphia near the corner of Arch-street; and such was its situation that it was either almost, or entirely inaccessible to fire-engines. I know a city in Europe larger than Philadelphia, that did not suffer so much by fire in fifteen years, as I have repeatedly seen the latter do in a single evening. Excuse this digression. I now return to my travels.

In coming back from New-York to this city, I preferred going by water.—The master of a stage-boat, which took us over an arm of the sea to New-Jersey, gave an eminent proof of attention to his duty. He suffered our boat to be very nearly run down on a smooth calm sea, in broad day light, by a vessel of much larger bulk than ours, that was coming up in full sail. At last, when within perhaps twenty yards of her, the shouting of her crew awaked him from his torpor; but after all, we missed only by a few feet, a stroke that inevitably would have sent us to the bottom. Thus were the lives of twenty or thirty people brought into the most imminent risk, because the boat was entrusted with a blockhead, who had not common sense enough to drive a dung cart.

At Amboy, part of our baggage was forgot, notwithstanding the injunctions which we gave, and the assurances which we received, that the whole would be carefully packed. So great was the politeness of the house, that though we had paid for seats over-night, the coach was on the point of setting off without giving notice to five or six of us, who were in considerable danger of being left behind.

In our passage across Jersey, the drivers did every thing in their power to kill the horses, by making them go at a hand gallop, for six or seven miles together, without stopping, over a deep sandy road, and in a very hot day. If the owners of these coaches had the least sense even of their own interest, they would flog such barbarous villains, in place of paying them wages.

At Bordenton, we went into a second boat, where we met with very sorry accommodation. This was about four o'clock in the afternoon. We had about twenty miles down the Delaware to reach Philadelphia. The *captain*, who had a most provoking tongue, was a boy about eighteen years of age. He, and a few companions, dispatched a dozen or eighteen bottles of porter. We ran three different times against other vessels that were coming up the stream. The women and children lay all night on the bare boards of the cabin floor. A little boy, one of the passengers from New-York, lingered at the brink of the grave, during several months, in consequence of this mode of travelling. We reached Arch-street wharf, about eight o'clock on the Wednesday morning, having been about sixteen hours on a voyage of twenty miles. Compared to such navigators as those two, whom I have just given you an account of, even poor Mitchell was an Anson or a Columbus.

Print the above. The press cannot do better than to describe scenes of inhospitality and swindling that seem to have been reduced to a national system, and that could hardly be expected in a Turkish caravansera.

The buildings of Baltimore, New-York, and Philadelphia, contain in their construction so great a proportion of wood, that if a flame has once fairly caught, nothing but the most vigorous efforts can stop its progress.

If the ground story of one of our houses catches fire, a family residing in the second floor, may run the utmost hazard of being either suffocated by the smoke, or burnt alive in the flames. Their only shift is to jump out of the windows, at the expence of breaking half their bones, unless, which does not always happen, ladders are brought to their assistance. Even in that case, from hurry and confusion, the risk is considerable. In many places, houses are heaped together in such a manner, that in case of a fire, either exit or access would be almost impracticable.

Every man who sees a conflagration in an American town, must remark the facility with which it spreads from one roof to another. This is one of the great and leading causes, which make our fires so generally destructive. The first reason is, that our houses are roofed with wood; and secondly, a most absurd and stupid practice among house-carpenters, has multiplied the hazard in a ten-fold proportion.

When two houses of equal height are built close together, it is very common for the planks of each roof *to cross over and join with those of the other.* By this means, whenever one roof kindles, the flame, if it gets not opposition, from a water engine, spreads immediately to the next. In Dublin, the houses are roofed with slate or tile, and each roof is separated from others by a little parapet of stone, which is raised about nine or twelve inches above the roof, being in fact, the top of the partition wall between the two buildings. This incombustible boundary makes the conflagration spread far more tardily than it otherwise would do.

When a traveller from Europe first lands in the United States, he is amazed at the blindness and infatuation of persisting in this practice of running the wooden roofs across each other, a practice so pregnant with danger and ruin. A few years of habit reconcile him to it, and if he builds a house for himself, he is not ambitious of looking wiser than other people.

We often hear of fires in London, and they are sometimes very terrible. But London is about seven or eight times more populous than the five largest sea-port towns in America put together, so that if we compare the number of buildings with the number of fires, in these different places, it will be found that those of London are of much inferior frequency.

In Edinburgh, the houses are far more durably built than either in London or Dublin. In the two latter, the walls are almost universally formed of brick, and the stairs of wood. In Edinburgh the walls and stairs are of stone, and every stair is arched quite round with stone, so firmly compacted, that the wooden parts of the house might be consumed twenty times over, and the stair-case itself remain without damage. No wooden roof is to be seen; and the slate roofs are invariably separated by a parapet wall. The result from this style of architecture is, that a well built house can hardly burn to the ground, on any account. A dirty chimney may kindle, cause occasional alarm, and produce petty damage; but the burning out of a family is a very uncommon accident.

CHAPTER VIII.

Proceedings of Congress.—Affair of Randall and Whitney.—Plan of appointing a short-hand writer.—Debates on the federal city.—Act of Appropriation.—Debates on the call for Jay's instructions.—Strange answer of the President.—Appropriations for the British treaty.—Explanation of the conduct of Mr. Muhlenberg.—Singular multiplicity of petitions in favour of appropriating for the British treaty.—Rise of the session.

THE preliminary and miscellaneous materials of this volume have swelled to a much greater bulk than had been foreseen or designed. After all, many articles are left out, which were originally propofed for infertion. Though not always in a regular feries, yet a confiderable part of the moft important events of the prefent year, have been related. Our maritime hiftory, that is to fay, an account of the French and Britifh depredations, for the firft five months of 1796, have been compiled with tolerable completenefs. The prefent chapter is to give a fketch of the principal proceedings in Congrefs, during that part of their feffion, which began with the 1ft of January, 1796. Of many of the moft interefting fpeeches, there have already been inferted large fpecimens.

The affair of Randall and Whitney belongs, moft properly, to the year 1795. A full account of it has been recently given in the American Annual Regifter. It is fufficient here to fay, that Robert Randall and Charles Whitney, did, in 1795, conceive a project, in conjunction with fome Britifh fettlers in Canada, for purchafing from Congrefs that fpacious peninfula, which lies between lakes Erie, Michigan, and Huron. It contains about twenty millions of acres. With this view they came to Philadelphia. Randall made fome improper advances to certain members of the Houfe of Reprefentatives, in order to gain their intereft. Having, no doubt, heard of the pilot-boat hiftory, he waited among others, upon Dr. William Smith. He was apprehended, brought to the bar of the houfe, and for a fhort time confined in prifon. Whitney had done nothing wrong. He was fent to jail, and then difmiffed without examination. In this bufinefs, the houfe acted without regularity, without judgment, and without juftice.

On the 19th of January, they took up the bill of appropriations for the current year. Mr. Williams moved to ftrike out of it all the fums allotted for the mint. After a very hard struggle, the mint protracted its existence, under the severest repobation of its management from every side of the house. The plan of this establishment came from Mr. Hamilton. Large sums had been expended to very little purpose. One design of it seems to have been the erection of a board of sinecures for the sake of increasing the executive influence.

On the 29th of January, the house went into a committee of the whole, on a report from a committee that had been appointed to find out a short hand writer who was to take down their debates at full length, and print them. A person had, for almost two preceding sessions, attended the house to take minutes of its proceedings for the Philadelphia Gazette. In this wilderness of scribbling, many particulars transpired, which members were ashamed to confess and afraid to deny. Four gentlemen were especially irritated, viz. Theodore Sedgwick, Dr. William Smith, Samuel Dexter, and Robert Goodloe Harper. Messrs. Dexter and Sedgwick were not able to forgive the figure that they had made in the nobility debates, as well as on some other occasions. Harper had disputed with col. James White, delegate from Tennessee, on the defence of the South-Western frontier; and the particulars, which were not to his advantage, had been related with unfeeling accuracy. But Dr. Smith, was by far more rancorous than the other gentlemen collectively. During the debate on Madison's resolutions, Mr. Abraham Clarke of New-Jersey said, turning round to his right hand, and *looking at Mr. William Smith*, that a stranger in the gallery might suppose there was a British agent in the house. The nickname of *British agent* became general. Mr. Smith was burnt in effigy at Charleston. On the rising of the session, he found it convenient to shun a meeting with his conftituents by a tour for the enfuing fummer, into the eaftern ftates. The blame of this whole fcandal was imputed to the pen of the guilty taker of minutes for the Philadelphia Gazette. Influence was employed, but in vain, to procure his difmiffion. This occurred in January, 1794.

But on the 2d and 3d of March, 1795, the Reprefentatives met in the evening, and fome of them being in a ftate of unufual vivacity, Smith and Dexter arofe and complained bitterly of the minutes in the Philadelphia Gazette. Neither of them faid, becaufe neither of them durft fay, that any thing of their own had been mifreprefented. The late Mr. Andrew Brown, knowing that miftakes were unavoidable, had uniformly advertifed that he was ready to receive and print corrections. The two members clofed by propofing a refolution for appointing a committee to examine a ftenographer. It paft by twenty-eight votes againft twenty-fix.

All this was in March, 1795. On the 29th of January, 1796, Mr. Giles and Dr. Smith, who had been appointed a committee, reported in favour of Mr. Robertfon, a Scotfman, from Peterfburg, in Virginia. He demanded four thoufand dollars. Congrefs were to give him two thoufand nine hundred, and Mr. Brown undertook for the reft of the fum. The debates were to be printed firft in his newfpaper. This would likewife anfwer the object of Mr. Smith in feparating Mr. Brown and his prefent reporter.

The plan was attacked from every part of the houfe, as impracticable, if ufeful; and as ufelefs if it could be practicable. Mr. Baldwin faid that he had feen many printed fketches of fpeeches made in that houfe, and which he would not wifh to fee better done. Mr. Swanwick had often heard of *miscellaneous compofitions*, but the ftrangeft of all mifcellanies that he ever heard of, was for the legiflature of a country to run fhares with a printer in the publication of their proceedings. Even Mr. Sedgwick, alfo, oppofed the plan. He honeftly faid, that gentlemen were apt to get into a paflion, and then they were angry at feeing their expreflions in print. Mr. Nicholas was for the appointment. He complained that a perfon who came often to that houfe, and who had a very good ftyle of writing, once publifhed a fpeech as his. "The language " was much better than I could have made," faid Mr. Nicholas, and here the member was miftaken. " The fpeech did not contain a fingle fentiment " that I would have difowned, but ftill the fpeech " was not mine." Mr. Harper attacked the debates in the Philadelphia Gazette, as difgraceful to the country, and full of falfehoods. He prattled away at this rate, for a confiderable time. He had never complained of inaccuracy but once ; and his correction was immediately adopted. Mr. Harper poffeffes a readinefs of invention, and a confidence of affirmation, which the public eftimate at their proper value.

Mr. Giles fpoke in favour of the report ; but he feemed to lofe courage on finding that a large majority in the houfe entirely difapproved of the plan. He expreffed regret at having been concerned in it. As an excufe, he complained, for the firft time, of the inaccuracy of the debates. He had never before dropt a hint of that nature. The prefumption is, that it was now brought forward to help him out with a lame argument. He felt evident chagrin at finding himfelf entangled in this prodigal and abfurd project. The committee rofe without a divifion. On the 2d of February, 1796, the fubject was difcharged by a refolution of the houfe. Mr. Robertfon had come fome hundreds of miles, from a lucrative employment, at the particular defire of the fpecial committee, and had ſtaid in Philadelphia waiting on this bufinefs, at a confiderable expence. He was difmiffed without compenfation. The houfe ought at leaſt to have paid the charges of his journey.

On the 8th of January, the Prefident had fent a meffage to Congrefs. It inclofed a memorial from the commiffioners appointed for infpecting the buildings at the federal city. The object was, to obtain a loan of money, under the fanction of government, in order to complete the public buildings at that place. The loan was to be fecured on the public property in the city. The United States were to pledge themfelves that, in cafe of the property proving inadequate for difcharging the loan, government was to make good the deficiency.

A committee was appointed to report on this meffage. After feveral difcuffions, a bill refpecting it paffed the Houfe of Reprefentatives, on the 31ſt of March, 1796. The Prefident was thereby authoriſed to borrow three hundred thoufand dollars on the plan above ſtated. The bill went through, by feventy-two votes againſt twenty-one. Thus a freſh bliſter is applied to the back of our national debt.

Mr. Coit, Mr. Sitgreaves, Mr. Havens, and Mr. Swanwick, did themfelves the honour of oppofing this *annihilation* of the public money; for, that thefe three hundred thoufand dollars will finally come out of the federal treafury, and never more return to it, is tolerably certain.

Mr. Coit faid, that, between three and four hundred thoufand dollars have already been expended; and, as he conceived, to *what was worſe than no purpoſe*. Ninety-feven thoufand dollars had been laid out on the Prefident's houfe, and it was eſtimated that nearly as much more would be wanted to complete it. When finished, he conceived that a house, which would cost only *fifty thousand* dollars, would better answer the purpose. About eighty thousand dollars had been expended on the capitol, and yet, *progress was scarcely made beyond the foundation*. He expected many *future* and *heavy* applications to *the public treasury* for those buildings, which he feared would be a lasting monument of the pride and folly of this country.—Ninety-seven thousand dollars for a presidential palace, that is not yet *more than half completed!* Thus the whole building will cost at least two hundred thousand dollars. If this is not deplorable waste of money, we should be happy to learn what name it deserves? Indeed, unless among the parties immediately interested in forwarding this house, there can hardly be two opinions about it. The absurdity is too enormous to be endured with tranquility by any man, unless his ideas are adulterated by self-interest, by prejudice, by the horror of *being left in a minority*, or by some other petty motive unconnected with the common exercise of his understanding. The capitol is another superfluous edifice, that, as came out in the debates, has already sunk *eighty thousand dollars*, and is scarcely raised beyond its foundation. Such things are encouraged to go on, while our most excellent of all governments can hardly raise money to pay the very interest of the debts which it is *annually* contracting. It is not a season to varnish the poop, when the wind is rending the shrouds, when the sea is bursting the seams, and driving in the cabin windows.

Mr. Sedgwick, in the debate on the 25th of February declared, with a convenient *rotundity* of assertion, that accommodations are to be made for government *without any expence to the public treasury*. It is certain that they will be erected at a very enormous expence, which must come in some shape from the purses of the people. Every newspaper is occasionally filled with advertisements about the *Washington lottery.* This is a tax on the public. In Europe it is universally agreed, that a lottery is the most ruinous of all methods for raising money, and, at the same time, the most injurious to the morals of the people. When we hear Mr. Sedgwick say, that these public buildings are to be raised *without expence to the public*, one might guess that, like the palace in an Arabian tale, they were to rise by enchantment.

It is amazing that any gentleman can stand up in Congress, and talk in such a way. Nay, Mr. Sedgwick went further. He said that the more magnificent these buildings were, so much the better. If they exceeded the splendour of the palaces of Europe, Americans ought to be *grateful*. It is highly wrong for any legislature to encourage, among its citizens, a taste for gambling. The lottery for *the federal city* does this in a considerable degree; it explains, what Mr. Coit justly said, that between three and four hundred thousand dollars have been expended *to what is worse than no purpose*.

Mr. Sedgwick may rant as much as he pleases, about the gratification that Americans must feel in contemplating the completion, and magnificence of these buildings in the federal city. A man with chaste ideas of political economy, and of national freedom, will consider them as an equal outrage on the one and the other. The pyramids of Egypt, the amphitheatre of Titus, the pillar of Trajan, and a thousand other edifices of a similar description, were durable and insulting testimonials of the slavery of mankind, with an impression more forcible than the pen or the pencil can convey. They attefted, that the property and induftry of millions of people had been facrificed to glut the caprice and vanity of a fingle man. *And who or what was this man?* Some jockey king, or cut throat emperor, who, if ftript of *a little brief authority*, would, ufually, have been one of the moft infignificant of his fpecies. But it is needlefs to enter into general declarations, or appeal to the mournful evidence of Rome and Egypt. The facts admitted in Congrefs fpeak with fufficient diftinctnefs.

If the money had been laid out on a canal between Newcaftle and Frenchtown, or on a high road between Philadelphia and Baltimore, or in penfions, to fome of the poor old foldiers, who fold their certificates for half a crown in the pound, there might be fome confolation. The cafh had, to be fure, been raifed in a bad way, but its expenditure had anfwered fome ufeful end; and, though no man of fenfe would ever have been highly pleafed by feeing the rapid fale of lottery tickets, yet the laudable application of the money, muft have ferved as an emolient to the ulcer.

It is hard to fay what was the original object of founding this federal city, or what benefit it could be fuppofed to anfwer to the country in general. The human faculties are as clear on the banks of the Delaware as on thofe of the Potomac. The Prefident had already a good houfe in Philadelphia, for which his very large falary, of twenty-five thoufand dollars, well enables him to pay a fuitable rent. The apartments wherein Congrefs at prefent affemble, in the fame city, are as roomy and elegant as can be defired. Philadelphia has a centrical fituation, and an atmofphere at leaft as healthy as the intended new metropolis. We afk then, what could be the use or object of these buildings? Or why did a government, encumbered with a debt of seventy millions of dollars, plunge its citizens into this unfathomable pit of architecture and of lotteries? An old London bookseller used to say, that the *title page* was half of the battle. In like manner, the *name* of this city has produced more than half the patience with which its expenditures have been endured.

Endured is the proper word, for this plan has never excited popular enthusiasm. It hardly could. Is there not already in the union a city good enough to accommodate Congress? No other city on the continent can expect the smallest advantage from this removal, and every one of them feels a certain loss. "On the same principle," said Mr. Swanwick, " the house might guarantee " loans for all the cities in the union? Why a loan " for the city of Washington in particular? Was " there any *reason* why the *different cities* in the " union should be *taxed for that city?*" He might have subjoined, is there any *justice* in such a tax? If Washington becomes an eminent commercial place, Alexandria, or Norfolk, or Baltimore, will not be one farthing the better for it, but they may chance to be the worse.

It is highly expedient that the legislature of a nation should assemble to do business in one of the largest of its cities. The reason is obvious. The eyes of the people are thus more effectually opened to its proceedings; and a legislature is much more safely to be entrusted when under such inspection.

The spirit of liberty, the penetration to discern and fortitude to resist despotism, have often been found to beat higher in the metropolis of a limited government than in any other place. Thus Charles the firſt was blamed for calling the long parliament at London, where his tyranny was deteſted, and conſequently where parliament were ſure of firm and effectual ſupport. His friends regretted that it had not met at Oxford; the miſtake coſt his majeſty the loſs of his head.

The French revolution began at Paris. The true character of government was much better underſtood there, by the common people, than by the ſame claſs in moſt other quarters of the kingdom. At Amſterdam, alſo, oppoſition to the corrupting influence of the ſtadtholder was always ſtronger than any where elſe. A very large city is, in almoſt every reſpect, a great nuiſance. Yet, as *it is a bad wind which blows good to nobody*, a ſubordinate advantage may often be traced in the midſt of a political evil.

Such immenſe capitals as London, Paris, or even Amſterdam, cannot ſubſiſt in America, for centuries to come, but if they did ſo, many reaſons would recommend that the ſeat of government ſhould alſo reſide in ſuch a ſituation. With ſo many obſervers to watch its motions, and whoſe very numbers inſpire them with peculiar confidence, the inſolence or corruption of office is more likely to be detected and expoſed than on a more limited field of enquiry. The preſent trifling oppoſition that the abandoned miniſter of England finds in the Houſe of Commons, would, by this time, have moſt likely dwindled altogether away, if the ſpirit of Sheridan and others had not been ſupported by their ſituation in the boſom of a numerous party of the citizens of London.

Theſe hints tend to point out the propriety of retaining the reſidence of the federal legiſlature in one of the larger cities of the union. On the ſtreets of New-York or Philadelphia, every member of Congreſs meets with fellow citizens as independent and well-informed as himself, and who, without ceremony, will tell him what they think of his conduct. In such a place, he has a thousand opportunities of learning public feelings, which he never could acquire in a sequestered desart, like the paper-built city of Washington, even supposing that he were to read all the newspapers in the United States. We have at this time about an hundred and twenty newspapers, if not more; and hence, that task is, in itself, impossible. It is by mixing with mankind that you learn how to legislate for them. *In the multitude of counsellors there is safety*, said the wise man; and in a limited sense, the maxim holds good. It is only by a collision of various sentiments, opinions, habits of thinking and views of life, the light of truth is finally to be struck out.

There is a large house in Philadelphia which the Assembly of Pennsylvania had designed for the President. Mr. Swanwick, in a debate about this federal city bill, noticed that twenty thousand dollars were granted to build it; but nearly twice the sum had been asked for it since, and the house is *not yet finished*.

Veterans who fought battles for America, were glad to accept, as all the world knows, of half-a-crown in the pound for the arrears of their dear-bought wages. Hundreds of petitions are, in the course of every session, presented to Congress from miserable objects of all sorts, who were reduced to decrepitude and beggary in the continental service. Government cannot relieve all these people, but still if they promoted lotteries for that end, the money would be more honourably bestowed than on a *capitol*, which has already cost *eighty thousand dollars*, though it is hardly *visible above ground!*

As for the palace of the President, the plan must

have originated with somebody, who wanted to set up a political idol. A President is the very last man in the community for whom the public ought to build a house, because he has a salary five times larger than that of any other public officer in the union; and hence can afford better than other public officer to pay the rent of his house.

The money expended on palaces at the federal city, is absolutely cast away. The President and Congress are already as well accommodated with lodgings as they need wish to be, or deserve to be. There is no use for such extravagant buildings. The raising of money by lotteries is the most pernicious resource within the range of political insanity. The erection of such fabrics tends to excite a tone of aristocracy and of royalty, to which mankind are already but too much addicted.

Dr. Samuel Johnson says, that "to build is to be "*robbed.*" We cannot expect that houses raised for a government will be carried on with more economy than those of private persons. Mr. Coit* says, that the buildings at Washington have been commenced on an extravagant plan, and that he hopes the commissioners will be obliged to *contract them.* Mr. Sitgreaves, in the same debate, also declares that the eventual expence of the buildings is not *within the reach of calculation, or even of conjecture.* What a miserable prospect is yawning before us!

Mr. Havens asked, what was meant when it was said that there existed an obligation of going to this new city at the year 1800? If room was not to be had in it, Congress might go to Georgetown. They *may just as well stay where they are.* What would they be at? Poor Richard says,

* See debate of the 31st of March, 1796.

> I never saw an oft removed tree,
> Or yet an oft removed family,
> Which throve so well, as those that settled be.

Let us make a supposition that, before the end of the year 1800, only two millions of dollars are expended on the federal city. The buildings, as has been already explained, are on an extravagant scale. The United States could do as well without them.

Put two millions of dollars into any rational scheme of domestic improvement in the country, such as a well contrived canal. The money will yield a clear profit of ten, twenty or thirty per cent. Take it at the lowest rate, and with ten per cent. of compound interest, a sum doubles itself in seven years, fifty-two days and an half. In fifty years, these two millions of dollars will double themselves seven times. They will amount to two hundred and fifty-six millions. In an hundred years, they will amount to thirty-two thousand seven hundred and sixty-eight millions of dollars, which, at that æra, will be the real expence of the city, even if restricted only to the original two millions. This computation shews the folly of sinking a capital on an object which is both unproductive and superfluous.

At the end of the nineteenth century, the federal *quarries above ground* will not be worth so great a sum; nor indeed worth *what they originally cost*. They cannot, like a high road, or an improved farm, pay a large interest. They are mere unproductive masses of brick and lime, and wood and stone, the spawn of lotteries and land jobbing, for all which fine articles Mr. Theodore Sedgwick imagines it our duty to be *grateful*.

This project of the federal city has been examined at some length, because the subject is very imperfectly understood, and because the plan, if completed, must end in destroying the American constitution. The monarchical party in the convention of 1787, had the following clause thrust into that paper. "The Congress shall have power to exercise EX-"CLUSIVE *legislation, in all cases whatsoever,* over "such district, not exceeding *ten miles square,* as "may, by cession of particular states, and the ac-"ceptance of Congress, become the seat of govern-"ment of the United States." A like clause was never heard of before in the constitution, or practical administration of any government in the world.

Suppose that, at the English revolution of 1688, the new parliament had declared themselves exclusive legislators over a square of ten miles, and of which St. Stephen's chapel was to be the centre. *Exclusive* legislation is but another term for arbitrary power, because it confounds the characters of judge and legislator. In so small a space, where parliament were sure to see every thing, magistrates would have been nothing but their tools; and jobs, despotism, anarchy, and revolt must have ensued. The citizens of London and Westminster would, in two or three years at the utmost, have laid the new government on its back. But it would be wronging the character of the English nation to put the supposition that a clause so absurd, so fantastical, so big with mischief, and confusion could ever have past in that country. Such an originality was reserved for the fertile brain of Alexander Hamilton. In the convention of bolted doors, this bauble was part of the compromise and sacrifice granted by Madison and his friends to the royal faction. Being combined with better materials, it was without reflection accepted by the citizens of America. As a parting appeal to their common sense, let us only figure this case, that the state of Pennsylvania had ceded to Congress a district of ten miles, *including this city.* There is not a man in Philadelphia who wishes to see Congress erected into its exclusive legislators.

Their ignorance, their caprice, the natural insolence of unlimited authority, would, in a few years, have thinned the streets of the city. If on the 4th of July, 1795, Congress had held exclusive legislation in Philadelphia the evening would not have closed with a shower of brick-bats. The dismounting and disarming of captain John Morrell; of the china ware-house, in North Front-street, and his being so basely pitched into Frog-pond at Kensington, might have produced a general massacre of the citizens. The sale of his sword for sixpence, on his declining to reclaim it, might have easily been turned into a high crime and misdemeanour. This inference becomes very probable, when we contemplate the bloody maxims of our American DUKE OF ALVA*. Thus much for the federal city.

On the 5th of February, 1796, the bill of appropriation for the current year, having gone

---

* Alexander Hamilton wished, "that the people, assembled at "Braddock's field, *had burnt Pittsburgh.*" Randolph's Vindication, p. 83. "One motive assigned in argument, for calling forth the mi- "litia, has been, that a government can never be said to be establish- "ed, until some SIGNAL DISPLAY has manifested its power of *mili-* "*tary coercion.* "This maxim," adds Randolph, "if indulged, would "heap curses upon the government. The strength of a government "is the affection of the people." Ibid p. 102. The maxims and wishes of Mr. Hamilton exceed any sentiment recorded from the hemp-crack-governor of the Netherlands. They rather approach to the comprehensive sublimity of Caligula.

It is extremely worthy of notice, that although the Gazette of the United States has been constantly railing at Randolph, yet no denial has ever appeared as to the accuracy of the passages above quoted. It is no wonder that, after such discoveries, the party hate him. They sometimes harp upon his stile. It is at least far superior to that of Mr. Fenno's auxiliaries. If Randolph is not so acute, so terse, so critical, and so brilliant, as Thomas Jefferson, yet, in his printed correspondence with Hammond, he writes like a man who meant well, and who felt for the wrongs of his country.

through both houses, was approved by the president. This approbation is an insignificant form. The worst laws, as well as the best ones, have, for several years past, constantly received the president's affirmative. In all cases of importance, however, his will is previously understood and strictly obeyed by a majority of the Senate. There may have been one or two exceptions to this rule, but none for a considerable time. In the case of Madison's first resolution, and of Mr. Clarke's bill for prohibiting commercial intercourse with England, the Senate were, indeed, equally divided, and the casting vote of Mr. Adams negatived both. But here it must be supposed, that Mr. Washington had kept himself in suspence. He had only just parted with Jefferson, and Hamilton was not yet completely fixed in the saddle. When the latter fact came to be known, every *federal* measure was bolted through by a large majority. After all, when two legislative bodies have agreed to a law, it is below their dignity to enquire for the opinion of any single man. By the constitution, a president who wishes to be troublesome, can raise considerable confusion. If he refuses approbation, the law is sent back to Congress; and, unless *two-thirds* of each house shall afterwards agree to it, the law becomes void. It is very seldom that so great a majority unites upon an important measure. The Senate consists, at present, of thirty-two members; and, by this clause of the constitution, Mr. Adams, supported by eleven senators, being more than one-third of the whole number, could prevent the passing of any bill which he did not like. Thus the veto of twelve persons, who are not wiser or better than their neighbours, might in every instance overweigh the whole House of Representatives, though supported by twenty-one senators. This is one of the mistakes in our constitution. If the citizens of America could, like the bees, create an animal of faculties superior to their own, this *veto* might be useful. But in the late and present mediocrity of presidential talents, it is at best an expensive excrescence. This subscription of the laws, and a trifling or inflammatory speech at the opening of each session of Congress, is almost the only real duty that a president has to perform. The business of state is divided among three secretaries, and we understand from Randolph that Mr. Washington used to hold a meeting with them on interesting points, and decide by the opinion of the majority. All this is no great matter. Jared Ingerfol, or the secretary of the state of Pennsylvania, or any counsellor of equal talents, would do the business fully as well, and think himself handsomely paid with an annual fee of a thousand dollars*.

---

* The account might stand thus:

    The UNITED STATES,   Dr.

To my trouble in writing and reading to the two houses of congress a speech against democratic societies, or against the citizens of the south western frontier, or against another speech made by a member of the French directory, or concerning my friendship with John Watts and Doublehead, or in praise of the gallant army who carried off one half of the pots and pans of the four western counties of Pennsylvania, and who burnt every rail fence within their reach,	25
To my secretary for a clean copy of ditto speech,	5
To my trouble in approving of sixty acts of congress, during last session, at five dollars each,	300
To my secretary, for announcing the same to the two houses, at twenty-five cents each,	15
For my attendance to count the votes of the triumvirate ministry, once a week, during fifty-two weeks, at eight dollars per time,	416
To a complete set of Cobbet's Gazette, of the Minerva, of the Columbian Centinel, of the Gazette of the United	
Carried over,	761

On the 9th of February, was presented the memorial above inserted from the snuff-makers of Philadelphia. The act of which they complained exemplifies the remark of Montaigne, that " there is " nothing so commonly or so grossly faulty as *the* " *laws.*" The first of the two statutes in question required the performance of impossibilities. For instance, the snuff maker was to swear to a *daily* journal of the snuff grinded. To be able to do so he must have taken down his mill at the end of every day's work, and another entire day was requisite for putting it again in order. Thus between *taking down* and *setting up,* the snuff-maker would have spent four or five days in the week in hard work, without grinding one ounce of snuff. Mr. Thomas Leiper, and his fellow sufferers, had not logic enough to convince Mr. Hamilton, Mr. Sedgwick, and Dr. Smith, of this rule producing a hardship. Other clauses were equally stupid, oppressive, and impracticable. A ruinous excise on refined sugar manufactured in America had been blended in the same law with snuff, and it still remains in force. In a proof sheet of the *short history of excise,* it was sta-

Brought over,	761
States, and of the works of Messrs. Harper and Cobbet, to be resorted to for occasional information,	100
To my trouble in signing recalls, and appointments of foreign ambassadors, e. g. the recall of my son from Holland, for which he had received an outfit of nine thousand dollars, to my trouble, at the same time, in appointing him ambassador to Portugal, with a second outfit of nine thousand dollars, of recalling him within six weeks, and sending him to Berlin, with a third outfit of nine thousand dollars, over and above his salaries,	120
To my loss of time in bowing on the street to the additional acquaintances whom I have acquired *since* my appointment,	19
Total dolls.	1000

ted that, after paying the duty, there would not remain to the refiners of sugar more than a clear profit of five per cent. upon the capital embarked in their business. This circumstance was related on the authority of some of the principal manufacturers in Philadelphia. But, on a revisal, they chose to strike it out of the publication, lest a disclosure might alarm their correspondents, and injure the general interest of the trade. This was in the fall of 1795. Matters have certainly been improved, or else the manufacture must have stopt, as that of snuff actually did. The sugar boilers could have got six per cent. for their money in the common rate of interest, and ten times that sum from an exporting flour merchant.

One would be apt to believe that the *federal* members of Congress wanted to destroy altogether American manufactures. The paper money system is chiefly theirs. Twenty millions of dollars, fabricated out of old rags, are now circulating about the continent. Of these, ten millions belong to the bank of the United States. The total dividend of all these banks, as stated in Congress by Dr. Smith and Mr. Gallatin, comes to two millions of dollars per annum. The expences of management can hardly be less than five hundred thousand dollars more. This enormous tax, for just nothing at all, and the scropholous abundance of money produced by the bank capitals, have tended extremely to impede the progress of American manufactures. Though not the sole cause, they have yet been among the chief causes that raise the wages of labour in America so extravagantly beyond its price in Europe. Some leaders of the federal party possess extensive concerns in the bank of the United States. But the maturity of American manufactures never can arrive, till wages fall, and that must be preceded by a reduction of the mass of paper. Hence these leaders wish to encourage the importation of British goods. The merchants who import them, also, and who, in general, detest American rivalship, are in constant habits of discounting at the banks, and it is of consequence to favour such valuable customers. These obvious motives tend to make the federal commanders anxious for the closest connection with England. The same scale of argument leads them to abhor the French, among whom paper currency has always been despised. Hence, among other reasons, we find their constant inclination to revile France*. Hence their enthusiastic zeal, for the completion of Jay's treaty to which the journal of Congress hath now brought us.

Nothing that excited general attention occurred in Congress from the trial of Randall till the 1st of March. On that day, the President sent a message to each house informing them that ratifications of the British treaty had been exchanged at London, on the 28th of October, 1795. " I have *directed* " the same to be promulgated," added the President, " and herewith transmit a copy thereof for " the *information* of Congress." This was clearly the style of a public officer, who considered his authority on this point, as independent and unques-

---

* Camden, in his history of Elizabeth, book iv. p. 443, has these words. " The French lawyers say, that whatsoever is once an- " nexed to the crown of France, doth inseparably adhere to it for- " ever." This vindicates the republicans from a suspicion of innovation, when they refuse to restore the Low Countries to the emperor.

During the time of the French league, Elizabeth was advised to attempt the conquest of Picardy and Normandy. " She heard it," says Camden, " with regret and dislike, and rejected it with much " indignation, saying, *whensoever the last day of the kingdom of France* " *cometh, it will, undoubtedly, be the eve of the destruction of England.*" Ibid. p. 444.

tionable. He had complied with every formality required by the constitution. He had selected an ambassador for England, and had given him instructions as a rule of conduct. The constitution says " he shall nominate, and by and with the advice " and consent of the Senate, shall appoint ambassa- " dors." The president had announced his nomination to that body. They were mean or stupid enough to acquiesce in the appointment, without once asking for what purpose Jay was to be sent to England, or demanding a copy of his instructions. This shewed that the message was but an empty form, and that, in the particular details of his negociation, the President scorned to hold any prefatory communications with them. Here, by the way, comes out, as before observed,* an evidence of hypocrisy towards Genet. Mr. Washington could not negociate with the French envoy, because the Senate were not in session. Yet, over their heads, he sent an envoy to England, without letting them understand one line of his directions. This was frankly telling the republic that he rejected their advances. He could not have taken a more ungracious, a more ungrateful or infatuated step. After such coldness and contempt on our part, we should speak with temper about the republic. Frenchmen have never been celebrated for patience; and it can least of all be expected in the midst of a blaze of victories, which reduce Belisarius and Hannibal to the rank and file of conquerors.

From this digression we go back to Jay. Receiving orders from the President, and a sanction from the Senate, he went to England and framed a treaty. On its arrival here, the Senate, and President, gave in due time, a ratification. They expressly

* Supra chap. 3.

took the whole burden upon themselves; and whether Jay obeyed his instructions, or broke them, was a question entirely between himself and the President, from whom exclusively he accepted of them. The Senate had, beforehand, resigned all right of thinking upon the subject. They possessed no future title to call for the instructions. The fit time for that demand had passed away. If the treaty proved to be a good one, it was quite a frivolous enquiry, whether the instructions were right or wrong. If it was bad, the President stood in the gap, and they could disappoint all bad effects by a rejection. They approved of the whole treaty, one article excepted. It was, thereafter, ratified by the President. Here the character of these two branches, or rather of these two sprigs from the trunk of *representation*, was completely embarked.

There does not appear any solid reason why the President, in the sequel, submitted Jay's instructions to the Senate, after the treaty had been ratified. The only time for such a communication was before Jay sailed for England. The instrument could only stand or fall, not by the tenor of the instructions, but by its own intrinsic value. The tardy production of Jay's orders resembled a Chinese marriage. The lover, it is said, does not see his mistress till after the wedding, but has leave to send her home again, if he does not like her. The President could only send this paper as a matter of civility. The Senate had lost their right of calling for the instructions. They had not even a decent pretence to have challenged Jay. He acted as private agent to Mr. Washington, and the Senate had, in plain justice, no more to do with him, than the President had with his secretary, Mr. Trumbal.

But farther, Jay was, upon a different ground, placed beyond the reach of personal consequences.

Admitting that he acted with the wildest deviation from his orders, yet he neither did nor could do any thing final. If the President disapproved of the treaty, still he had only to refuse it. He could have sent Grenville a copy of his instructions to evince that Jay had entirely contradicted them. This must have been a full apology for his negativing the treaty.

There still remained one point of view in which Jay might be regarded as responsible. Suppose that, while he carried on a negociation contrary to the spirit of his orders, the relative condition of the two parties had altered, that Britain had become stronger, and America weaker, or that some change in the condition of a third party had produced a similar effect. In that case, the House of Representatives might have addressed the envoy in terms like these:

" It is true that you acted as an immediate agent
" for the President, that he had legal authority to
" employ you, and that he, along with the Senate,
" has taken upon himself the total responsibility for
" your conduct. In common matters an employer,
" by vindicating his agent, *completely covers him*
" *from enquiry ;* but, in your affair, there is some-
" thing particular to be said. We *believe* that you
" disobeyed your orders, that you treacherously en-
" tangled the President in a bargain for which you
" had no powers, and that you thus forfeited that
" impunity annexed to the character of HIS agent.
" He received your production with every feeling of
" shame, of alarm, and indignation. Agreeable to
" law he assembled the Senate; and they and he suc-
" cessively ratified the treaty, under the dread that
" if they rejected it, their perfidious and formidable
" enemy would pervert their refusal into a pretence
" for declaring war. So standing the case, we con-

"tend that in substantial equity, you have not been
"the agent of Mr. Washington, but of lord Gren-
"ville; and that the compulsive operation created
"by your perfidy on the minds of the Senate and
"President, transferred the constitutional responsi-
"bility from them to you. The charges here
"made against you are matters of strong suspicion,
"but not of certainty. We are in want of evi-
"dence either to support or to refute them. We
"can only get that evidence by resorting to your
"instructions, for you can only be *impeached* on the
"head of having disobeyed them, and of your diso-
"dience having thereafter shackled the delibera-
"tions of the President and Senate. For the pur-
"pose of ascertaining your guilt or innocence,
"we are going to solicit the President. He has
"sent these papers to the Senate. He cannot,
"therefore, in common civility, or even decency,
"deny our request. Yet we have no constitution-
"al right of demanding the paper. The power of
"*making treaties* has been exclusively and jointly
"vested in the Senate and in him. No part of
"the constitution requires that he should explain
"to our house his motives, or divulge, unless by
"his own free will, your instructions and subsequent
"correspondence. If he withholds these means of
"information and impeachment, we can only grum-
"ble into silence, and blush at the contemptible in-
"cense of adulation that, for seven years past, we
"have piled on the altar of Mount Vernon."

The above is apprehended to contain a summary of the arguments that might have been employed in favour of impeaching Jay. The stress lies on ascertaining that the President disliked the treaty, and gave it a reluctant ratification. On this point, Randolph affords a copious evidence. " My opinion," says Mr. Washington, " respecting the treaty, is "the same now that it was, that is, *not favourable to it*, but that it is better to ratify it in the manner the Senate have advised, than to suffer matters to remain, as they are, unsettled.—I find endeavours are not wanting to place it in *all* the odious points of view of which it is susceptible, and in some which it will not admit." [This is plain enough.] "I have never, since I have been in the administration of the government, seen a crisis, which in my judgment has been so pregnant of interesting events, nor one from which more is to be apprehended: whether viewed on *one side or the other*.—Scarcely a day passed, that he (the President) did not *enumerate many objections to it*; objections going not only to the commercial part, but also to the Canada article,— to the omission of compensation for the negroes and property plundered, and to some other parts of less consequence." It would be useless to heap up farther testimony that the President disapproved of Jay and his treaty, and that he agreed to it only to prevent some worse consequences.

Having settled this point, we proceed with the journal of the Representatives. On the 7th of March, 1796, the house took up a resolution moved by Mr. Livingston. It was in these words:

"*Resolved*, that the President of the United States be requested to lay before this house, a copy of the instructions to the minister of the United States who negociated the treaty with the king of Great Britain, communicated by his message of the first of March, together with the correspondence and other documents relative to the said treaty, excepting such of said papers as any existing negociation may render improper to be disclosed." As one

* Randolph, p. 35, 36, 38.

reason for this motion, Mr. Livingston said that the production of the papers would determine the house whether " an impeachment would be deem "ed adviseable*." But his chief reason was " a "firm conviction that the house were vested with " a discretionary power of carrying the treaty into " effect, or refusing it their sanction. To guide " them in an enlightened determination as to that " point, the papers are necessary; they would cer "tainly throw light upon the subject, and enable " the house to determine whether the treaty was " *such* as that it ought to be carried into effect*." Mr. Livingston calls the latter his *principal* reason. He did not speak exactly what he thought. The papers called for could not be needful to guide the determination of the house, as to whether they should sanction the treaty, for nothing but its individual merits could decide for or against it. But, second, if the papers were needful, the house, before this time, had virtually, though not officially seen them. They had been lying for some time on the table of the Senate. Many Representatives had gone up stairs and read them, and every member was acquainted with the essence of their contents. Hence, they could not be wanted for the purpose of determining an opinion about the treaty, even had its fate rested on such a disclosure.

Mr. Livingston well knew that his former reason for wanting the papers was almost equally hollow. He knew, or he well might have known, that an impeachment was *not* adviseable. The sequel of the debates discovered the real sense of his party. The project of impeachment was but rarely and faintly dwelt upon. But the democratical members had other and good reasons for desiring an of-

---

* Bache, vol. i. p. 4.   † Ibid. p. 5.

ficial communication of the inſtructions. This would have fixed the perfidy of Jay in departing from them. Popular reſentment at his behaviour would have riſen to the higheſt pitch. His alledged preceptor, Mr. Hamilton, would have been involved in the clamour. The treaty muſt, on freſh grounds, have become an object of jealouſy and diſguſt; and this addition to the force of its enemies was to have enſured, in the Houſe of Repreſentatives, a refuſal of money for its fulfilment.

By an impeachment of Jay, nothing, in common ſenſe, could be expected, but an enormous waſte of time and of congreſſional wages, a pernicious and endleſs delay in the routine of private buſineſs, and finally, a triumphant acquital of the envoy. In defiance of all imaginable teſtimony, the Britiſh treaty majority in the Senate were ſure to have pronounced him guiltleſs. Look at their extruſion of Albert Gallatin, at their fraternal embrace of Meſſ. Gunn and Marſhal!

Thus it appears that Mr. Livingſton could hope for nothing from an impeachment, and he as little needed the inſtructions* to complete his opinion of the treaty. *That* opinion had been long ſince matured. It is difficult to keep from ſmiling when we perceive an intelligent legiſlator ſtanding up, and giveing all reaſons but the real one, in defence of his reſolution. The debate laſted, with ſome intervals, from the 7th of March to the 7th of April, both incluſive; and the report occupies three hundred and eighty-ſix cloſe printed octavo pages. This is the

---

* In the debate of the 21ſt of March, Mr. Williams obſerved that "for the ſpace of ten weeks, any member of that houſe "might have ſeen them," Bache, vol i. p. 236, But the great loſs was, that no member could, from ſuch inſpection, venture to quote them in the Houſe of Repreſentatives. He would have been called to order, and obliged to ſit down.

American mode of managing legislative debates. In a British House of Commons, the question could hardly have been protracted beyond six o'clock on a second morning.

Mr. William Lyman rose next after Mr. Livingston. He defended the resolution. One of his arguments was, that possibly the papers " might throw " such light as to produce a very great degree of " unanimity relative to that instrument (viz. the " treaty). Such circumstances might possibly be " disclosed as to reconcile those now opposed to it, " and who might otherwise remain irreconcilable. " If the resolution tended only to this object it was " effecting a valuable purpose." Mr. Lyman held the treaty in notorious detestation, so that this argument was mere hypocritical canting. The *unanimity* which he desired and expected from a production of the papers was not *for* the treaty, but, *against* it. As to impeachment, Mr. Lyman spoke not one word. Mr. Giles on the same side, followed. He did not contemplate impeachment " as the " *probable* issue, but the information might tend, " perhaps, to reconcile those now averse to the in- " strument." This gentleman spoke with as little sincerity as the two former. We may observe how very soon the Madisonians began to file away from their impeachment.

Mr. Murray succeeded Mr. Giles. He opposed the resolution. He denied the right of the house to intermeddle in treaties, unless these were alledged to be *unconstitutional*. He objected the general impolicy of exposing secrets of state. Mr. Murray is a moderate and sensible speaker; but, with all his fondness for secrecy, he would certainly have voted *for* the resolution, if its real object had been to promote the success of the treaty.

Mr. Buck, another friend to Jay, took the same side, " but not from an apprehension that the pa-

"pers referred to will not *bear the public scrutiny*, or from a belief that there would be the least reluctance on the part of the executive to *deliver them.*" Here the first sentence of Mr. Buck's harangue contained two direct untruths. He knew that the papers would not *bear scrutiny**. He knew, and and so did every person in the house, that Mr. Washington would be ashamed and unwilling to give them up. It was for these very reasons, which Mr. Buck set out with disowning, that he opposed the resolution.

Thus the combatants went on. They interpersed much extraneous matter, with pretended arguments on each side, which, as in the five cases already cited, the orator himself held in sovereign contempt, and which every man who heard him knew that he despised. Some speeches deserved a better character, but the limits of this volume do not permit farther criticism. At a future time it may be convenient and instructive to trace the obliquities of congressional discussion. The pompous petulance and Iscariot-like malignity of Buck†, the plausible stupidity and self-important ignorance of Sedgwick, the pregnant

---

* Such as the two cards upon impressment. Supra chap. 5. "Was it unknown, that *thousands* of our sailors have been occasionally enslaved by the impress tyranny of the British government? Or, that *thousands* have lost their lives in noxious prisons, while their vessels were carried into British ports for *legal ajudication?*" Features of Jay's treaty, section 3d.

"In all my vast reading," as Dr. Wagtail says, this pamphlet, both as to stile and matter, is considerably the best which has appeared either for Jay or against him. Candid, elegant, comprehensive, and concise, its accuracy gratifies the most informed, while its perspicuity convinces the plainest reader. Yet Mr. Dallas has a material defect. His extreme reserve and delicacy are entirely cast away upon such enemies as Wilcocks, Webster, Curtius, and Camillus, on the stupid malignity too frequent in Mr. Fenno's Gazette, and on the illiterate brutality of the Columbian Centinel.

† A short memoir of this gentleman, transmitted from Vermont, has, for the present volume, been laid aside.

vacuity, and elegant loquacity of Harper, often approaching to good sense, yet almost never getting up to it, hold out prominent materials for amusing illustration. But the number of respectable speakers was greatly superior to that of such phantoms as these. In general, a member of Congress hath sufficient prudence either to hold his tongue, or to tell his sentiments in a way which does not make him ridiculous.

On Thursday, the 24th of March, 1796, a division took place in a committee of the whole house on this resolution to call for Jay's instructions and correspondence. It passed by sixty-one votes against thirty-eight. This was a majority unusual on great political questions. When some victim who has been reduced to beggary by the late war, or some French officer, who neglected to call, in due time, for his arrears of pay, has the weakness to solicit Congress, a negative passes with unanimity, or something like it. But in matters of high political import, the majority runs, for the most part, very close. The resolution past in the house by sixty-two votes against thirty-seven. On the 25th of March, it was presented to the President. On the 30th, he sent a refusal of the papers. His message misquoted and perverted the request of the house into a positive *demand*, and then pretended to refuse what had not been asked†. Their behaviour gave Mr. Washington reason to despise them. The debates that lasted for eight, ten, or twenty days about an answer to his annual speech dishonoured the whole body. His refusal of the instructions was to conceal the disobedience of Jay, and his own tameness in bearing it.

The majority of sixty-two ought to have received the message with silent disdain, and prohibited their

† See American Annual Register, chap. xi.

clerk from inserting it on the journals. Without oftensible interference they could have sent to press a copy of the instructions. These would have darted through the newspapers with the velocity of lightning. An abortive attempt to conceal this paper must have ensured its universal perusal. A victory to the publishers was the natural consequence. The people would have resented the disobedience of Jay, the pusillanimous acquiescence of the President, and his ill-concerted scheme for suppressing information. While they sympathized with the affronted representatives, a few well written essays might have matured into effective service the germ of indignation; and the treaty and its allies had sunk into the dust.

But the majority possessed not one man with the resources, firmness and activity of colonel Hamilton. The party seemed studious to display more than their usual inferiority of address and boldness. Never was a critical moment more miserably cast away. Instead of a glowing declaration that they contemned the refusal, instead of some spirited harangues to animate their partisans without doors, their tremulous and trimming measures towards a faction whose animosities are immortal, betrayed their total want of energy, depressed their friends, encouraged their enemies, and paved the way for their own approaching downfall. They did not perceive that the public had become tired of these debates, that farther haggling and wrangling would only increase that disgust, and raise the message to an unmerited importance, and that silent contempt was the plainest way to render it despicable.

On the 6th of April two resolutions* were brought forward. The meaning of the first was, that the majority, if they could hold themselves together,

---

§ See them in Bache's Debates, vol. i. p. 374.

would refuse money for fulfilling Jay's treaty. The second implied, that when the house desired the executive to let them have the instructions, they were not obliged to tell for what purpose the paper was wanted. Madison explained and enforced the resolutions with that superior knowledge, ingenuity, and eloquence, which have so often illustrated and adorned the transactions of Congress. Next day, they were past, ayes fifty-seven, noes thirty-five. They were not worth one half of the trouble which they cost. To illuminate and brace the minds of the people it would have been better to propose the striking twenty thousand dollars from the president's salary. Mr. Adams, as a premium for his two British negatives, might have been restricted to twelve dollars per day during the sitting of Congress. This is the allowance to a speaker of the representatives, a character of more real use, and who bears more actual drudgery than the Senate and their vice-president put together. Such resolutions could not have been carried, but the bare proposal would have conveyed an important hint. A contrast might have been run between an old soldier with the palfy and seven dollars and an half per annum, or his widow with six ragged children, and Mrs. Washington gossipping for a whole evening at the national expence, with fifty or an hundred and fifty women, while snuff-mills and sugar-bakeries were cast idle by the *approbation* of her husband.

Treaties had, within a short time, been entered into by the United States with Britain, with Algiers, with Spain, and with those Indians whom Wayne defeated at fort Miamis. On the 13th of April, 1796, Mr. Sedgwick moved a resolution that provision should be made for carrying these treaties into effect. He meant that the house ought to vote sums of money for that end, and his view in bundling the whole four treaties into one resolution was that they might stand or fall together. This resolution produced warm debates. Several amendments were suggested and discussed. Of these a particular detail can hardly interest an ordinary reader. The whole proceedings have been minutely compiled by Mr. Bache, and deserve to be studied by every future candidate for a seat in Congress. For this place, it is enough to set in one luminous point of view the actual objects of the opposite parties. The news of the Spanish treaty had been received in America with universal exultation. It was to open the navigation of the western waters, of which the king of Spain had hitherto been the jailor. The Indian and Algerine treaties were rather convenient than advantageous, but as their terms gave general satisfaction, no doubt was entertained that money would be voted to fulfil them. A refusal was, of necessity, to subject the union to immediate piracy and warfare. But it was, in all respects, quite otherwise with the British treaty. A general and violent opposition had appeared against it. A complexity of principles was involved in its discussion. Hitherto, most representatives had professed to dislike it, and a delay, or even a rejection, could not reasonably be supposed to produce war, when, by the conquest of Holland, the extirpation of her armies in Europe and the West-Indies, the scarcity of money, and the discontent of her people, England was evidently staggering on the brink of ruin.

The scheme of the federal members was to blend these negociations in one mass. Their arguments and motives, when stript of the loquacious masquerade common to both parties, might be expressed thus:

"We have on the table before us four treaties.
" Of these, three are equally acceptable to the whole
" house; but you want to fulfil them, and to reject

" the fourth. We are as defirous as you can be
" for friendfhip with Spain, and for peace with Al-
" giers and the Indians. But our Britifh treaty,
" that you propofe to deftroy, is of infinitely grea-
" ter importance in our eyes than all the others col-
" lectively, and the intereft and independence of our
" country into the bargain. Grenville has adver-
" ted to you, as American jacobins, and has affu-
" red the toad-eating Thomas Pinckney that a Bri-
" tifh army fhall, if we requeft it, be fent over to
" crufh you. But if we reject this treaty, that aid
" cannot be expected; and that twilight of our po-
" litical millenium fhall be forever extinguifhed,
" while fo fignal a defeat on the floor of Congrefs
" will give a mortal blow to the power which we at
" prefent poffefs. Mankind will begin to think
" and act about us with common fenfe. They will
" demand *a publication of the books of the treafury.*
" They will no longer pay intereft for forty mil-
" lions of dollars of domeftic debt to creditors, till
" they fhall have learned *who thefe people are?* And
" whether William Smith, or Izard, or Hillhoufe,
" or Sedgwick, has waded fartheft into the funds?
" This profpect is terrible. To avert it we fhall
" fall or conquer by the fide of the treaty. If that
" cannot be carried, we fhall rejoice in blocking
" up the Miffiffippi, in whetting the tomohawk, in
" glutting the pirates of Barbary with the plunder
" of our commerce."

The refolution was negatived. The three treaties were agreed to. A fecond feries of debates occurred as to the granting of money for fulfilling Jay's
treaty. This ended on the firft of May, 1796. The
appropriations paft, in committee of the whole, by
the cafting vote of the chairman, Mr. Muhlenberg,
the votes of members being forty-eight on each
fide. In the houfe, this appropriation paft by fifty-

one votes against forty-eight. Some even of this narrow majority, declared their entire disapprobation of the treaty. The general zeal excited in its favour, and the probability that the six per cent. citadel of Connecticut would have burst into actual rebellion*, were forcible reasons in favour of adoption. The multitude and stile of the addresses to Congress in its behalf were sufficient to make thoughtful members doubtful as to rejecting it. Mr. Muhlenberg has been highly blamed for his vote on this question. By an uniform tenor of conduct, since 1789, he had already offended the opposite party beyond all hope of forgiveness. But on this emergency, he preferred the security of internal peace, even to the approbation of his constituents. He had candidly stated his ideas in several private meetings of members previous to the final vote.

The session rose on the 1st of June, 1796. British depredations did not, as had been fondly foretold, cease after the appropriations had past for the treaty. As one of its consequences the French began soon after to disturb our trade. The western posts were, however, delivered up. The general election for Congress, and that for a President, the difference between the French minister and the American executive, were among the chief events which occurred till the next meeting of Congress, which was on the 5th of December 1796.

* Supra, chap. 2d. See also, the spirit of some people in that state, in the American Annual Register, chap. 6th.

ERRATA.

On p. 164, third line from the bottom, read "the American *monied* interest."——In the note on page 232, eleventh line from the bottom, read "A minority declined *to pass an act for the calling of a* "*convention, in order to its* acceptance," &c.——On page 260, third line from the bottom, read "amounted, *in* 1794, to," &c.

www.ingramcontent.com/pod-product-compliance
Lightning Source LLC
Chambersburg PA
CBHW030751230426
43667CB00007B/920